Continuity and Change:
From the Warren Court
To the Burger Court

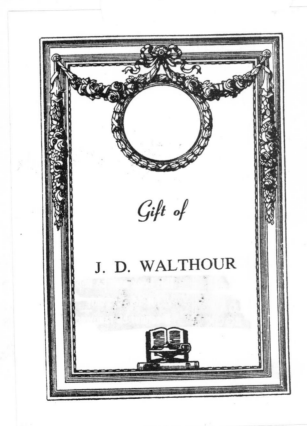

Gift of

J. D. WALTHOUR

GOODYEAR SERIES IN AMERICAN POLITICS AND PUBLIC POLICY
Joel B. Grossman, Series Editor

RACIAL EQUALITY IN AMERICA: IN SEARCH OF AN UNFULFILLED GOAL
Charles S. Bullock, III and Harrell R. Rodgers, Jr.

ONE ENVIRONMENT UNDER LAW: A PUBLIC-POLICY DILEMMA
Lettie McSpadden Wenner

CONTINUITY AND CHANGE: FROM THE WARREN COURT TO THE BURGER COURT
Stephen L. Wasby

Continuity and Change:

From the Warren Court
To the Burger Court

STEPHEN L. WASBY
Southern Illinois University at Carbondale

Goodyear Publishing Company, Inc.
Pacific Palisades, California

Library of Congress Cataloging in Publication Data

Wasby, Stephen L
    Continuity and change.

      (Goodyear series in American politics and public policy)
      Includes index.
      1.   United States.   Supreme Court.   I. Title.
KF8748.W32   347′.73′26   75–20808
ISBN 0–87620–163–X

Library of Congress Catalog Card Number: 75–20808

ISBN: 0–87620–163–X
Y–163X–1

Current Printing (last digit):
10 9 8 7 6 5 4 3 2 1

Printed in the United States of America

To my parents,

Milton and Pauline Wasby,

and to all Court-watchers,
whether "liberal" or "conservative,"
"strict" or "loose" in their construction.

Contents

The Transition to the Burger Court: A Final Look   206

Epilogue   212

Index   227

Preface

Like most Court-watchers during the late 1960s and early 1970s, I watched with fascination as Earl Warren retired, President Nixon struggled with the Senate, and a new set of justices joined the Supreme Court. I was also aware of the media's tendency to overplay the change occurring in the Supreme Court, and had an opportunity to sharpen my thoughts on the Warren Court–Burger Court transition while teaching a course on the law of civil liberties. The opportunity to write on the subject was therefore welcomed. I hope I have presented the material in this book so that it will be of interest not only to college students but also to that general readership that seeks to know more about the Supreme Court.

I owe debts of gratitude to quite a number of people. Joel Grossman, editor of this series, provided the impetus for the project, much sage advice, and appropriate language that serves to make matters clearer; his harrassment of my stylistic tendencies was appreciated. David Adamany's reading of the entire manuscript was, as usual, thorough and perceptive, provoking numerous clarifications. Russ Austin of the *Milwaukee Journal* asked me to write an "op ed" page piece ("Nixon/Burger Court: How Sharp a Turn?") that helped clarify my thinking early in the project. My students have provided considerable feedback and deserve a retroactive medal (but no grade changes!) for enduring my lectures; Jacqueline Ratermann Hunt, who read the entire manuscript, was particularly helpful. Susan Crain, "Colonel" Ed Griffith, Tyler Young, and my son Robert recorded, sorted, and counted cases, searched bibliography, and abstracted articles. Once the manuscript was initially completed, Lucille Grimes, Terry Nelson, and Susan Ritch provided invaluable typing help on numerous occasions. Most important, my friends and colleagues Tom and Joann Paine provided their house in Oregon overlooking the ocean, giving the undisturbed and idyllic location for writing about which every author dreams; Oregon's famous fog and mist also kept me indoors often enough to let me write.

These people provided the stimulus, some of the information, help in preparation, and the setting in which it was written. As the author, I must take the responsibility for what may have happened after that.

Continuity and Change:

From the Warren Court
To the Burger Court

Introduction

The Supreme Court of the United States is both highly revered and controversial. The latter is particularly likely when the Court's decisions differ from prevailing public views about policy. During the early 1930s when President Franklin D. Roosevelt tried to establish the New Deal and the Supreme Court invalidated much of the resulting legislation, economic policy was at the heart of the conflict enveloping the Court. During Earl Warren's term as Chief Justice (1953–1969), the Court turned unprecedented attention to civil liberties and civil rights, handing down decisions on individual rights far more liberal than those of any other Supreme Court in the nation's history. Those civil liberties rulings on equal rights for blacks, strict enforcement of separation of church and state, and procedural protections for criminal defendants not only made the civil liberties policy area the most controversial but also focused attention on the recurring question of how the Court was to fit into a democratic political system. People again asked whether a court whose members were appointed for life should have the power of judicial review, the authority to invalidate acts of other branches of the national government and of the state governments.

In 1968, Richard Nixon promised to name to the Court "strict constructionist" justices who would adopt a "law and order" stance on criminal procedure. That pledge alone makes it worthwhile to look at what occurred as the Court shifted from the tutelage of Earl Warren to the Chief Justiceship of Warren Earl Burger. Whether the Court did what President Nixon hoped or expected and whether, how, and at what pace the Court changed are subjects worthy of study. Those questions provide reasons for this book. New patterns take time to develop. We need to see the ways in which a transition takes place in a political institution like the Supreme Court and the new policies that may result. Thus the subject of this book is the Supreme Court's transition

1

from the late 1960s through the early 1970s. No attempt is made to provide a complete history of the Warren Court's sixteen terms. Instead, we examine what the Warren Court did and did not do, particularly in its last years. This is followed by an extended exploration of policy during Chief Justice Burger's first terms in office.

The Warren Court did not suddenly materialize when Earl Warren became Chief Justice, and there were several Warren Courts, that is, several identifiable periods during Warren's tenure. Similarly, the Burger Court, which with its four Nixon-appointed justices was complete only with the October 1972 Term, is not likely to have taken on its final complexion. Yet by mid-decade the Burger Court had an identity sufficiently clear to allow an examination of its configuration and policies. The period we cover is that when the new justices came to the Court, as well as the first years of the full "Nixon/Burger Court."[1] We end our detailed examination with the conclusion of the 1973 Term in July 1974, at the end of which—and with the Court's help—President Nixon was out of office. Important decisions from the 1974 Term will be discussed in a brief Epilogue.

COURTS IN TRANSITION

A court in transition, whether the Supreme Court under Chief Justice Burger or some other court, is "divided, uncertain, and adrift";[2] its doctrinal path is "sawtooth rather than linear."[3] The Burger Court has been said to be

> a transitional Court accepting much of the received doctrine as it happened to stand at the end of the preceding era, a Court gnawing at the fragile ends of the heritage without confronting its underpinnings, by and large a Court standing pat and surer about where it does not want to go than about articulating new directions.[4]

Whether the Burger Court suffers more from the infirmities of a transitional court than have other courts in transition is unclear. However, this transition, of interest in any event, could be compared with others, like the 1937 change from the conservative-dominated Court that invalidated much of FDR's New Deal to a Court more accepting of economic regulation. It could also be compared to the shift from the post–World War II Vinson Court (1946–1953) with its generally conservative civil liberties record, to the more civil liberties–minded, more liberal, and far more activist Warren Court.

The Supreme Court's role in the nation's political system considerably affects its action during a period of transition. The Supreme Court has been said to legitimize policy for the nation.[5] Certainly the Court commands respect because it is part of the political system and may even "command some additional respect because of the American devotion to 'law' and to the Constitution."[6] It has also been suggested that the Supreme Court is not for long out of line with dominant policies and public opinion and "is inevitably a part of the dominant national alliance."[7] However, when the public's policy preferences change, the Supreme Court faces a problem.

When political realignments occur, some time may pass before the new national policy directions are reflected on the Supreme Court. That was largely President Roosevelt's problem, because public opinion is more likely to be reflected by a responsive Congress and President than by the Supreme Court. The conflict then was made more severe because not only was the political shift major but FDR had to wait an inordinately long time to name any members to the Supreme Court. The situation when President Nixon took office was quite different, however. Nixon's election by a narrow margin in 1968, the lack of change in the public's partisan identification, and the Democrats' retention of control of Congress suggested that there had been no major political realignment. Furthermore, the Democrats in Congress, reflecting a shift in public opinion, underwent a change in views on civil liberties, so that many of them shared with the President an orientation more moderate or conservative than that of earlier days. Had the Warren Court continued intact, conflict could well have escalated as a liberal Court found itself further and further away from Congress' and the President's positions. Instead, President Nixon was able to name a new Chief Justice immediately and filled three other seats on the Court within two years. As a result, the President's views were soon evident in the Court's rulings. President Nixon's nominees reflected the change in the nation's tone, producing a policy coalition loosely aligned across all three branches of the national government instead of a situation with one policy coalition dominating both Congress and the executive branch while another held the Supreme Court.

In the past, such divided control led to increased instances of judicial review.[8] However, the use of that power by the Burger Court has not been frequent. The transition has passed so far without frequent major conflict between the Supreme Court and elected officials, although the executive branch's powers have been constrained in important instances. The level of conflict between Congress and the Court would certainly rise were the Congressional majority to turn more liberal on civil liberties issues. Yet even then the likelihood of intense conflict would be decreased by the Court's continuing post-1937 general deference to Congress on *most* matters of policy, a posture adopted because a Court that objects to or blocks policy reached by law-making majorities is likely to hurt its own legitimacy. Thus the Supreme Court has come into line with the public's and Congress' views on policy willingly, not because it is surrendering in the face of certain defeat, as was more nearly the case in the 1930s. Conflict may continue *within* the Court, as the remaining liberal justices "tough it out" until 1976 in hopes of a Democratic President to name their replacements, but conflict between the branches of government has been reduced from the days of the Warren Court.

POLICY IN THE TRANSITION

What can happen on the Supreme Court during a time of transition? Put another way, what can a Court do with the doctrinal legacy of its predecessor? Sometimes, little, in policy areas where only one Court or the other ruled. One Court may have drained or closed off old areas, as the Warren Court did with school prayer and civil rights demonstrations. A policy area, such as prison regulations, may be entered for the first time by the new Court, or it may deal with an area the previous Court had barely touched. (Claims that the Warren Court left little untouched are exaggerated.) However, even if cases in certain policy areas have not been heard by both Courts, the general thrust of each Court in a liberal or conservative direction can still be noted, and we can talk of differences in their general tone.

In most policy areas, both the old and new Courts in a transition decide cases. The newer Court may revive an older, and temporarily quiet, policy area, as the Burger Court did with government employees' rights, a policy area with which the early Warren Court had dealt. What accounts for the largest number of cases is that policy questions raised at the end of one Court may continue to be raised in the next. When this occurs, we may find the newer Court extending or advancing the older Court's rulings, or it may merely maintain, consolidate, and perhaps clarify those decisions. On the other hand, the new Court, to the extent it represents a different point of view, may curtail, erode, or even overturn its predecessor's work either directly or indirectly.

A successor Court is likely to *extend* or *advance* earlier rulings in at least some policy areas, because the new Court will find that its predecessor has set the basic premises for its rulings. The

Burger Court extended policy in taking due process protections introduced by the Warren Court for the trial and applying them to parole- and probation-revocation. Similarly, the Burger Court took the Warren Court's church-state doctrines and extended their thrust to legislative attempts to aid parochial schools. A successor Court may also simply *maintain* the earlier Court's work, perhaps *consolidating* doctrinal developments in the process. Examples of consolidation are the Burger Court's reinforcement of lower court judges' discretion to fashion remedies for previously separate school systems and its broad reading of the coverage of the Civil Rights Act public accommodations section and of the Open Housing Act of 1968. Maintaining may also be more passive, as when the successor Court finds ways of keeping new issues from coming to the Court and thus avoids having to deal with existing doctrine. Here the Court simply does not step forward.

Clarification of earlier doctrine is another possibility, quite likely when the old Court has handed down many broad decisions. Examples are the Burger Court's declarations that *local* community standards could be used in judging obscene material and that a state's obscenity standard had to be spelled out in either a statute or judicial construction of a statute. Although "the new Court ... has shown no inclination directly to overturn *clear, carefully explained* precedent,"[9] such as the exclusionary rule on improperly seized evidence or the *Miranda* rule on police interrogations, clarification can, however, be a guise for limiting earlier vague policy. The Warren Court's failure to provide specific standards for measuring malapportionment made it easier for the Burger Court to say that different, looser standards would be acceptable for state legislative reapportionment than for congressional reapportionment.

This suggests that a Court may retreat from past doctrine, *curtailing, eroding,* and *overturning* what has gone before. While this may come through direct challenges, the justices may instead initiate a less direct process of eroding precedents or their legitimacy; the previous Court's rulings thus wither away without being explicitly overruled. For example, the Burger Court ruled that improperly seized evidence could be used in grand jury proceedings and that confessions obtained without warnings could be used to try to discredit a defendant's testimony. This process of cutting back is gradual, but it can serve to dispose of disliked precedent. As Howard suggests, the Burger Court's strategy appears to be "a whittling away of precedents ... to the point that overruling them may be unnecessary."[10] Because the cumulative effect of such quiet undercutting can be devastating, we need to

examine trends as well as individual cases in order to see changes
in policy.

THEMES

As we look at what occurred during the Court's transition,
primarily from 1967 through mid-1974 (the end of the 1973 Term
of Court), in addition to dealing with the question of whether
President Nixon was able to accomplish what he set out to do with
the Court, we will stress several themes. They are the degree and
character of the Court's restraint, the Court's liberalism and conservatism, and the question of continuity and change.

Self-Restraint

The theme of judicial self-restraint is brought to the fore by
charges that the Warren Court had been excessively activist and
by President Nixon's claims of the corrective need for "strict constructionist" judges. Activism and restraint have several mean-
ings, and a court restrained on one dimension may not be so on
others. For a conservative, the Court is activist when it disturbs
the status quo and promotes social change; for the liberal who
finds the Court not taking expected positive steps, the Court is too
restrained. Among the aspects of strict construction and judicial
self-restraint to be examined are whether the Court has interpreted statutory and constitutional provisions narrowly and how
it has dealt with social problems. We will also look at the Supreme Court's deference to actions of state officials, the lower
courts, and other branches of the national government.

Liberalism

Another of our principal concerns will be to portray why and
where the Supreme Court has become more and/or less liberal.
The distinction between liberalism and conservatism is ambiguous because liberalism, like conservatism, has several dimensions. In the context of evaluating Supreme Court policies,
liberalism means essentially deciding for the individual against
the government, or supporting government economic regulation
against business claims. In some cases, however, determining the
liberal result is not easy. For example, when the conflict is between a labor union and an individual union member, one could
say a decision favoring the individual is liberal or conservative
(the latter because it weakens the union). Students of judicial
attitudes have found two types of liberalism—an economic

liberalism[11] and a political liberalism (or "civil liberties liberal-ism"), not simply a "general liberalism."[12] Political liberalism was an underlying factor in cases in such areas as freedom of speech, criminal procedure, and equal protection for minorities; economic liberalism affected most Warren Court rulings on economic regulation.[13]

Terms like "liberalism" and "conservatism" can be useful in understanding the Supreme Court. They are least useful when applied to the Court's overall record, and most useful in describ-ing particular policy decisions. As this suggests, the Court may be liberal in some areas and conservative in others. Statements about individual justices—which generally suggest only how each stands in relation to the others—must also be made in terms of defined sets of cases. Thus a judge may be conservative in some areas, for example, generally voting against programs of economic regulation, and liberal in others, for example, deciding for the individual against the government in civil rights cases.

Continuity and Change

"Continuity" and "change" are also relative terms. Different ana-lysts of the Supreme Court's work, looking at the same cases, can see either—or both—continuity and change. Both were stressed by President Nixon in his speech at the Supreme Court swearing-in of Chief Justice Burger. The President, having stressed change from the Warren Court during his campaign, was later to play it down when he nominated Powell and Rehnquist. In this volume, the stress will be on continuity rather than discontinuity, an em-phasis reinforced by the fact that social change in America usually comes gradually.

Perhaps because of the fanfare President Nixon made over his desire to change the Court's direction, the tendency of many commentators has been to *expect*—and from that to *see*—much change, particularly in the area of criminal procedure. Starting from a presumption of *dis*continuity, they have tended to em-phasize discontinuities with the Warren Court's rulings:

> Trend watchers readily proclaimed sharp breaks in constitutional direction and unquestionable emergence of absolutely firm voting blocs. There was a widespread yielding to obvious temptations—to strain descriptions in order to match preconceptions, to voice dramatic appraisals that obscure the subtler nuances.[14]

A close look at what occurred through the 1973 Term does *not* produce such a picture. There has indeed been change. However, the importance of maintaining earlier rulings has been underestimated, areas of noticeable continuity have been missed, and areas where the Burger Court has advanced along the paths first marked by Earl Warren and his brethren have been set aside. Growth has been ignored, while the amount of erosion that has occurred has been played up. Similarly, prominent new areas of law have also been ignored. Differences between the two Courts have been exaggerated because the Burger Court has been judged in terms of whether it matched the Warren Court's path-breaking, liberalness, and forthrightness. The contrast between the last years of the Warren Court, with their extremely liberal rulings, and the first, uncertain years of the Burger Court presented in this book is likely to heighten the differences we see, but those differences, instead of being consistently earthshaking, are revisionist and incremental.

THE COURT'S POLICY-MAKING ROLE

The principal emphasis of this book is on *policy outputs*, the results of the Court's deliberations. Policy-making is

> . . . a problem-solving endeavor or enterprise in which the actors . . . make conscious or unconscious choices regarding the removal or change of conditions which form an identifiable problem, or in which the actors respond by making such choices as are necessary to preserve the status quo, or in which the actors consciously or unconsciously refrain from actions which disturb the status quo.[15]

In these terms, although it may make policy in ways different from those utilized by other governmental institutions, the Supreme Court *is* a policy-making institution, and its outputs *are* policy. Because the Supreme Court develops policy only in the course of deciding cases involving specific controversies, we will draw on major and representative cases that seem to show most clearly what the Court has done, sketching the broad lines of policy development that the other cases produce cumulatively. Merely to present a summary of the policy without reference to the cases would be to misrepresent the slow, case-by-case, issue-by-issue process in which the Court is involved and which has as one of its natural results—even for a highly activist Court—the uneven and incomplete development of policy in any subject area.

Our exclusive attention to the Court's policy-making role and its outputs does not, however, mean the Court is the most crucial element in the American policy-making process or that its policy, once enunciated, is final. Studies of the *outcomes* ("impact") of the Court's decisions and the feedback from them[16] indeed suggest that neither may be the case. Thus we must keep in mind:

> The Justices are of primary importance to the policy-making process; but they are not the whole process. . . . Policy outputs of the Supreme Court are just one of many factors considered by participants in the policy process. . . . It is as if the Justices decided on the size and shape of the ball and the dimensions of the park but could neither determine the directions in which the ball would be batted or thrown nor, in general, could control the game until someone had thrown the ball back to the Court.[17]

This book begins with attention to the personnel of the Court and the situations surrounding their appointment. We will pay particular attention to the process by which Chief Justice Warren and Justice Fortas left the Supreme Court and the "Nixon Four" came to it. We will also provide a brief picture of each of the justices who served during the transition.

The process by which the Court reaches decisions next receives our attention. This includes "managing the Court." Here we will look at the size and content of the Court's docket, the justices' selection of cases, and proposals for change in that selection process, as well as at the Court's internal dynamics—the patterns of interaction among the justices—which include voting alignments among the justices and the Chief Justice's opinion-assignment practices.

Turning to the policy the Court develops—the results reached in cases and the justices' opinions—we begin with an overview of changes and non-changes in policy outputs, and then proceed to an examination of specific issue-areas. For each subject covered, we begin with an examination of the Warren Court's later years to provide a baseline against which to examine the Burger Court's work, occasionally looking at public opinion, an important input in the Court's work whether or not, in Mr. Dooley's phrase, the justices "follow the election returns." We look in some detail at the following policy areas: access to the courts; separation of powers; equality, particularly race relations; the First Amendment, including church-state relations and free speech; and finally, the most controversial, criminal procedure. As this listing suggests, the greatest share of our attention will be devoted to civil liberties and civil rights, matters at the heart of the controversy over the Warren Court.

NOTES

1.   Said one federal judge of the Nixon/Burger Court, "I'll take mine with onions."
2.   Gerald Gunther, "The Supreme Court, 1971 Term: Foreword: In Search of Evolving Doctrine in a Changing Court," *Harvard Law Review*, 86 (November 1972), 1.
3.   J. Woodford Howard, Jr., "Is the Burger Court a Nixon Court?" *Emory Law Journal*, 23 (Summer 1974), 747.
4.   Gunther, 6.
5.   For the basic argument, see Robert A. Dahl, "Decision-Making in a Democracy: The Supreme Court as a National Policy-Maker," *Journal of Public Law*, 6 (Fall 1957), 279–295. An incisive criticism is David Adamany, "Legitimacy, Realigning Elections, and the Supreme Court," *Wisconsin Law Review*, 1973, 790–846. Adamany argues that the Court cannot legitimate, given the low knowledge the public has of what the Court decides, and that the elite's approval of the Supreme Court stems from general policy orientations and ideology, not from the Court's decisions. He even suggests that the elite legitimize the Court more than the other way around. Ibid., 819.
6.   Adamany, 844.
7.   Dahl, 293.
8.   Stuart Nagel, *The Legal Process from a Behavioral Perspective* (Homewood, Ill.: Dorsey Press, 1969), 248.
9.   Gunther, 3; emphasis supplied.
10.   Howard, 762.
11.   Economic liberalism has as its subcomponents fiscal claims, governmental regulation of business, union-management disputes, freedom of competition, and constitutionality of state taxation. Two distinctive subscales of economic liberalism can be produced, "a general subscale . . . and a pro-union component." Glendon Schubert, *The Judicial Mind* (Evanston, Ill.: Northwestern University Press, 1965), p. 170. If one shifts from attitudes to what Schubert calls ideologies, economic conservatives are divided into pragmatists (conservative on economic matters) and dogmatists (political conservatives). Ibid., pp. 272 ff.
12.   "General liberalism . . . was not a scalable variable for the voting behavior of Supreme Court justices" during 1946–1963. Ibid., pp. 97–98. For discussions of scaling, in addition to Ibid., pp. 31–37, see also Schubert, *The Quantitive Analysis of Judicial Behavior* (Glencoe, Ill.: Free Press, 1959), pp. 269–290, and Schubert, "Civilian Control and Stare Decisis in the Warren Court," in Schubert, ed., *Judicial Decision-Making* (New York: Free Press, 1963), pp. 55–77. A discussion of factor analysis, which Schubert uses in his later work, can be found in *Judicial Mind*, pp. 22–31. Schubert has also suggested that liberalism encompasses "the inherently contradictory . . . goals of equalitarianism (social equality, political equality, economic equality) *and* individualism (individual rights to privacy of the mind, body, and spirit . . .)." Schubert, *The Constitutional Polity* (Boston: Boston University Press, 1970), p. 52. Elsewhere, Schubert writes that "The central component of liberalism is equalitarianism . . . defined by the issues of racial integration, legislative reapportionment, and the right to citizenship." *Judicial Mind*, p. 280.
13.   Thus a study of the early Warren Court years (the 1953–1959 Terms) showed that

the justices' attitudes toward business were part of a larger value, defined as economic liberalism, in which the liberally-oriented justice is anti-business, pro-competition, and pro-union. . . . In its decision-making, the Court was shown to be liberally oriented—somewhat more so in its regulation of business than of unions. (Harold J. Spaeth, "Warren Court Attitudes toward Business: The 'B' Scale," in Schubert, ed., *Judicial Decision-Making*, p. 100.)

Other values that might have affected the operation of this economic liberalism, such as federalism and attitude toward the courts or administrative agencies, had little effect; they were overriden by the economic liberalism. Such potential overriding values are examined with respect to an individual justice in Joel Grossman, "Role-Playing and the Analysis of Judicial Behavior: The Case of Mr. Justice Frankfurter," *Journal of Public Law*, 11 (1962), 285–309, where the denial of judicial responsibility (DJR) factor ("judicial self-restraint") is examined in relation to civil liberties position. Frankfurter's civil liberties scale position was not affected by removing DJR cases.

14.   Gunther, 2.

15.   Grossman, "A Model for Judicial Policy Analysis: The Supreme Court and the Sit-in Cases," in Grossman and Joseph Tanenhaus, eds., *Frontiers of Judicial Research* (New York: John Wiley, 1969), p. 408.

16.   For studies of impact, see Stephen L. Wasby, *The Impact of the United States Supreme Court: Some Perspectives* (Homewood, Ill.: Dorsey Press, 1970); Theodore Becker and Malcolm Feeley, eds., *The Supreme Court's Impact: Empirical Studies*, 2nd ed. (New York: Oxford University Press, 1973); and Samuel Krislov et al., eds., *Compliance and the Law: A Multi-Disciplinary Approach* (Beverly Hills, Cal.: Sage Publications, 1972).

17.   Grossman, pp. 417, 422.

CHAPTER ONE

The Burger Court:
A Collective Portrait

MR. NIXON'S WISHES

Presidents generally name to the Supreme Court those they believe share their ideological persuasions. There are exceptions,
such as Eisenhower's choice of William Brennan, and other
motivating factors, such as friendship or political debts, but ideology seems to be the key factor.[1] Thus we should not be surprised
that President Nixon named conservatives to the Court. We have
not had more conservative justices in recent years for the "man-
ifest reason that from Coolidge until Nixon we had no conservative Republican presidents, such as Taft or Harding, to appoint
right-wing Republican justices."[2]

That Presidents try to choose those of compatible ideology
does not mean that they are always successful. A President may
assume that someone of the same political party will share his
ideology. He may appoint a friend, assuming he will exhibit the
proper point of view as a judge (Kennedy with Byron White[3]). Yet
nominees often turn out to be more conservative (Frankfurter,
White) or more liberal (Warren) than expected.

However, President Nixon was strongly committed to having
persons on the Court who would pursue certain goals. Barry
Goldwater had made the Supreme Court an issue in 1964, and the
Republican platform that year supported amendments to override
the reapportionment and school prayer rulings. But in 1968 the
Court's posture was a *major* element in a presidential campaign
for the first time since Franklin D. Roosevelt. Candidate Nixon
explicitly stated he wanted judges who would be "strict constructionists" of the Constitution and who would not encroach on areas
belonging to Congress and the President. Nixon said, after his
nomination, "I think some of our judges have gone too far in

assuming unto themselves a mandate which is not there, and that is, to put their social and economic ideas into their decisions."[4] The type of judge he preferred, as he put it later in nominating Powell and Rehnquist, was a judicial conservative who would "not twist or bend the Constitution in order to perpetuate his personal, political and social values."[5] Such appointments would satisfy the Court's critics, who disliked "judicial law-making," particularly that in which the Warren Court had engaged. The George Wallace–stimulated "law-and-order" atmosphere had also produced calls for the Court not to substitute its views on desegregation for those of local school boards and to be more sympathetic to law-enforcement needs.

"Strict construction" has a nice ring to it. Because it is a code word, what Nixon meant by its use was not always clear. For example, he said that judges should not inject their values into the Constitution, but he also criticized the Warren Court's criminal procedure rulings: "From the point of view of the criminal forces, the cumulative impact of [the Court's criminal procedure] decisions has been to set free patently guilty individuals on the basis of legal technicalities."[6] So he wanted at least certain law-and-order values to govern judges' choices. Yet the overall *thrust* of the President's wishes was that the Court should be less activist, more "subdued," "restrained" at least where other branches of government were involved. Such a Court would give more credence to legislative judgments instead of subjecting them to a strict scrutiny test and would give more leeway to the executive branch on questions of executive privilege and national security. A restrained Court would also be more respectful of States' Rights. State governments would thus be allowed more flexibility to develop their own rules of criminal procedure instead of being subjected to one national standard. In short, Nixon wanted judges who by reading constitutional language and statutory provisions appropriately, in a way that could be called "strict," would produce conservative results.

That the President said what he had in mind does not, however, mean that he gave—or could give—the nominees a specific charge to reform the Warren Court's decisions.[7] However, they could hardly have been unaware of his views nor of his implied understanding of their values. This was particularly true with Chief Justice Burger. As a Court of Appeals judge, he had criticized fellow judges for nit-picking on criminal procedure and had made known his dislike of the use of the judicial process for solving social problems. Justice Rehnquist's strongly conservative ideological position was also well known.

OPPORTUNITIES AND "WHAT HE DONE WITH THEM"

Within his first term, President Nixon had the opportunity to name four justices of the Supreme Court, starting with the Chief Justice. Unlike Franklin Roosevelt, whose frustration with the Court resulted from an inordinate wait to replace some of its members, Nixon was given his first Supreme Court opportunities immediately.

President Kennedy, without much controversy, had named two members of the Court: Byron White, his Deputy Attorney General, to replace Charles Whittaker, and Arthur Goldberg, to fill the seat on the Court left vacant by Felix Frankfurter and usually held by somebody Jewish. Those appointments were crucial, because the two "assumed a position between Brennan and Stewart, in their support of civil liberties . . . and Goldberg did provide the fifth reliable liberal vote in favor of civil liberties for the first time in our political history."[8] Only with Goldberg's appointment was the Warren Court set free to do its most important work.

In 1965, Lyndon Johnson persuaded Goldberg to leave the Court to become Ambassador to the United Nations, and named Abe Fortas to his position.[9] (Had Goldberg remained on the Court, he would likely have been part of a core of four liberal justices outnumbering Nixon's replacements for Warren, Black, and Harlan; liberal majorities could still have been created with the vote of either Stewart or White.) The Senate Judiciary Committee did delay the nomination of Thurgood Marshall, and there was also some objection to Fortas' closeness to the President and his role in helping suppress the story of the assistant to the President who had been arrested for homosexual behavior. However, neither nomination caused serious controversy.[10] In fact, there had been relatively little controversy over nominations to the Supreme Court since the early Eisenhower years, when Senator Joseph McCarthy's anti-Communism, Southern senators' desegregation concerns, and Eisenhower's penchant for recess apointments (Warren, Brennan, Stewart) had combined to increase resistance to the President's choice. But even that controversy was not much by current standards; only two of the Eisenhower nominees received more than ten negative Senate votes.[11]

Controversy began in earnest in 1968, after Chief Justice Warren indicated his intention to retire when a successor was found. President Johnson nominated Fortas to be Chief Justice. The Republicans, anticipating victory in the 1968 presidential elections, wanted to be able to name the Chief Justice and re-sisted. They attacked Fortas' liberal position and the help he had given the President. Their charge of "cronyism" was only rein-forced by Johnson's nomination of Judge Homer Thornberry, a former congressman and another friend, to succeed to Fortas' old seat. The Republicans were joined in their efforts by conservative Democratic senators upset about Court rulings on obscenity and other civil liberties issues. Republican Senator Robert Griffin led an attack on the right of a "lameduck" President to name the new Chief Justice, and Senator Sam Ervin (D–N.C.) claimed there was no vacancy to be filled since Warren had not actually re-signed or retired. Fortas was not helped by the discovery, a har-binger of his later troubles, that he had accepted a $15,000 fee, raised by friends, for conducting a law school seminar. His oppo-nents, by dragging out the nomination, were able to block it. When the Senate refused to cut off debate, President Johnson withdrew the nomination at Fortas' request.

After President Nixon took office in 1969, Warren submitted a retirement with a definite date. President Nixon's nomination of Judge Warren Earl Burger of the Court of Appeals for the District of Columbia, the first Chief Justice to be appointed di-rectly from the lower courts, was confirmed with only three oppos-ing votes, despite liberal dissatisfaction with Burger's criminal procedure record. Even before Burger could take his seat for the October 1969 Term, the Fortas ethics issue broke into the open. Fortas had received money from financier Louis Wolfson, in trou-ble with the government, as part of a lifetime contract as a con-sultant to the Wolfson Foundation. While he had given the money back before the end of the year, so that he had no tax obligation, he had not done so immediately. As it looked to then Assistant Attorney General Will Wilson, "Fortas was guilty either of prac-ticing law on Wolfson's behalf or, even worse, trying to influence the outcome of the government's prosecution."[12] The question of possible violation of the law was unresolved, but the American Bar Association's ethics committee found that the Canons of Ju-dicial Ethics, which stated that "A judge's official conduct should be free from impropriety and the appearance of impropriety" and that "A judge should not undertake inconsistent duties . . . which will in any way interfere or appear to interfere . . . with his devo-tion to . . . his official functions," had been violated. The pressure for Fortas to explain or resign, or to resign anyhow, was helped along by the Nixon administration, which decided against at-tempting to impeach Fortas and took its information to Chief Justice Warren. Fortas then resigned in May 1969, but the liber-als remained furious at the administration's not-well-hidden role.

The ethics issue was soon to rise again, to haunt the administration's first nominee for the Fortas position, Fourth Circuit Court of Appeals Chief Judge Clement F. Haynsworth, Jr.[13] He was opposed by the NAACP as a "foot-dragging segregationist" and by the AFL-CIO for being anti-labor, but the ethics issue was crucial. In a case where he appeared to have a financial interest, Haynsworth had not withdrawn from participation. In another case, he had purchased stock, in one of the corporations involved as litigants, before the decision was announced, although after the case was decided. Several years before, he had been cleared of charges of unethical conduct,[14] but the standards applied after the Fortas incident were much higher. The nomination might have cleared the Senate without the ethics issue, but that provided many senators a cover for their ideological opposition.[15] The nomination was defeated, 55–45, the first Supreme Court nomination rejected by the Senate since that of Judge John Parker in 1930.[16]

The President dispelled any doubt that the Haynsworth nomination was part of his "Southern strategy" by his nomination, several months later, of Fifth Circuit Judge G. Harrold Carswell. While the fatigued Senate would probably have confirmed a prompt nomination (unless, as one senator said, the nominee had just raped a small child—in public), as time passed the opposition regained strength and solidified its organization. While Judge Haynsworth had been accused of not moving fast enough to implement *Brown* v. *Board of Education*, Carswell was accused of being a racist—on the basis of a 1948 campaign speech (which some would have been willing to forget if it stood alone), his role (while U.S. Attorney for the Northern District of Florida) in transforming the Tallahassee municipal golf course into a private club to avoid desegregation, his signing of a racially restrictive covenant on some property, and his alleged in-court treatment of black attorneys and civil rights workers.[17] His lack of candor with the Senate Judiciary Committee, reinforced by the Justice Department's failure to arrange a meeting between him and several undecided senators, also hurt. So did the opposition of lawyers and law professors, some of whom clearly distinguished between him and Judge Haynsworth both as to racism and judicial temperament.[18] They pointed out that, as a district judge, Carswell had been reversed by his own Court of Appeals far more frequently than all but a few other district judges in the circuit and that his opinions were cited infrequently by other judges.[19] (An irony is that Assistant Attorney General William Rehnquist, later to be nominated himself, had made a review of Carswell's rulings.) The nomination finally was defeated, 51–45, provoking the President's statement, "I cannot successfully nominate to the Supreme Court any federal appellate judge from the South who believes as I do in the strict construction of the Constitution." That nine southern and border state senators voted against Carswell, coupled with the later confirmation of Lewis Powell, suggested that this was not really the case.

President Nixon had become the first President since Grover Cleveland to lose two consecutive nominations to the Supreme Court. He had actively supported both, but his heavy presence in the Haynsworth nomination, including holding a special news conference to make a detailed refutation of the conflict-of-interest charges, had irritated some senators, who objected to the "arm-twisting" they said had been used. During consideration of Carswell, Nixon maintained a low profile, even when the administration was caught inadequately prepared to deal with the allegations of racism. However, this low profile disintegrated at the end.[20] The President had urged earlier that senators should not take a judge's philosophy into account in deciding how to vote on confirmation and should not vote against a nominee on the basis of legal or political philosophy. However, trying to convince Senator (later Attorney General) William Saxbe (R–Ohio) to vote for the nomination, he sent Saxbe a letter saying:

> What is centrally at issue in this nomination is the constitutional responsibility of the President to appoint members of the Court— and whether this responsiblity can be frustrated by those who wish to substitute their own philosophy or their own subjective judgment for that of the one person entrusted by the Constitution with the power of appointment. The question arises whether I, as President of the United States, shall be accorded the same right of choice in naming Supreme Court Justices which has been freely accorded to my predecessors of both parties. . . .
>
> . . . If the Senate attempts to substitute its judgment as to who should be appointed, the traditional constitutional balance is in jeopardy and the duty of the President under the Constitution impaired.[21]

Bad history (nominees had been regularly rejected in the nineteenth century) and even worse politics, the letter helped seal Carswell's fate, as ambivalent senators rejected the presidential challenge to their authority.

After the Carswell defeat, things moved more smoothly. Judge Harry Blackmun, a member of the Court of Appeals for the Eighth Circuit and, like Burger, from Minnesota, was the next nominee. He was unanimously confirmed. An attempt to impeach Justice Douglas on the basis of his foundation connections and outside writings, led by House Minority Leader Gerald Ford, and not restrained by President Nixon, failed when it was not supported by the House Judiciary Committee. However, it did produce Ford's famous statement that an impeachable offense "is whatever a majority of the House of Representatives considers it to be at a given moment in history," with "few fixed principles" to guide deliberation.[22]

In the fall of 1971, Nixon had two more opportunities to fill positions on the Court when Justices Black and Harlan retired from the Court (and died) within a short time of each other. Initial speculation centered on several people, including Little Rock attorney Herschel Friday and Los Angeles Judge Mildred Lillie, but the American Bar Association's attitude toward both was cool. Then President Nixon, in a nationwide television announcement, nominated Lewis Powell of Virginia, former president of the American Bar Association, and Assistant Attorney General William Rehnquist, who Nixon said rated "at the very top of government lawyers as a constitutional lawyer and legal scholar."[23]

Here the timing of the nominations, toward the end of the Senate's session, helped the President. Powell perhaps received less attention because of his age (the ABA had earlier considered him too old for nomination to the Court). Despite opposition from the Black Caucus in Congress because of his service on the Richmond (Va.) School Board and the Virginia Board of Education, Powell was approved with only one negative vote. Rehnquist, drawing far more fire, was attacked for his conservative views, opposition to public accommodations ordinances,[24] and earlier public defense of the Carswell nomination. His positions on matters like electronic surveillance and mass demonstrations also provoked the wrath of the American Civil Liberties Union, opposing a Supreme Court nominee for the first time in the organization's history. However, Rehnquist weathered the opposition and was approved, 68–26. Thus, in all, Nixon had a batting average of four nominations confirmed of six submitted, poor by twentieth-century standards.

THE PRESIDENT'S MEN AND THE OTHERS

We must remember that when we talk about the Burger Court, we mean all the justices, not just the four who most recently joined the Court. (Similarly, we must be careful not to attribute to Warren all the opinions during his tenure, although "As a judge, he represented vastly more than the sum of his opinions."[25]) Furthermore, not until early 1972 were all four Nixon appointees sitting. In the October 1969 Term, Chief Justice Burger joined seven members of the old Court. When Justice Blackmun put the Court back at full strength, he and the Chief Justice provided only two votes and with Harlan, Stewart, and White, could barely form a majority. Then the Court operated at less than full strength for much of the 1971 Term, making the 1972 Term the first in which the Burger Court was at full strength.

Two carryover justices were to be with the Court for only two terms after Chief Justice Burger took his position. John Marshall Harlan, an Eisenhower appointee and perhaps the Court's most respected opinion-writer, had a generally conservative bent, reflected in the extremely high number of dissents he cast during the height of the Warren Court. He was also the justice most openly concerned about judicial self-restraint and the operation of our system of federalism; he tried to allow the states considerable leeway to experiment with policy. However, Harlan was not without a liberal spirit, which showed in one of his last opinions, a case where someone had been arrested for "offensive" behavior for wearing a jacket saying "Fuck the Draft." While he could easily have disposed of the case on the ground that no one could define "offensive," Harlan made the most of the case's free speech aspects in reversing the conviction.[26] Showing that the application of conservative and liberal labels is at best hazardous, he asserted, "That the air may at times seem filled with verbal cacophony is . . . not a sign of weakness but of strength." When Harlan left the Court, it lost a scholar with an open mind; it was no insult to his colleagues or successors when people remarked that the quality of the Court's work was likely to be less after his departure.

Justice Hugo Black, a New Deal senator when named to the Court, was still in the late 1960s considered "the senior New Dealer in American public life."[27] Although he had once been associated with the Ku Klux Klan, Black had developed a reputation as a staunch civil libertarian, prompting the comment that "Hugo Black used to go around in white robes, scaring black people. Now he goes about in black robes, scaring white people."[28] Toward the end, however, observers began to question whether Black's position in support of civil liberties and civil rights had deteriorated with age.[29] In the 1962–1964 Terms, Black regularly voted with several other justices to form a liberal grouping or bloc, but in the last four Warren Court terms, he moved away from them toward the center of the Court. "His increasing conservatism on many civil liberties and economic questions was countered by his continuing positive support for others, thus bringing him into disagreement, on one issue or another, with everyone else."[30]

Increasingly, Black upheld restrictions states placed upon demonstrators and picketers. He also showed very little sympathy for the rights of welfare recipients. He became increasingly strident in tone, demanding in *Tinker* v. *Des Moines School District* that teachers be allowed to make school children keep their minds on their work, free of distractions like black armbands worn to protest the Vietnam dead. He wrote:

> If the time has come when pupils of state-supported schools . . . can defy and flout orders of school officials to keep their minds on their own schoolwork, it is the beginning of a new revolutionary era of permissiveness in this country fostered by the judiciary.[31]

Yet a case can be made that Black always opposed certain actions connected with speech, and that his ultimate position may have been evident early in his career.[32] Black was, in this view, no absolutist but was "searching for the requisite balance between liberty and order and [was] willing, if the circumstances are serious enough, to allow restrictions on First Amendment rights," particularly if he were writing for the Court and not merely expressing himself in dissent.[33] He was such a "strict constructionist" of the First Amendment that he would not let anything new be written into it, just as he had earlier objected to the justices' writing their views of reasonableness into the Constitution in the economic realm.[34] What produced the seeming change in his position may have been not Black so much as the type of cases coming to the Court.

Despite possible shifts in his position, Black left the Court in a blaze of First Amendment glory, writing in the *Pentagon Papers* Case:

> The press [is] to serve the governed, not the governors. . . . Only a free and unrestrained press can effectively expose deception in government. And paramount among the responsibilities of a free press is the duty to prevent any part of the government from deceiving the people and sending them off to distant lands to die of foreign fevers and foreign shot and shell. . . . Far from deserving condemnation for their courageous reporting, the New York Times, the Washington Post, and other newspapers should be commended for serving the purpose that the Founding Fathers saw so clearly. In revealing the workings of government that led to the Vietnam war, the newspapers nobly did precisely that which the Founders hoped and trusted they would do.[35]

Of five other holdovers, the three justices who were to form the Burger Court's "liberal bloc" came to the Court at widely differing times. Justice William O. Douglas, who left the Court in late 1975, now holds the Court's record for length of service; he was appointed in 1939. He is the most consistent liberal on the Court, as predictable at one end of the ideological spectrum as Justice Rehnquist is at the other. Douglas is also the Court's most frequent dissenter, both on the merits and with respect to the Court's refusal to hear cases. Off the bench, he is also a prolific writer on a wide variety of environmental and political subjects.[36] However, Douglas is not considered a skilled judicial craftsman and has been criticized for being reckless and irresponsible in tax cases, in which he was said to display less care and more emotional language in his opinions as well as increasing distrust of the government's position.[37]

William Brennan, a former member of the New Jersey Supreme Court, is a liberal, Catholic Democrat, who satisfied President Eisenhower's need for a nominee with judicial experience after he had been criticized for naming former Republican Vice-Presidential candidate Earl Warren, who had no previous judicial experience, to be Chief Justice. Consistently an adherent of the Warren Court's liberal positions, Brennan was seldom in dissent. However, as the Court's ideological position shifted during the transition, he spoke out more and more frequently along with Justices Douglas and Marshall. During the Warren Court, Brennan attempted to develop a coherent position on the standards by which allegedly obscene material should be judged, although his success in gaining a majority to support his position was not great. Because of the difficulty in defining obscenity, Brennan has now moved toward a position of deregulating it.

Thurgood Marshall came to the Court with a distinguished record. The Court's first black member had argued many race relations cases before the Court for the NAACP, including *Brown* v. *Board of Education*. He had also argued other cases for the government while Solicitor-General. Before assuming that position, he had been a member of the Court of Appeals for the Second Circuit. In his first couple of years on the Supreme Court, his performance was disappointing, partly because he withdrew from participation in many cases and did not speak out strongly in others. Now he seems to have found a niche as a dissenter rather than as a weak member of the majority and is a firm member of the "liberal bloc." He is a particularly firm spokesman for fair treatment for welfare recipients and the poor and against retreat from earlier positions on school desegregation.

The other two holdovers, at the center of the Burger Court, were Potter Stewart and Byron White. Stewart is an Eisenhower appointee from Ohio, who came to the Court in 1958. Generally moderate, he has become increasingly willing to criticize his colleagues for departures from what he considers proper procedural practices and constitutional interpretation. He also came to look more and more liberal, in part because of the Court's increasingly conservative tone, thus reminding us that a justice's ideological label is largely relative to the positions of the Court's other members.

Byron White is perhaps best known because of his "swing" position, a result of more conservative colleagues coming to the Court. During the Warren Court years, he often differed with colleagues "over timing, public acceptance and the effectiveness of the Court over time."[38] He dissented frequently, both in criminal procedure cases and on other civil liberties issues. When he joined the majority, it was often only on extremely narrow grounds. At best a moderate, White leans toward the government's position in a great many cases. "His opinions show great sympathy for the official—whether cabinet officer or patrolman—who is given a messy complicated job without the resources or the training he really needs and then is second-guessed by judges after the event."[39] Portrayed less favorably, he is said to have a "tendency to sacrifice rights when they clash with government actions" and worse, "an icy aloofness" toward those in the civil rights movement.[40] Such a justice, even if appointed originally by Kennedy, certainly fits well into the Nixon mold.

Nominations to the Supreme Court are a way of keeping the Court current with the public's policy preferences, as we have noted, and roughly three-fourths of the justices perform about as the Presidents who nominated them expected.[41] On the whole, President Nixon, even after his particularly difficult time getting his preferences onto the Court, did better than the average. However, although they occasionally ruled against President Nixon's position, sometimes on extremely crucial matters, all four of his nominees adopted positions generally ranging from moderate to conservative.

The second Nixon appointee, Justice Blackmun, is thoughtful and restrained in position and tone. Like Justice Harlan, although expressing his reluctance, he will follow even those precedents he dislikes. Blackmun often makes use of a distinction between what he would do as a legislator and what he can do as a judge, where he cannot substitute his own wisdom for the legislators'. This position was expressed most clearly in his dissent from the Court's invalidation of the death penalty. Blackmun said he "yield[ed] to no one in the depth of my distaste, antipathy, and, indeed, abhorrence, for the death penalty, with all its aspects of physical distress and fear and of moral judgment exercised by finite minds," and found that "capital punishment serves no useful purpose that can be demonstrated," and "violates childhood's training and life's experiences." As a legislator, he said, he would sponsor legislation and vote to repeal the penalty and might, as a governor, use the pardon power. But, he said, "There—on the Legislative Branch of the State or Federal Government, and secondarily, on the Executive Branch—is where the authority and responsibility for this kind of action lies,"[42] not on the federal judiciary. Despite the clarity of this stance, Blackmun did not use it in the abortion cases, where he wrote for the majority in invalidating anti-abortion laws. Off the bench, freed somewhat of his institutional responsibilities, Blackmun has spoken out on Watergate, calling for removal of the "taint and corruption in our public life" and citing the "misplaced loyalties, . . . strange measures of the unethical, . . . unusual doings in high places, and by lawyer after lawyer after lawyer," as a result of which "The very glue of our ship of state seems about to become unstuck."[43]

Justice Powell is also like Harlan in his views of states' rights and judicial self-restraint. Quiet and reserved, he thinks the Court overworked. He has made a strong plea for applying the same standard to both North and South in school segregation cases. Although presumed to be conservative, he is in some ways an old-fashioned liberal, concerned about invasions by the government of citizens' rights. While president of the American Bar Association in 1965, he called the Warren Court's criminal procedure decisions "significant milestones" in protecting the individual from "arbitrary or oppressive government."[44] On the Court, while conceding the necessity of electronic surveillance, which he called an unwelcome development, Powell has stressed the need for free public and private discussion, saying, "The price of lawful public dissent must not be a dread of subjection to an unchecked surveillance power." Powell also unhesitatingly defended the Court when it was challenged by the President. He quickly turned aside the administration's argument that "internal security matters are too subtle and complex for judicial evaluation" with the response that federal judges can comprehend and be sensitive to domestic security issues, adding, "If the threat is too subtle or complex for our senior law enforcement officers to convey its significance to a court, one may question whether there is probable cause for surveillance."[45]

William Rehnquist became the most controversial of the four Nixon appointees because he is so strongly and trenchantly conservative, and because he refused to withdraw from participating in several close cases involving policies he helped develop as a member of the administration. The hope that he might change his views once he became a judge did not last long. In the criminal procedure area, his conservative views are particularly strong, and the general tone of his opinions quickly became evident in a prisoners' rights case: "None of our holdings under the First Amendment requires that, in addition to being allowed freedom of religious belief, prisoners be allowed freely to evangelize their views among other prisoners."[46] Taking a "strict construction" or "restrained" view, he presumes the validity of state legislative acts; he also feels that constitutional decisions should be more open to re-examination than should precedents that involve only statutory interpretation, because the latter can be corrected more easily by the legislature.[47]

Chief Justice Warren Burger is strongly task-oriented and businesslike. On reaching the Supreme Court, he did not delay before assuming a position toward the right side of the Court, thus contradicting claims that a justice is likely to take a middle position at first, moving to a "polar" position only after several terms.[48] In the criminal law area, where his own jurisprudential ideas were most developed, Burger took a position favorable to the government in 70 percent of the cases available in his first term, a rate which climbed the next term to 81.6 percent, the highest figure for the period extending all the way back to 1937.[49] (By comparison, Warren voted for the government 19 percent of the time in criminal law cases over sixteen years.)

Burger's statements reflect adherence to conventional values, a dislike of indecent language—one can imagine he was appalled by the "expletives deleted" in the presidential tape transcripts—and a lack of sensitivity to those of unconventional values and lifestyles. Thus in the Amish school attendance case, Burger stressed the fine law-abiding record of the Amish and made offhand remarks about those who have discovered new and "progressive" ways of bringing up children. In cases involving the rights of aliens to public employment or to practice law, the tone is one of nativism, stressing the virtues of those who have become naturalized citizens and objecting to others who choose not to do so.[50]

More important is the Chief Justice's far-from-restrained attitude toward precedent, which he values less than his own strict interpretation of the Constitution. Rejecting the idea "that what the Court said lately controls over the Constitution," he has said, "I do not acquiesce in prior holdings that purportedly, but nonetheless erroneously, are based on the Constitution."[51] This position supports earlier findings that Supreme Court justices with prior judicial experience are more likely to depart from precedent than those who did not have prior experience and that "a greater percentage of judges with lower judicial experience voted contrary to their value position than did judges with high judicial experience."[52] Burger also appears quite willing to engage in loose rather than strict construction when it suits his purposes. For example, on the question of whether the mail fraud statute could be used to reach fraudulent use of stolen credit cards, he argued in dissent that the law should be used to deal with new frauds as a "stop-gap device . . . until particularized legislation can be developed and passed to deal directly with the evil."[53]

In his role as Chief Justice, Burger has devoted much energy to reforming court administration in both state and federal courts and has also worked hard to reduce the flow of litigation to the Supreme Court. He has spent more time on such matters than any Chief Justice since William Howard Taft. So extensive has been his commitment to administrative efforts that he has asked for an administrative deputy, and has said the United States needs to have a lord chancellor to handle court administrative tasks.[54] Unlike Warren, who needed a few terms to grasp the full dimensions of his job, Burger did not wait before beginning his administrative emphasis, but then he was already familiar with the role of a federal appellate judge.

Burger has used several devices, including delivery of an annual State of the Judiciary address at American Bar Association meetings, numerous other appearances, and magazine articles,[55] in stressing the importance of court administration. He has given strong support to the Federal Judicial Center (the research and development arm of the Administrative Office of the Courts); helped substantially in establishing the National Center for the State Courts; supported the idea of a National Institute of Justice to disburse public and private funds to upgrade both federal and state courts; encouraged the establishment of federal-state judicial councils; worked closely with the Institute for Court Management, which trains court administrators; and pushed successfully for a new position of court executive for each of the Courts of Appeals.

The new Chief Justice's attention to administrative matters fits in with his conception of the Court, which he feels should "take a less active role than it did during the Warren years, assume a low profile, and keep hands off more decisions of other branches of Government."[56] Thus as a lower court judge, Burger ruled that courts should not decide Representative Adam Clayton Powell's claim that Congress had acted improperly in refusing to seat him, because Congress was to judge the qualifications of its own members, while Chief Justice Warren wrote the opinion reversing Burger and deciding the claim.

Burger may wish the Court to keep a low profile. He may wish results that will reduce the Court's profile and be more acceptable to the public. However, his own early harsh dissents, quite unlike Chief Justice Warren's more diffident early approach to cases, may interfere with that result. They also suggest a conflict between the Chief Justice's policy goals and the Court's institutional goals, better met when the Court is unanimous or nearly so. Burger, while succeeding in massing a cohesive bloc, has devoted less attention to massing the entire Court than did Chief Justice Warren.

The Supreme Court tends to have a social leader, who helps keep the Court socially cohesive, and a task (or intellectual) leader, who concentrates on the Court's opinions. The Chief Justice may fulfill one of these roles, both of them, or neither. For example, Chief Justice Taft appears to have been a social leader while Justice Vandevanter was the task leader; Chief Justice Hughes performed both roles, thus decreasing conflict and increasing the Court's production; on the other hand, Chief Justice Stone performed neither role and the level of conflict on the Court rose substantially.[57] Chief Justice Burger's general posture as Chief Justice and the flow of his interests into administrative matters seem to suggest that he is performing neither role for the Court as a whole, although he may be performing both for the Nixon appointees. Who is performing those roles for the Court in Burger's place is not clear.

CONCLUSION

The mid-1970s find a Supreme Court of widely diverse membership, with a new Chief Justice who gives considerably greater emphasis to the administrative side of his job than had his immediate predecessor and indeed more than his predecessors for several decades. Three of the new justices were in their late fifties or early sixties, and the three carryover members of the Warren Court were still older. Of the two remaining Roosevelt appointees, Justice Black served into mid-transition and Justice Douglas remains on the bench, while appointees of Eisenhower, Kennedy, and Johnson also remain.

Lyndon Johnson, who ultimately chose not to run for renomination, tried to leave a lasting image through the Court in his effort to have Abe Fortas, his nominee to the Court, become

Chief Justice. Growing reaction to the Court's liberal decisions, the Republicans' desire to choose their own Chief Justice, and Fortas' missteps gave Richard Nixon the opportunity to change the Court's membership substantially in a very short period. Despite his difficulties in getting his nominees confirmed, four now sit on the Supreme Court. Whether that four-judge core he placed on the Court will get new additions of comparable ideology or whether there will be a Democratic President to create a new transition is something we cannot yet know.

NOTES

1. See Robert Scigliano, *The Supreme Court and the Presidency* (New York: Free Press, 1972), particularly pp. 85–160; and Henry Abraham, *Justices and Presidents: A Political History of Appointments to the Supreme Court* (New York: Oxford University Press, 1974).

2. Glendon Schubert, *The Constitutional Polity* (Boston: Boston University Press, 1970), p. 137.

3. It has been observed that liberals' complaints should be directed not at President Nixon's appointments but at Kennedy for picking a crony instead of a Harvard law professor.

4. James Simon, *In His Own Image: The Supreme Court in Richard Nixon's America* (New York: David McKay, 1973), p. 8.

5. Quoted at ibid., p. 227.

6. Quoted at ibid., p. 7. See also Robert Shogan, *A Question of Judgment: The Fortas Case and the Struggle for the Supreme Court* (Indianapolis: Bobbs-Merrill, 1972), p. 9. What was a "technicality" to Nixon was, of course, a matter of important individual constitutional rights to others.

7. Kohlmeier suggests, however, that Burger had conversations with the President and then Attorney-General Mitchell on important issues if not specific cases. Louis Kohlmeier, *This Honorable Court* (New York: Charles Scribner's Sons, 1972), p. 259.

8. Schubert, pp. 116–117.

9. That Johnson had to be mightily persuasive to get Goldberg to leave the Court is clear from the latter's statement: "I shall not, Mr. President, conceal the pain with which I leave the Court after three years of service. It has been the richest and most satisfying period of my career." Shogan, p. 108. Johnson also had to overcome Fortas' resistance to being named. "Now he had given Fortas his marching orders and he expected Fortas, like Arthur Goldberg, to be a good soldier and obey." Ibid., p. 112. For LBJ's reasons for selecting Fortas, see ibid., p. 109.

10. Marshall was confirmed by a vote of 69–11.

11. Harlan, 71–11; Stewart, 70–17.

12. Shogan, p. 228.

13. The following material draws on Joel B. Grossman and Stephen L. Wasby, "The Senate and Supreme Court Nominations: Some Reflections," *Duke Law Journal*, 1972 (Summer), 557–591.

14. We earlier indicated that an investigation of Judge Haynsworth had been undertaken "at the behest of Attorney-General Robert Kennedy by Chief Judge Sobeloff. . . ." Grossman and Wasby, 577. Judge Haynsworth has graciously

28   CONTINUITY AND CHANGE

pointed out our error. The investigation was undertaken by Judge Sobeloff after he and Judge Haynsworth, discussing allegations that had been made, "came to the joint conclusion" that such an investigation should be undertaken. After it was completed, the investigative file was sent to Attorney-General Kennedy, who acknowledged receipt and indicated he "share[d] your expression of complete confidence in Judge Haynsworth." Kennedy to Sobeloff, February 28, 1964. Judge Haynsworth to Joel Grossman and Stephen Wasby, October 31, 1972.

15.   "While most senators who voted against Judge Haynsworth publicly attributed their opposition to the conflict of interest issue, it is reasonable to speculate . . . that the issue provided a convenient justification for opposition generated in fact by ideological or political considerations. . . . A recent study of the roll-call votes on the Haynsworth and Carswell nominations. . . suggests that the liberal-conservative orientation, not party or region of the voting senators, was the important determinant of voting behavior." Grossman and Wasby, 577.

16.   For examination of the many parallels between the two rejections, see Grossman and Wasby, "Haynsworth and Parker: History Does Live Again," *South Carolina Law Review*, 23 (1971), 345–359. Judge Haynsworth's service on the Fourth Circuit began while Parker was still Chief Judge. Parker arranged to have the circuit judicial conference program committee, which he had asked Haynsworth to chair, meet in Washington so Haynsworth could meet members of the Judicial Conference of the United States, and Haynsworth was with Parker in Washington then when Parker died. That Judge Parker continued his work as a judge for many years after the rejection of his nomination also served as an example to Haynsworth. Clement F. Haynsworth, Jr., to Stephen L. Wasby, November 29, 1972.

17.   In his unsuccessful campaign for U.S. Senator after his resignation from the Court of Appeals, Carswell seemed to prove beyond all doubt what his critics had charged.

18.   Joseph Rauh said that Carswell was "Judge Haynsworth with a cutting edge . . . with a bitterness and a meanness that Judge Haynsworth never had." 116 *Congressional Record* 2415 (1970).

19.   See the summary at Grossman and Wasby, "The Senate and Supreme Court Nominations," 571, note, and sources cited there.

20.   For discussion of the nominations in terms of the President's style of operation, see James David Barber, *Presidential Character* (Englewood Cliffs, N.J.: Prentice-Hall, 1972), pp. 426–429.

21.   Richard M. Nixon to William Saxbe, March 31, 1970, at 116 *Congressional Record* 10158 (1970).

22.   Raoul Berger, *Impeachment* (Cambridge, Mass.: Harvard University Press, 1972), p. 53.

23.   But see the tape references to "Renchburg" as a "clown." "Transcript Reveals View on Rehnquist," *Portland Oregonian*, July 19, 1973, p. 11.

24.   He was also attacked for a memo he had written, while law clerk to Justice Robert Jackson, supporting the "separate but equal" doctrine of *Plessy* v. *Ferguson* at the time *Brown* v. *Board of Education* was being considered. However, this probably reflected Jackson's position at the time. Grossman and Wasby, "The Senate and Supreme Court Nominations," 576.

25.   Simon, p. 69.

26.   *Cohen* v. *California*, 403 U.S. 15 (1971).

27.   John Frank, "Justice Black and the New Deal," *Arizona Law Review*, 9 (Summer 1967), 27.

28.   Quoted at Fred Graham, *The Self-Inflicted Wound* (New York: Macmillan, 1970), p. 49.

29. Schubert, pp. 124 ff., examines aging and senescence as explanations for Black's behavior. See also S. Sidney Ulmer, "Parabolic Support for Civil Liberties," *Florida State University Law Review*, 1 (Winter 1973), 131–153.

30. Schubert, p. 125.

31. 393 U.S. 503 at 518 (1969). Compare Fortas' statement in the same case:

In our system, undifferentiated fear or apprehension of disturbance is not enough to overcome the right to freedom of expression. Any departure from absolute regimentation may cause trouble. Any variation from the majority's opinion may inspire fear. Any word spoken, in class, in the lunchroom, or on the campus, that deviates from the views of another person may start an argument or cause a disturbance. But our Constitution says we must take this risk.

32. In one of the early Jehovah's Witnesses doorbell-ringing cases, Black, while subsequently reversing himself, had initially circulated a memo that the community could forbid doorbell-ringing altogether to protect its privacy. See J. Woodford Howard, Jr., "The Fluidity of Judicial Choice," *American Political Science Review*, 62 (March 1968), 48. The case is *Martin* v. *Struthers*, 319 U.S. 141 (1943).

33. Solomon Resnik, "Black, Douglas, and Absolutes: Some Suggestions for a New Perspective on the Supreme Court," *Journal of Urban Law*, 47 (1970), 794. Resnik takes essentially the same position as to Douglas.

34. "He could not abide doctrines that allow judges to impose their own predilections upon a reluctant community. Thus no one surpassed his early efforts to destroy substantive due process and substantive equal protection. At the same time he led the movement to incorporate the Bill of Rights into the Fourteenth Amendment. Obviously these were complementary efforts directed at the same target: judicial free wheeling." Wallace Mendelson, "From Warren to Burger: The Rise and Decline of Substantive Equal Protection," *American Political Science Review*, 66 (December 1972), 1232.

35. *New York Times Co.* v. *U.S.*, 403 U.S. 713 at 717 (1971).

36. William O. Douglas, *Points of Rebellion* (New York: Random House, 1970) and *The Three Hundred Year War: A Chronicle of Ecological Disaster* (New York: Random House, 1972).

37. Bernard Wolfman et al., "The Behavior of Justice Douglas in Federal Tax Cases," *University of Pennsylvania Law Review*, 122 (1973), 235–365.

38. Lance Liebman, "Swing Man on the Supreme Court," *New York Times Magazine*, October 8, 1972, p. 97. Liebman was once White's clerk. While White is a former football All-American, no one challenges his brilliance. A Rhodes Scholar, he certainly didn't play without a helmet.

39. Ibid., p. 95.

40. Robert Zelnick, "Whizzer White and the Fearsome Foursome," *Washington Monthly*, December 1972, p. 50.

41. Scigliano, p. 146.

42. *Furman* v. *Georgia*, 408 U.S. 238 (1974). Compare Frankfurter's "but as judges we are neither Jew nor Gentile, neither Catholic nor agnostic." Dissenting, *West Virginia Board of Education* v. *Barnette*, 319 U.S. 624 at 647 (1943).

43. "Justice Deplores 'Watergate Pall,'" *Milwaukee Journal*, August 6, 1973.

44. Lewis Powell, "An Urgent Need: More Effective Criminal Justice," *American Bar Association Journal*, 51 (1965), 439.

45. *U.S.* v. *U.S. District Court*, 407 U.S. 297 at 314, 320 (1972).

46. *Cruz* v. *Beto*, 405 U.S. 319 at 324 (1972). Blackmun and Burger both concurred with the Court.

30   CONTINUITY AND CHANGE

47. See his dissent in *Weber* v. *Aetna Casualty & Surety Co.*, 406 U.S. 164 at 177 (1972), on the rights of illegitimate children.

48. Eloise Snyder, "The Supreme Court as a Small Group," *Social Forces*, 36 (March 1958), 232–238. Justices may also move toward the center over time, however, as true of Justice Black.

49. Ulmer, "Supreme Court Justices as Strict and Not-so-Strict Constructionists: Some Implications," *Law & Society Review*, 8 (Fall 1973), 13–14.

50. See his dissent in *In Re Griffiths*, 413 U.S. 717 at 730 (1973); similar views are evident in Justice Rehnquist's dissent covering *Griffiths* and *Sugarman* v. *Dougall*, 413 U.S. 634 at 649 (1973).

51. *Coleman* v. *Alabama*, 399 U.S. 1 at 22 (1970).

52. Respectively, John Schmidhauser, "*Stare Decisis*, Dissent, and the Background of the Justices of the Supreme Court of the United States," *University of Toronto Law Journal,* May 1962, 194–212; Stuart S. Nagel, "Off-the-Bench Judicial Attitudes," in Glendon Schubert, ed., *Judicial Decision-Making* (New York: Free Press, 1963), p. 41.

53. *U.S.* v. *Maze,* 414 U.S. 395 at 405–406 (1974).

54. For a critical view utilizing this theme, see Arthur S. Miller, "Lord Chancellor Warren Earl Burger," *Society*, 10 (3, March–April 1973), 18–27. For a more helpful and thoughtful discussion, see Arthur R. Landever, "Chief Justice Burger and Extra-Case Activism," *Journal of Public Law*, 20 (1971), 523–541. See also William F. Swindler, "The Chief Justice and Law Reform, 1921–1971," in Philip B. Kurland, ed., *The Supreme Court Review 1971* (Chicago: University of Chicago Press, 1971), pp. 241–264.

55. See Warren Burger, "The Chief Justice Talks about the Court," *Reader's Digest,* 102, (610, February 1973), 95 ff. See also Burger's statements, "The State of the Federal Judiciary—1972," *American Bar Association Journal,* 58 (October 1972), 1049–1053, and "Report on the Federal Judicial Branch—1973," *American Bar Association Journal*, 59 (October 1973), 1125–1130.

56. "Toward a Burger Court," *Time*, 95 (April 13, 1970), 50.

57. David Danelski, "The Influence of the Chief Justice in the Decisional Process of the Supreme Court," in Walter Murphy and C. Herman Pritchett, eds., *Courts, Judges, and Politics* (New York: Random House, 1961), pp. 498–500. Blocs may also have such leaders; perhaps that is the present situation.

CHAPTER TWO

Access to the Court:
Implicit and Explicit Policy

More and more cases come to the Supreme Court each year. The number of cases in which the justices write opinions has increased only slightly. This means that the justices must do more sorting before they can concentrate on those cases where they explicitly develop policy. Before we turn to them, we need to look at the overall size and content of the Court's docket and the Court's acceptance and rejection of cases.

DOCKET VOLUME

In 1935, fewer than 1,000 cases were filed in the Supreme Court, and fifteen years later the Court still had fewer than 1,500 cases on its docket. Filings increased only gradually in the 1950s, but after 1960 the annual growth became substantial so that by 1971 filings had reached 3,600. In 1972 over 4,500 cases were filed, and the figure continued to grow, climbing to over 5,000. This meant that the justices had to consider over 1,000 cases during their conferences in the 1974 Term's first week alone. Despite this increase, the Court's basic work calendar—from October through mid-June, with Christmas, Easter, and opinion-writing recesses—has remained roughly the same. However, the Burger Court terms have been somewhat more extended. In 1971, the *Pentagon Papers* Case, which did not arise until June, was the cause; in 1972, the Court adjourned on June 29, the latest ever, only to reconvene on July 7 for a Special Session to hear the Democratic National Convention delegate challenges. In 1974, the Court remained in session without a break until late July to hear argument early in the month in the Nixon tapes case, on which the Court ruled on July 24, followed the next day by the Detroit busing case.

The number of cases argued in recent years has varied from roughly 140 to 180; for each of the 1971–1973 Terms, over 175 cases were argued. However, time devoted to oral argument dropped from 103 hours in the 1970 Term to 73.5 hours in the 1972 Term, less than half of the time so devoted less than ten years before.[1] This decrease was a result of allowing only 30 minutes of oral argument per side instead of one hour. The Court also decided more cases *without* oral argument, although it usually gave them shorter written treatment than the others.

As input increased, so did the Court's output: from almost 2,700 cases disposed of in the 1965 Term, the number climbed unevenly to over 3,100 in the last year of the Warren Court. During Chief Justice Burger's first year, over 3,400 cases were decided, and the number continued to increase with each successive term. The number of cases handed down with signed opinions, that is, identifying the justice writing them, remained at roughly 100 per term through the early part of the transition, in addition to 15–20 *per curiam* (unsigned) decisions announcing substantive law. After a drop to 88 signed cases in the 1969 Term, Chief Justice Burger's first, perhaps a result of a missing ninth justice, the number climbed to over 125 and did not fall even when the Court was short two justices for the first part of the 1971 Term.[2] For the 1972 and 1973 Terms, the figure was 140. The number of summary rulings also increased substantially with the Burger Court.[3]

Because the output did not increase as rapidly as the input, there was an increase in the carryover from one term to the next. Because with few exceptions the Court decides within a term all cases argued within that period, this carryover is primarily of undecided petitions for review. The number of cases remaining on the docket actually decreased from 1965 to 1966, but rose to over 600 at the end of the 1967 Term and at the end of the Warren Court stood at 767. After Burger's second year, the figure jumped again, to almost 900, where it has stayed. There were also some cases carried over from one term to the next for reargument, but these were largely a result of the absence of personnel, reinforced by the controversial nature of the cases.[4]

The overall result was an increase in the size of the Court's docket from just under 3,300 cases (1965 Term), to over 3,900 in the 1968 Term, to 4,200 cases in the first year of the Burger Court. Thus by the beginning of the 1972 Term, the Court had a total docket seven to eight times the size of its docket in 1925, the year the Judges Bill gave the Court discretionary jurisdiction in most appellate cases.

SCREENING OF CASES

The Supreme Court's grant of review can come in several ways, the most important being certiorari or appeal. Through them, the Court has substantial control over its docket. The writ of certiorari is an order to a lower court to send up the records in a case, and is granted by a vote of four justices. The power to grant or deny it is fully discretionary—that is, the Court can grant or deny as it sees fit, without giving reasons. On the other hand, the Court is supposed to take all cases in the appeals category, that is, its appeals jurisdiction is technically obligatory. However, the Court has also made review of appeals cases discretionary by dismissing those which lack a "substantial federal question." About half of the cases falling in the appeals category are accepted and account for a large proportion of the cases decided, but only one-twentieth of those in the much larger certiorari jurisdiction are accepted.

The Court must screen cases because it could not possibly consider fully all of the cases people bring to it. This leads the Court to refuse to exercise even its original jurisdiction. For example, when states have brought environmental cases directly to the Supreme Court rather than going through the lower courts, the justices generally turned the cases away. When Ohio tried to bring before the Court its complaint against several companies for mercury pollution of Lake Erie, the justices said that not only were several national and international bodies already looking into the problem, but Ohio courts could deal with it in terms of local law.[5] Justice Harlan's opinion was a full-blown argument for judicial self-restraint:

> Changes in the American legal system and the development of American society have rendered untenable, as a practical matter, the view that this Court must stand willing to adjudicate all or most legal disputes that may arise between one State and a citizen or citizens of another, even though the dispute may be one over which this Court does have original jurisdiction.

The Court took the same stance in two other rulings, with Justice Douglas writing for the Court despite his frequent arguments against the Supreme Court's not exercising its responsibilities. The Court, saying it wanted to avoid impeding disposal of cases on its docket, refused to accept the antitrust and conspiracy case that several states brought against automobile manufacturers for not developing pollution control equipment; other federal courts were available to hear the case.[6] In Illinois' suit against Milwaukee for polluting Lake Michigan, the Court also pointed out that water pollution issues could be tried on nuisance law in the lower federal courts.[7]

Policy Implications of Screening

The Court's almost complete control of its docket has policy implications. While our basic interest is in explicit policy, implicit policy deriving from the Court's screening of cases is also important. Put another way, while the discretion to grant and deny review is *intended* as a screening device to let the Court concentrate its efforts, it also allows the Court to avoid issues and serves a latent policy-making function. As such it is closely related to explicit policies—on standards litigants must meet to get into court, the exhaustion of remedies requirements for prisoners seeking federal habeas corpus, and its restrictions on the use of three-judge federal courts in challenging state laws—that also serve to deflect cases and allow avoidance of issues. And the effects on litigants and policy development are clear and have been recognized. As Chief Justice Warren stated after leaving the Court,

> Denials [of certiorari] can and do have a significant impact on the ordering of constitutional and legal priorities. Many potential and important developments in the law have been frustrated, at least temporarily, by a denial of certiorari.[8]

In recent years, the percentage of cases in which the Court grants review has been decreasing, dropping steadily each decade with the increase in the Court's docket, from 17.5 percent in 1941 to 11.1 percent in 1951, 7.4 percent at mid–Warren Court (1961), and 5.8 percent in 1971. Of the cases that come to the Court with relatively complete records and briefs, higher percentages are accepted, while as few as *1 percent* of petitions written by prisoners may be accepted. Granting of certiorari petitions in the more fully prepared cases dropped slowly from 13.9 percent (1963) to 11.2 percent (1966). After a rise to 14.4 percent, the figure fell to below 10 percent in the Warren Court's last year. For the first two Burger Court years, it was down to 7.8 percent, where it stayed.[9]

The official judicial interpretation is that denial of review means only that the Court has not decided cases. The lower court ruling is left standing and no inference is to be drawn other than that the Court did not hear the case. Citing Frankfurter, Justice Douglas recently remarked, "Our denial of certiorari imparts no implication or inference concerning the Court's view of the merits. . . . "[10] However, the meaning of the Court's denial of review has been a matter of controversy ever since the Court was given the authority to utilize the discretionary writ of certiorari, and the controversy even broke into the open during the 1972 Term. When Justice Blackmun speculated that dissents from an earlier certiorari denial were "not without *some significance as to* [the justices'] and *the Court's attitude* . . . ,"[11] Justice Marshall strongly disagreed. He said justices may simultaneously agree about an issue's importance and feel the case was not appropriate for deciding the issue, and attacked speculation about reasons why certiorari is denied. However, even if the Court does not want its certiorari denials to be interpreted as meaning the Court has dealt conclusively—or at all—with the issues presented, observers will continue to make inferences to the contrary. As Adamany has noted, "When the Court consistently leaves undisturbed decisions at variance with principle, or when it denies certiorari in a notorious case, . . . the public may well believe that the Court is implementing an unspoken constitutional judgment."[12]

Certainly the issues not decided *are not* insignificant. Examples from the 1973 Term are a claimed underrepresentation on a jury of blacks, women, and those twenty-eight to thirty years old; a libel judgment based on a claim that an election poll was corrupt, dishonest, and rigged; discharge of a teacher whose views that compulsory school attendance was improper was stated *not* in the classroom but at home; a judge's refusal to allow a heroin seller the advantages of the Narcotics Addict Rehabilitation Act; claimed double jeopardy from continuation of a criminal trial after a not-guilty-by-virtue-of-insanity verdict and a commitment; and the suspension from school of Pawnee Indian males, hair parted in the middle with a long braid on each side, for violation of "long hair" rules.[13]

Drawing of inferences about denial of review is further stimulated by continued citation of certiorari denials by lawyers and the justices themselves to support their positions and by the Court's failure to tell us why it refuses review. The infrequent reasons given for denying certiorari are almost never substantive,[14] and the reason for denial of appeals is usually an opaque "lack of a substantial federal question."

We also find many of the dissents coming from justices who have the same ideological positions, for example, the liberals Douglas, Marshall, and Brennan. This further reinforces the idea that denials of review are implicit policy decisions. Along these lines Ulmer suggests that while a liberal justice will rule for the criminal defendant in fully reviewed cases and the conservative justice would vote for the government, the former will also vote to grant review where the government has won in the lower courts and the latter will vote not to grant certiorari where the government has already won.[15]

If we turn from reasons for denying review to reasons for granting certiorari, policy implications seem even clearer. The Court's own Rule 19 indicates that the Court will consider the importance of the case, conflicts in interpretation between circuits, interpretation of an important federal law question counter to past Supreme Court rulings, and departure by a federal court from "accepted canons of judicial proceedings." Individual justices have stated that the Court does not grant review merely to correct lower court errors, but wants cases of broad importance. Thus Justice Harlan has argued that

> the certiorari jurisdiction was not conferred upon this Court "merely to give the defeated party in the . . . Court of Appeals another hearing," . . . or "for the benefit of the particular litigants," . . . but to decide issues, "the settlement of which is of importance to the public as distinguished from . . . the parties."[16]

Rule 19 and the justices' comments, while suggesting a high degree of judicial discretion in the granting or denying of review, stress *legal* considerations. An alternative explanation, drawn from studying the Court's patterns in dealing with cases to which they do grant review, emphasizes *policy* considerations in the Court's exercise of discretion. Howard puts it forcefully: "The Justices supported whoever agreed with them in whatever interested them in appeals before them. . . . The high court appears to have given priority to its law-making . . . functions."[17]

Certainly the Court's "informed discretion" or "informed arbitrariness"[18] are key factors in its choice of cases to accept. In Chief Justice Warren's words, "The standards by which the justices decide to grant or deny review are highly personalized and necessarily discretionary. Those standards cannot be captured in any rule or guideline that would be meaningful."[19] When the Court does decide cases, it seldom tells us much about why it has taken them. Reasons for granting certiorari were given in about two-thirds of the full opinion cases in the 1956–1958 Terms, but in 20 percent of the cases the reason was only "to decide the issue presented." In the remaining 46.7 percent of the cases, the only often-mentioned reasons were a conflict between the circuits, the importance of the issue (mentioned more frequently), or both, but *why* the case was important was not indicated.[20]

Certain cues may, however, help explain granting or nongranting of certiorari. The source of the case might be one. However, Schubert found little difference in the Court's treatment of state and federal certiorari petitions, although the latter were somewhat more likely to be granted. Federal appeals, however, were given much better treatment than state appeals: only about 10–15 percent of the former were dismissed.[21] In cases from 1947–1958, in the absence of other cues, when the federal government favored review, certiorari was granted at a rate of 47.1 percent; when all other parties sought review, the rate was only 5.8 percent, the same rate as when no cue was available. Certiorari was granted in 12.8 percent of cases where the sole cues were dissension between lower courts or between judges in a single lower court. Presence of a civil liberties issue, including race, but no other cue, was significant, but presence of only an economic issue had little effect.[22] (Note that, even with certain cues present, far from all cases with that cue are given review.)

Reanalysis of the data confirms the decisive nature of the federal government's favoring review, but suggests little cue effect from civil liberties issues.[23] One set of scholars found that the Court "primarily heard cases in which the district and circuit courts agreed . . . [and] hears many more unanimous appeals than split ones. . . . " Another observer found, however, that "The Justices were inclined to hear reversed decisions more than affirmed decisions, non-unanimous decisions more than unanimous decisions, and en banc decisions more than panel decisions" from the Courts of Appeals,[24] with disagreement *within* a Court of Appeals providing a stronger signal to the Supreme Court than did disagreement *between* levels. Regardless of the findings, it is clear that "The Supreme Court . . . is not primarily guided by lower court agreement—either intercourt or intracourt—in deciding the cases it will hear or reverse."[25]

In addition to this data, we find that when the court accepts a case on certiorari, it is quite likely to reverse the lower court, particularly true for its summary dispositions. Among the cases in the appeals category, state court cases were more likely to be reversed than were federal court cases. Appeals cases from the federal courts were particularly likely to be reversed when the Supreme Court decided them with formal opinions, so that the Supreme Court, which has supervisory power over the federal courts, could explain the law to the lower federal courts. The patterns of affirmances and reversals are, according to Schubert, "too definite to have arisen by sheer happenstance," and he concluded that the Court is implicitly even if not formally deciding them on the merits.[26] More recently, Howard has confirmed that certiorari is granted primarily so lower court decisions can be reversed. This is done whether the federal district courts and Courts of Appeals agree or disagree, and is done so the Supreme Court can state its own values and develop its own policy.[27]

Overload (?) Screening Remedies

The new justices, particularly the Chief Justice, and many observers are concerned that the Court is overloaded with work. Some efforts to deal with the problem have already been initiated. For example, to help with screening petitions for review before a decision is made to accept or reject them, Justice Powell and four other justices share their law clerks. Hiring experienced permanent staff lawyers in place of some of the younger law clerks, who stay for only a year, has also been initiated. Justice Rehnquist says the issue is the need for adequate time "for careful deliberation and reasoned decision of the very important types of cases which are the staple of [the Court's] business today."[28] Because the Court is current in its docket with respect to argued cases, these claims have been challenged. Chief Justice Warren and Justices Stewart and Douglas have said the Court is capable of doing its work. Douglas thinks the Court "if anything, underworked, not overworked,"[29] and he and Stewart have needled their colleagues for taking certain cases. As they said about one case:

> The only remarkable thing about this case is its presence in this Court. For the case involves no more than the application of well-settled principle to a familiar situation, and has little significance except for the respondent. Why certiorari was granted is a mystery to me—particularly at a time when the Court is thought by many to be burdened by too heavy a caseload.[30]

The Chief Justice has made several proposals to deal with the Court's docket, for example, suggesting that prospective appellants get approval to appeal. He has also recommended that all new federal statutes carry a "court impact statement" indicating how many more judges and related staff would be required to handle litigation produced under the statute.[31] This idea caused the Chief Justice some trouble in late 1972. After Rowland Kirks, Executive Director of the Administrative Office of the Courts, visited House Speaker Carl Albert in the company of an interest group lobbyist, Burger was accused of sending a lobbyist to Congress to argue against pending product safety legislation. Denying the charge, Burger said his only concern was in terms of the bill's effect on the court system.[32]

A more far-reaching proposal fits closely with the Court's 1971 rulings limiting the use of three-judge district courts for injunctions against pending state criminal prosecutions. Three-judge courts are now required for injunctions against state statutes; appeals from their decisions come directly to the high court.

Those courts would be eliminated, forcing cases to come to the Supreme Court only through the Courts of Appeals. The impact for the Supreme Court would be substantial, because in the 1972 Term, the Court heard 37 cases from three-judge courts, almost a third of the cases it heard. The Court also wanted to eliminate direct appeals in antitrust cases, and in a recent decision openly suggested to Congress that the jurisdiction be taken away and elaborated the reasons against its retention;[33] in 1974, Congress took such action, and eliminated as well direct appeals of Interstate Commerce Commission orders.

Perhaps the most far-reaching suggestion for change—a National Court of Appeals that would screen cases going to the Supreme Court—came from a Study Group the Chief Justice appointed.[34] The judges of this "mini–Supreme Court" were to be chosen for fixed terms from the present Courts of Appeals. They would sort through the cases people wanted the Supreme Court to hear, selecting 400 or so most worthy of the highest court's attention. The Supreme Court would still have selected 120–150 of those cases for full consideration. The National Court of Appeals' denial of review would have been final, as would its determinations on conflicts between the Courts of Appeals.

Critics have stressed that, while offered as an administrative reform, the proposal was really far more and had considerable potential policy implications.[35] In exercising final determination as to whether a case will be *heard*, the new court would have had the final power to determine what *policy* ruling remained in effect. Such a proposal would thus have diminished not only the Supreme Court's workload but also its authority. The Supreme Court's ability to pick a *particular* case on an issue and "the more subtle power to decide when, how, and under what circumstances an issue should or should not be accepted for review," to determine "the kind, nature, and timing . . . of issues,"[36] would be vitally affected. Judges of the new court, without a Supreme Court justice's feel for a case's "certworthiness,"[37] might emphasize different areas and could potentially have screened out entire policy areas. Because, as Justice Douglas has stated, "Selection of cases across the broad spectrum of issues presented is the very heart of the judicial process,"[38] such proposals must be watched carefully. So should others, for example, one for a special division drawn from the present Courts of Appeals to deal with cases where uniformity would appear useful, with review available in the Supreme Court,[39] or the more recent one for a National Court to take cases sent from the Supreme Court or the Courts of Appeals, with review in the Supreme Court. These are not as far-reaching as the Study Group's original proposal and the latter proposal does not make great inroads on the Court's policy discretion, but their policy implications should not be ignored.

ACCESS TO THE COURTS

In addition to the discretionary screening of cases presented to the Supreme Court, the justices also have other ways in which they control the flow of cases. One form of this gatekeeping involves the adoption of substantive doctrinal rules that indicate that consideration of policy in a particular area is closed so that it would not be worth bringing cases. Such areas would now include state economic regulation and welfare benefit levels and allocations. Another way of closing off cases is through the development of doctrinal rules concerning what is necessary before disputes may be heard by the federal courts. The Supreme Court can't tell state courts what cases to hear, but it is not always bound to accept the state courts' determinations that cases should be heard. Because the rules the justices develop (what we might call the "doctrine of procedure") help determine the ways in which courts can be used to solve social problems, they have important policy implications in addition to being indications of the justices' judicial and perhaps political ideology. Of particular importance are cases dealing with the jurisdiction of the courts (the legal power to hear cases) and justiciability (whether a case is appropriate for courts to decide).

The Supreme Court makes policy, yet we must remember that it is a *court*, that is, a policy-making body that makes decisions within an adjudicatory framework, one different from that used by legislatures and executive branch agencies. For example, the Constitution limits the courts to dealing with "cases or controversies." That leads to the requirement that, at a minimum, the party bringing a case have the proper standing to sue, that there be two parties to a case with interests adverse to each other, and that the case not have been collusively manufactured to get a ruling from the courts. While any individual could take a complaint about existing policy to Congress to ask that the policy be repealed or altered, to get into a court a person must show that he or she has sustained—or is likely to sustain—some injury from the policy. If using rules like these, the justices of the Supreme Court consistently limit jurisdiction or interpret narrowly what types of cases judges may hear, major policy claims may never reach even the lower federal courts, much less the Supreme Court itself.

Presumably, the Supreme Court could discard some (if not all) of these limitations on its policy prerogatives. However, judges believe in them. They are also embodied in the expectations of the court's most watchful publics (particularly lawyers). These are expectations based on the idea that the courts are not intended to be the primary policy-makers in our political system.

The justices are not unaware of such expectations, which affect the way they think they should go about doing their work. Yet they vary in interpreting their policy-making roles. Some do not allow these rules of access to prevent them from ruling on major policy questions. This was particularly true of the Warren Court, which showed a concern with many social problems the Supreme Court had not previously considered. However, in terms of our nation's history, the Warren Court's concerns were in a way an aberration, and the great amount of attention the Warren Court's rulings focused on the Supreme Court distracted us somewhat from the many other agencies in society—public and private, formal and informal—where disputes are also resolved.

The Burger Court's more restrictive readings of the rules controlling which cases come to the Supreme Court are closely related to its screening of appeals papers and certiorari petitions. Such interpretation puts the Court squarely within the pattern followed by the Supreme Court between 1925 and the Warren Court. In short, the Burger Court makes much policy but does so within more self-imposed constraints than the Warren Court used. Cases that could come to the Court have been limited primarily by vitiating class action suits, reviving the Eleventh Amendment, and limiting access to federal courts for declaratory and injunctive relief against state statutes, all jurisdictional matters, and by taking a conservative approach to other matters such as standing to sue and mootness, which contain elements of both jurisdiction and justiciability.

Class Actions

A class action is a suit brought by one or more individuals sharing the same legal problem. An example would be all black children seeking admission to an all-white school in a particular city. The suit is brought on behalf of the plaintiffs and "all others similarly situated." An old device intended to reduce repeated litigation on the same facts, the class action suit has recently come into vogue, particularly in connection with consumer and environmental matters. The Warren Court had, toward the end, put a crimp in the use of federal courts for class action suits by ruling that a person could not join his claims with those of others to reach the $10,000 jurisdictional amount required by statute.[40] When Vermont lakefront property-owners sued a New York corporation for damages from industrial discharges, the Burger Court further said that *each and every member* of the class must satisfy the $10,000 amount; those with smaller claims were to be dismissed from the case, which could then not be maintained as a class action.[41] Brennan, Douglas, and Marshall argued that this decision would not help reduce the number of court cases, because not only would remaining federal court claimants have to litigate separately the issues common to their cases, enlarging rather than diminishing the burdens of the federal judiciary, but many more suits would be produced if the state did not have a class action device for those not eligible for the federal case. Furthermore, some people might be entirely out of court if their claims, although valid, were not large enough to warrant the expense of litigating, an exclusion that would not do the judicial system credit.

In 1974, in a class action antitrust and securities suit brought by New York Stock Exchange odd-lot buyers, the Court went even further. Because of the substantial cost (over $200,000) of complete notification to all members of the class, the district court had approved notification of only a sample of members of the class, as well as requiring those being sued to pay 90 percent of the notification costs. By a 6–3 vote, the Court disapproved, saying that petitioners must bear the notice costs and that individual notice must be sent to all class members who could be identified through reasonable effort.[42] The dissenters' principal concern was that important issues would not be litigated and that one of the small claimant's few legal remedies against "those who command the status quo" was being disabled so that consumers with small claims would lose their practical recourse for injury.

Suits Against States

The Eleventh Amendment bars suits against a state by citizens of another, and has also been held to bar suits against a state by its own citizens. The Burger Court revived this latter use. The Warren Court, with atypical self-restraint, had not decided what to do if state employees sued a state for minimum wages not paid.[43] The Burger Court, left with the issue, held in 1973 that Congress had not intended to deprive the states of their old common-law immunity to federal suits, so the employees couldn't sue. However, they were not left without a remedy, because the Secretary of Labor could bring cases in their behalf. The Eleventh Amendment was not at the heart of the case but was clearly brought into the picture.[44]

The Court then extended its position and made the amendment more central. By a 5–4 vote, the Court said that retroactive payment of *improperly withheld* welfare benefits was barred by the amendment if the state did not consent to be sued.[45] An agreement to participate in a federal welfare program was not, said Justice Rehnquist, a grant of such consent. The dissenters stressed the incentive that state officials now had in not complying with regulations and in depriving welfare recipients of what was properly due them. The Court seemed to be saying that suit was barred where recovery of direct payments from the state treasury was being sought, although other rulings indicated the states could be sued for injunctions that might require payments in the future.

Other claims against state officials also came before the Court. In a unanimous ruling resulting from the killings at Kent State University, the Court allowed suits for damages against state officers who violated the federal Constitution while acting under state law. The violation would strip an official of his official character and make him *personally* liable. Despite the holding, Chief Justice Burger showed considerable deference to state executive officials. The higher the officials and the broader the range of their discretion, he said, the greater the executive immunity to which they would be entitled.[46] However, where federal officers were involved, the Court allowed suits to be brought under the Fourth Amendment for damages when federal agents made improper searches and seizures; Burger, dissenting, said the remedy should have come from Congress.[47]

Federalism: Abstention, Injunctions, and Federal Habeas Corpus

If federal judges do not wait to rule on challenged state laws until state courts have had an opportunity to determine the validity of those laws, the touchy question of interference by federal judges in state judicial proceedings arises. Yet the issue must be faced if litigants initiate federal court challenges to state laws before turning to the state courts or before state court proceedings are complete. The Supreme Court has developed the policy of *abstention* to help with this problem. Federal courts are to stay their hand until state courts have ruled, in order to remove a possible irritant in federal-state relations, because state courts might rule in such a way as "to avoid or significantly modify the federal questions appellants raise."[48]

The Burger Court reinforced this abstention doctrine in several rulings.[49] However, the Court does not always follow the abstention doctrine, and individual justices sometimes set it aside depending on the policy challenged. When nude dancing in bars was the issue, Justice Rehnquist, writing for the Court in sustaining California's regulation, refused to accept Justice Douglas's argument that the issues needed to be more particularized by the state courts before the Supreme Court could rule.[50]

The abstention doctrine is definitely implicated in the crucial question of whether the federal courts should issue injunctions against state prosecutions either threatened or already in progress. In the Warren Court's leading case on the subject, *Dombrowski* v. *Pfister*,[51] improper raids on a civil rights organization had already occurred and the prosecutor was making public use of illegally seized documents. Such action invited a remedy; the Court said a federal injunction was proper. The result of the ruling, which added to lawyers' growing tendency to turn first to the federal courts, was a multitude of cases seeking injunctions in circumstances not as severe. State judges were not being given "a fair chance to clean up their own statutory deficiencies" first,[52] and were "being largely deprived of a role in enforcing the Constitution they have sworn to support,"[53] even where they might well have enforced the claimed federal constitutional rights.

As one might expect, the Burger Court tried to curtail such federal court injunctions. In 1971, the Supreme Court ruled in *Younger* v. *Harris* that federal courts were not to enjoin pending state criminal prosecutions except under unusual circumstances —where great and immediate irreparable damage was threatened and damage to civil rights could not be prevented by the normal process of raising constitutional claims at trial or on appeal.[54] Even when the challenged statute was clearly unconstitutional, no injunction could be sought. The Supreme Court was trying to decentralize the making of judicial decisions and was clearly saying that most cases could be handled, at least initially, in the state courts.

Despite the seeming clarity of this ruling, the Court was not consistent in dealing with other requests for declaratory and injunctive relief. When prosecution was *threatened* (but not yet initiated) and the threat was real and not speculative, declaratory relief was held to be available, even if one could not demonstrate the irreparable injury necessary for an injunction.[55] However, the justices were divided over whether granting declaratory relief in such a situation would lead to subsequent issuance of an injunction. Justice Rehnquist accurately described the law in this area when he said it was one "through which our decisions have traced a path that may accurately be described as sinuous."

Further inconsistency seemed to occur when the Court ruled on the question of whether injunctive-relief actions under the civil rights statute (42 U.S.C. 1938) were barred by the federal anti-injunction laws or allowed as expressly authorized exceptions. Here the Court said that the suits *were* allowed.[56] This decision served to *increase* rather than diminish access to federal courts, as did a ruling that civil rights actions could be brought for violation of *property* and not merely *personal* rights.[57] That the Chief Justice could not carry the Court in his effort to limit use of the courts was made even more clear when the Court, by a 5–3 vote, decided that farmworker organizations could obtain a federal injunction against the Texas Rangers and a sheriff's department for conspiring to deprive them of their constitutional rights by harassing, assaulting, detaining, arresting, and jailing them, particuclarly where a continued pattern of activity was involved.[58]

At least prior to the Warren Court, federal courts had generally refused to review state convictions where there was an adequate independent state ground for upholding them. However, those who had fully but unsuccessfully pursued their state post-conviction remedies often went to federal courts with petitions for a writ of *habeas corpus* in order to test their convictions further. The Warren Court had expanded the circumstances in which such actions could be brought by saying that a prisoner need not first exhaust his state remedies where the remedy was no longer available, even when he had failed to use it earlier.[59] This decision led to a flood of prisoners' petitions. The Burger Court did not help the prisoners get out of jail faster. The justices did say that prisoners' complaints about prison conditions (rather than their convictions) could be handled under the Civil Rights Acts, which did not require exhaustion of remedies.[60] However, in 1973, the Court ruled that the prisoner's *only* avenue was habeas corpus where the complaint, for example, about a reduction of "good time," would result in immediate release; that way, the exhaustion of remedies doctrine would apply.[61] This ruling came over the dissenters' complaint that the Court destroyed the earlier ruling and rewrote a federal statute as well as increased rather than diminished federal-state court friction.

Standing and Mootness

Even if all the jurisdictional hurdles discussed above are surmounted, others remain. One is whether a person has the requisite *standing* to bring a case; if there is no standing, the court lacks jurisdiction to hear a case. While standing is part of the question of a court's jurisdiction—and thus can be established or limited by statute—it also partakes of justiciability, the set of judge-made rules on whether a case is proper for judges to decide. As such it is quite flexible in nature and subject to manipulation by the judges for policy reasons.

The Warren Court had started to liberalize the standing requirements by saying that federal taxpayer suits, previously prohibited, would now be allowed if a specific constitutional prohibition was said to have been violated, and if the general taxing and spending power (Art. I, Sec. 8, Cl. 1) was involved.[62] However, in two 1974 rulings the Burger Court resisted extending this development. Speaking through the Chief Justice, the Court turned aside a suit to force an accounting of the Central Intelligence Agency's receipts and expenditures.[63] Burger, saying taxpayers could not use a federal court to assert general grievances, found no connection between taxpayer status and Congress' failure to require more detailed reports of the CIA under the Constitution's Statements and Accounts Clause. He also rejected as too generalized the claim that, without such information, a petitioner could not pursue his duties as a voter. Concurring Justice Powell, arguing that "Allowing citizens to settle all their claims in court would mean a shift away from a democratic form of government," said that such claims should be taken to the legislature. The Court also turned aside a group of armed service reserve officers trying to prevent congressmen from holding reserve commissions by claiming a violation of the Incompatibility Clause (no executive official should be a member of Congress). The Chief Justice said they, too, had failed to establish a "nexus" between their taxpayer status and their claim, their interest being no different from the generalized interest of all citizens; thus the issue was abstract and did not present a case or controversy.[64]

Earlier, however, the Burger Court, noting that "the trend is . . . toward enlargement of the class of people who may protest administrative action,"[65] had participated in relaxing the requirements on standing. However, the Court refused to grant the state of Hawaii standing to sue on behalf of its citizens under the antitrust laws for injury to the state's economy. Individual consumers suing for themselves could recover for much of the general economic damage.[66]

When a claimant did not allege injury to itself, the Court was unwilling to grant standing. The Sierra Club, seeking to block a large recreational project in northern California, spoke only of its special interest in conservation of the nation's parks and of its service as a representative of persons with that interest. Justice

Stewart said that "aesthetic and environmental well-being" could be protected, but ruled that the complaining party had to be among the injured in order to bring the case.[67] Because the group had not claimed adverse effects to its members, it did not have standing to bring this case.

When this requirement of injury *was* met, the Court was willing to grant standing. For example, a group of law students attacked railroad freight rate surcharges applied to recyclable materials. They claimed that the rates would discourage the use of such materials, promote the use of new materials, and thus adversely affect the environment, causing economic, recreational, and aesthetic harm. They had bolstered this with the further claim that *they* would have to pay more for finished products and that their use of forests and streams would be impaired. The Court granted them standing even though the injury claimed was rather general and tenuous to reach from the challenged rate surcharge.[68]

However, the Court did refuse to hear the controversy about Army surveillance of civilian political activity, because only a subjective "chill" to First Amendment rights rather than objective harm had been shown, depriving complainants of standing as well as making the case too speculative.[69] And, through use of the injury-to-oneself idea, the Nixon Court majority kept out of the federal courts important claims of racial discrimination in the criminal justice system. An attempt by black and white citizens of Cairo, Illinois, to obtain relief from claimed illegal bonding, sentencing, and jury fee practices of state judges was turned aside largely because "None of the named plaintiffs is identified as having himself suffered any injury in the manner specified." In order to obtain the injunction, they would have to show continuing injury; "past exposure to illegal conduct" was not enough.[70] Although the Supreme Court warned the state judges by saying they were subject to action under federal criminal statutes for willful discrimination, the Court also said that to enforce the plaintiff's requested injunction, undesirable continuing intrusion into the state judiciary would be necessary. Douglas, dissenting, would have allowed a federal judge to intervene in what he called a "more pervasive scheme for suppression of Blacks and their civil rights than I have ever seen," because the pattern of behavior was difficult to see in reviewing individual cases.

Most of the law of standing is judge-made, but it occasionally has a statutory basis. The statute establishing the National Railroad Passenger Corporation (Amtrak) gave the Attorney-General exclusive authority to enforce its provisions and did not provide for private causes of action. The Court, interpreting the law, said a railroad passenger group did not have standing to protest a passenger train discontinuance.[71] Similarly, when an individual union member sought to intervene in a Landrum-Griffin Act union election case brought by the Secretary of Labor, the Court allowed him to intervene but limited his claims to those presented by the Secretary's complaint. Justice Marshall said Congress had made the Secretary's suit the exclusive post-election remedy in order to centralize litigation in a single proceeding and to protect unions from frivolous litigation.[72] In both these cases, the Court was showing its deference to legislative judgment. Similarly, when the issue was whether white tenants of an apartment complex could sue under the 1968 Civil Rights Act because of racial discrimination in housing, the Court allowed the suit, saying the statute defined standing broadly.[73]

Part of standing is the question of whether a case is moot, that is, brought too late to apply a remedy. The Warren Court relaxed the rules of mootness. That issue frequently arose in connection with elections, where a candidate's case would normally not get to the appellate courts until after the election. (Because it would not be clear that he would run again, a challenge to future application of a law was often thought speculative.) However, the Warren Court ruled on a challenge to state election rules brought by independent presidential electors even after the 1968 election, recognizing that the rule's burden remained for the future and that the problem was "capable of repetition, yet evading review."[74] The Warren Court also ruled that a prisoner's release from prison did not moot his habeas corpus petition, because disabilities accompanying the conviction would still remain.[75] The Nixon appointees generally tried to limit these expansions of the mootness rules, but the exceptions were many.

Representative of the Burger Court's work was the case in which a stockholder group sought to include an anti-napalm amendment in Dow Chemical Corporation's charter. The group was initially denied a vote on the proposal and the refusal was upheld by the Securities Exchange Commission (SEC). When Dow on its own allowed a vote, the Court ruled the issue moot over Douglas' objection, although Dow's action would hinder the group's subsequent efforts to place the matter before the stockholders again.[76] Similarly, in the *DeFunis* affirmative action case (to be discussed in Chapter Six), the Court said that because DeFunis was about to graduate from law school, his complaint of discrimination in admission was moot. Among the exceptions were the abortion cases. There, Justice Blackmun pointed out that pregnancy could never be reviewed on appeal under usual mootness rules because the pregnancy would already have ended;

such a situation called for a ruling on the basic issue, which would recur frequently, he said. In another case, Blackmun, abandoning his colleagues, said the courts should rule on a company's challenge to state laws providing welfare relief to strikers, even though the strike was over, because the law "by its continuing and brooding presence casts what may well be a substantial adverse effect on the interests of the petitioning parties."[77] Also of note is a case in which the "Nixon Four" plus White refused to use mootness where it was the simplest solution. Challenges to the Ohio National Guard's riot control rules had been sought by Kent State University students after the killings there. Four justices (Douglas, Brennan, Stewart, and Marshall) thought the challenges moot for the obvious reasons that the plaintiffs had graduated from school and the rules had been changed. However, the majority wrote new law that made it more difficult for others to bring cases to court, by saying that deciding the case would involve the judiciary in constant supervision of the executive branch.[78]

Under the rules of justiciability, cases also cannot be heard if they are premature. In addition to the surveillance case already noted, the Court rejected as premature a challenge to Ohio provisions requiring signing of a loyalty oath before a "minor" political party could appear on the ballot; nothing in the record showed injury to the complainants.[79] (Douglas, however, would have held the oath unconstitutional as a denial of equal protection because it was not required of all parties.)

The area falling most clearly under the heading of justiciability is that of "political questions," those thought best left to other branches of government or other political institutions for resolution. It is also the area with the fewest guidelines, leaving the justices the greatest flexibility. The major political question issues to be decided by the Warren Court were reapportionment and Congress' refusal to seat Adam Clayton Powell, to be examined later. In both, the justices substantially relaxed the limitations the "political question" doctrine had earlier been used to establish. A major political question issue and one of the toughest justiciability questions to face the Burger Court was posed by some delegates to the 1972 Democratic National Convention when they attacked a Credentials Committee recommendation for their unseating. The appeals court had ruled in favor of McGovern's California delegates and against Illinois machine delegates, and the Supreme Court was faced with the need to act before the convention acted. Taking special action, the Court stayed the Court of Appeals' judgment, saying a political convention had a traditional right to act on its committees' recommendations.[80] However, the Court did say the appeals court was probably wrong, leading to Douglas' remark that the Court had really decided the case in "an oblique and covert way." Justice Marshall would have been more direct; he said at least prompt declaratory relief was appropriate because the question was not a political one to be avoided. He also thought intervening later would cause more serious problems than intervening immediately and argued, "Our duty lies in making decisions, not avoiding them," particularly where participation in the process of nominating the President was involved.[81]

CONCLUSION

The Burger Court's position on access to the courts, and particularly jurisdiction and justiciability, has potentially, although not necessarily, conservative implications. If one cannot bring cases, the status quo is maintained. Thus it will be both difficult and expensive for consumers to bring challenges to business practices and for welfare recipients to receive benefits improperly withheld by the government. However, the prerequisites for obtaining standing to sue have not been made particularly difficult to satisfy, and the Court's interpretation of the civil rights laws at times has allowed more rather than fewer cases.

The Burger Court's deference to legislative and executive officials also has led the Court to tighten up on challenges to government actions generally. Suits against state and local *governments* for violations of civil rights still are not possible, although one will be able to sue their *officials* as persons. Challenges to the national government's actions will remain difficult, particularly for the individual citizen or taxpayer. However, where deprivations of individuals' civil rights have been particularly blatant, Warren Court policy has not been substantially curtailed by the Burger Court. Individuals will still be able to obtain their rights under state statutes, if they are not yet under prosecution. And they will be able to get injunctions against these state laws in extreme circumstances. So one finds overall that there is some movement in a conservative direction and retention of some earlier restrictions. Otherwise, we have a mixed set of rules that certainly does not prevent most challenges to government policy. The justices want to be able to make decisions; they do not wish to give up the opportunity to affect policy. Thus they will keep open the channels of litigation.

NOTES

1. Erwin Griswold, "The Supreme Court's Case Load: Civil Rights and Other Problems," *University of Illinois Law Forum*, 1973, 624.

2. That number is well below those of earlier years when the Court had to take all cases coming to it. In 1889, there were 265 signed opinions, and the 1923 Court had 208 signed opinions.

3. For statistics, see the articles by Paul Bartholomew summarizing the work of each term of the Supreme Court, in *Western Political Quarterly*, and the tables in the *Harvard Law Review*'s annual November summary. Each of the latter is preceded by a thematic article by a distinguished law professor.

4. Over a half-dozen cases were carried over from the 1968 Term to the Burger Court, while fifteen cases from the 1969 Term required reargument. The 1971 Term produced nine cases for reargument, but four were decided in the same term when Powell and Rehnquist were seated.

5. *Ohio* v. *Wyandotte Chemical Co.*, 401 U.S. 493 (1971).

6. *Washington* v. *General Motors*, 406 U.S. 109 (1972).

7. *Illinois* v. *City of Milwaukee*, 405 U.S. 91 (1972).

8. "Retired Chief Justice Warren Attacks, Chief Justice Burger Defends Freund Study Group's Composition and Proposal," *American Bar Association Journal*, 59 (July 1973), 728.

9. Review is granted to as many as one-third of the cases remaining after the Chief Justice has exercised his discretion and indicated which are more important. S. Sidney Ulmer, William Hintze, and Louise Kirklosky, "The Decision to Grant or Deny Certiorari: Further Consideration of Cue Theory," *Law & Society Review*, 6 (May 1972), 640. Until recently, the Chief Justice "dead-listed" those cases he thought unimportant; affirmative action by one of the justices was required before such cases could be discussed in conference. Now a "discuss list" of cases the Chief Justice considers more important is used; the other justices can add to this list; otherwise, review is automatically denied.

10. *Farr* v. *Pitchess*, 409 U.S. 1243 (1973), citing *Maryland* v. *Baltimore Radio Show*, 339 U.S. 912 at 919.

11. *U.S.* v. *Kras*, 409 U.S. 434 at 443 (1972); emphasis supplied.

12. David Adamany, "Legitimacy, Realigning Elections, and the Supreme Court," *Wisconsin Law Review*, 1973, 801, drawing on Jan Deutsch, "Neutrality, Legitimacy, and the Supreme Court," *Stanford Law Review*, 20 (1968), 207.

13. *White* v. *Georgia*, appeal dismissed, 414 U.S. 886 (1973), Brennan-Douglas-Marshall for granting certiorari; *Patrick* v. *Field Research Corp.*, 414 U.S. 922 (1973), Douglas dissent; *Meinhold* v. *Taylor*, 414 U.S. 943 (1973); *Lee* v. *U.S.*, 414 U.S. 1045 (1973), Douglas and Marshall dissenting; *Ex Parte Kent*, 414 U.S. 1077 (1973), Douglas-Brennan-Marshall to hear; and *New Rider* v. *Board of Education, Pawnee County, Oklahoma*, 414 U.S. 1097 (1974), Douglas-Marshall dissent. Douglas thought the result "especially repugnant" because of our treatment of Indians. The Tenth Circuit Court of Appeals had upheld the school regulation as "instilling pride and initiative . . . leading to scholarship attainment and high school spirit and morale."

14. A sample of more than 3,000 unsuccessful certiorari applications over a twenty-year period yielded fewer than forty instances with an explanation; the most common was dismissal on motion of the parties or failure to timely file. Joseph Tanenhaus, Marvin Schick, Matthew Muraskin, and Daniel Rosen, "The Supreme Court's Certiorari Jurisdiction: Cue Theory," in Glendon Schubert, ed., *Judicial Decision-Making* (New York: Free Press, 1963), p. 114. An exception is

52   CONTINUITY AND CHANGE

Chapman v. *California*, 405 U.S. 1020 (1972), the Court saying, "It appearing the state court decision is not final . . . ," but such an explanation does not deal with substantive matters.

15.   Ulmer, "Supreme Court Justices as Strict and Not-so-Strict Constructionists: Some Implications," *Law & Society Review*, 8 (Fall 1973), 27–28. See also Ulmer, "The Decision to Grant Certiorari as an Indicator of Decision "On the Merits,' " *Polity*, 6 (1971), 429–447. For the path-breaking exploration of justices' certiorari votes in relation to their votes on the merits, using game theory on FELA cases, see Glendon Schubert, "The Certiorari Game," in *The Quantitative Analysis of Judicial Behavior* (Glencoe, Ill.: Free Press, 1959), pp. 210–254.

16.   *Jones* v. *Mayer*, 392 U.S. 409 at 478–479 (1968).

17.   J. Woodford Howard, Jr., "Litigation Flow in Three United States Courts of Appeals," *Law & Society Review*, 8 (Fall 1973), 49. Howard's personal comments on this section are much appreciated.

18.   Eugene Gressman, "The National Court of Appeals: A Dissent," *American Bar Association Journal*, 59 (March 1973), 255.

19.   Earl Warren, statement in "Retired Chief Justice Warren Attacks . . . ," 728.

20.   Tanenhaus et al., p. 114.

21.   Schubert, *Quantitative Analysis*, pp. 53–55.

22.   Tanenhaus et al., p. 123.

23.   Ulmer, "Revising the Jurisdiction of the Supreme Court," *Minnesota Law Review*, 58 (November 1973), 154; Ulmer et al., "The Decision to Grant . . . ," *Law & Society Review*, 6 (May 1972), 640–641. The federal government's presence as petitioner also makes it more likely that the cases will be "special-listed" rather than "dead-listed." Ibid., 642.

24.   Richard J. Richardson and Kenneth N. Vines, *The Politics of Federal Courts* (Boston: Little, Brown, 1970), pp. 153, 155.

25.   Howard, 47.

26.   Schubert, *Quantitative Analysis*, p. 66. For 1953–1956, Ibid., pp. 55–67; for 1967–1972, from analysis by the author of data coded by David Gruenenfelder, Southern Illinois University at Carbondale.

27.   Howard, 42, 48. See also Richardson and Vines, pp. 153–157.

28.   William H. Rehnquist, "The Supreme Court: Past and Present," *American Bar Association Journal*, 59 (April 1973), 363. Douglas instead argues that case-screening is more important.

29.   *Tidewater Oil* v. *U.S.*, 409 U.S. 151 at 176 (1972).

30.   *Butz* v. *Glover Livestock Commission Co.*, 411 U.S. 182 at 189 (1973).

31.   Warren Burger, "The State of the Federal Judiciary—1972," *American Bar Association Journal*, 59 (October 1972), 1050.

32.   See "Burger and Rehnquist," *New Republic,* 167, 17 (November 4, 1972), pp. 8–9.

33.   *Tidewater Oil* v. *U.S.*, 409 U.S. 151 at 169–170 (1972). Direct appeals also add to the Court's summary decision-making. Feeling compelled to take the cases, the Court in many instances (about fifty per term) decides them without full opinion. See Rehnquist, op. cit.

34.   Paul Freund, "Why We Need the National Court of Appeals," *American Bar Association Journal*, 59 (March 1973), 250. The report of Freund's study group is at *American Bar Association Journal*, 59 (February 1973), 139–144.

35.   See James Kilpatrick, "A Supreme Minicourt is Not the Answer," *Milwaukee Journal*, May 14, 1973, p. 17; Henry Friendly, *Federal Jurisdiction: A General View* (New York: Columbia University Press, 1973), pp. 49–54; Nathan Lewin, "Helping the Court with Its Work," *New Republic,* March 3, 1973, pp.

15–19, as well as the debates in the pages of the *American Bar Association Journal*. I want to express my thanks to Carol Welch and Irv Gottschalk, University of Wisconsin–Milwaukee, for their ideas and comments on this subject.

36.   Gressman, 256, 257.

37.   For examples of such "feel," see Lewin, p. 18.

38.   *Tidewater Oil* v. *U.S.*, 409 U.S. 151 at 175 (1972).

39.   Shirley M. Hufstedler, "Courtship and Other Legal Arts," *American Bar Association Journal*, 60 (May 1974), 547.

40.   *Snyder* v. *Harris*, 394 U.S. 332 (1969).

41.   *Zahn* v. *International Paper Co.*, 414 U.S. 291 (1973).

42.   *Eisen* v. *Carlisle & Jacquelin,* 417 U.S. 156 (1974).

43.   *Maryland* v. *Wirtz,* 392 U.S. 183 (1968), upholding the law's extension.

44.   *Employees of Department of Public Health and Welfare of Missouri* v. *Department of Public Health and Welfare,* 411 U.S. 279 (1973).

45.   *Edelman* v. *Jordan*, 415 U.S. 651 (1974).

46.   *Scheuer* v. *Rhodes*, 416 U.S. 232 (1974).

47.   *Bivens* v. *Six Unknown Federal Narcotics Agents,* 403 U.S. 388 (1971). This case provided Burger's basic argument, in dissent, against the exclusionary rule because of its ineffectiveness.

48.   *Lake Carriers Assocation* v. *MacMullan*, 406 U.S. 498 at 512 (1972).

49.   See, for example, *Reetz* v. *Bozanich*, 397 U.S. 82 (1970), on Alaskan salmon fishing licenses; *Fornarnis* v. *Ridge Tool*, 400 U.S. 41 (1970), on a state school funding provision.

50.   *California* v. *LaRue,* 409 U.S. 109 (1973).

51.   380 U.S. 479 (1965).

52.   Personal communication from a federal judge, who observes that "law students are being trained to 'seek ye first the kingdom of the federal court,' with the consequent denigration of the state courts."

53.   Friendly, p. 125. He added, "I am by no means convinced that state judges cannot be relied upon to enforce constitutional rights when asserted as defenses, subject to Supreme Court review." However, the Warren Court had clearly said that federal courts cannot abstain simply because state courts have a responsibility to uphold the Constitution and that a suitor's choice of forum must be respected. *Zwickler* v. *Koota*, 389 U.S. 241 (1967).

54.   *Younger* v. *Harris*, 401 U.S. 37; *Samuels* v. *Mackell*, 401 U.S. 66; *Boyle* v. *Landry*, 401 U.S. 77; and *Perez* v. *Ledesma*, 401 U.S. 81 (1971). Only in the last, involving free speech questions, was there more than one dissent.

55.   *Steffel* v. *Thompson*, 415 U.S. 452 (1974).

56.   *Mitchum* v. *Foster*, 407 U.S. 225 (1972), reinforced by *Gibson* v. *Berryhill*, 411 U.S. 654 (1973).

57.   *Lynch* v. *Household Finance*, 405 U.S. 538 (1972).

58.   *Allee* v. *Medrano,* 416 U.S. 802 (1974). Burger, concurring in part and dissenting in part, restated the *Younger* requirements.

59.   *Fay* v. *Noia*, 372 U.S. 391 (1963); see also *Townsend* v. *Sain*, 372 U.S. 293 (1963).

60.   *Wilwording* v. *Swenson,* 404 U.S. 249 (1971).

61.   *Preiser* v. *Rodriguez*, 411 U.S. 475 (1973).

62.   *Flast* v. *Cohen*, 392 U.S. 83 (1968). The case had been based on provisions of the Elementary and Secondary Education Act providing certain assistance to parochial schools. When a subsequent case on ESEA's Title I requirements that certain services be provided to nonpublic schools reached the Court, the justices at least temporarily avoided the church-state questions by saying no order directing on-premises instruction in the parochial schools was yet in effect,

although the Court seemed to say that the parochial schools suing to obtain services under the Act were entitled to relief, and Justice Blackmun suggested a number of options they might use to obtain that relief. *Wheeler* v. *Barrera*, 417 U.S. 402 (1974).

63. *U.S.* v. *Richardson*, 418 U.S. 166 (1974).

64. *Schlesinger* v. *Reservists Committee to End the War*, 418 U.S. 208 (1974).

65. *Data Processing Service* v. *Camp*, 397 U.S. 150 at 154 (1970); *Barlow* v. *Collins*, 397 U.S. 159 (1970).

66. *Hawaii* v. *Standard Oil of California*, 405 U.S. 251 (1972).

67. *Sierra Club* v. *Morton*, 405 U.S. 727 at 734–735 (1972).

68. *U.S.* v. *S.C.R.A.P.* (Students Challenging Regulatory Agency Procedures), 412 U.S. 669 (1973). SCRAP's victory was only partial. Stewart held that the Court lacked jurisdiction to issue an injunction against the rates, as the ICC had final and exclusive power to suspend rates, and that the National Environmental Policy Act (NEPA), the basis for SCRAP's claim that the ICC had not complied with its provisions, was not meant to repeal other statutes.

69. *Laird* v. *Tatum*, 408 U.S. 1 (1972).

70. *O'Shea* v. *Littleton*, 414 U.S. 488 at 495–496 (1973).

71. *National Railroad Passenger Corporation* v. *National Association of Railroad Passengers*, 414 U.S. 453 (1974).

72. *Trbovich* v. *Mine Workers*, 404 U.S. 528 (1972).

73. *Trafficante* v. *Metropolitan Life Insurance Co.*, 409 U.S. 205 (1972).

74. *Moore* v. *Ogilvie*, 493 U.S. 814 (1969).

75. *Carafas* v. *Lavallee*, 391 U.S. 234 (1968). The Burger Court held that a person released on personal recognizance is still in "custody" for purposes of habeas, because of restraints on his movement, so that he has standing to bring a petition for the writ. *Hensley* v. *Municipal Court*, 411 U.S. 345 (1973).

76. *S.E.C.* v. *Medical Committee*, 404 U.S. 403 (1972).

77. *Super Tire Engineering Co.* v. *McCorkle*, 416 U.S. 115 at 122 (1974).

78. *Gilligan* v. *Morgan*, 413 U.S. 1 (1973).

79. *Socialist Labor Party* v. *Gilligan*, 406 U.S. 583 at 589 (1972).

80. *O'Brien* v. *Brown*, 409 U.S. 1 (1972).

81. In October, bearing out Douglas' prediction that "everyone knows the cases will be moot" by the beginning of the Court's regular term, the Court did grant certiorari, then vacated and remanded the cases to have them dismissed as moot. *O'Brien* v. *Brown* and *Keane* v. *Democratic National Party*, both 409 U.S. 816 (1972).

CHAPTER THREE

Internal Dynamics

The focus of this book is on the policy developed by the Supreme Court. Before we can examine that policy in detail, we need to know something about the decision-making process by which it is developed, just as we need to know about the process by which the Court accepts cases. Both are affected by the justices' values and the collegial nature of the decision-making process.

When a group of individuals interact frequently over an extended period of time, their interaction becomes patterned. This does not mean that it is fully determined, but regularities do occur. Thus we find justices voting quite frequently with certain other justices, so that there are references to the "liberal bloc," the "Nixon Four," or the "Minnesota Twins" (Burger and Blackmun); other justices may remain more independent of their colleagues, perhaps performing the function of being the "swing voters" on the Court. The way in which the justices vote is largely a matter of the values or ideologies that they bring to the Court and that develop in the course of their careers there, but where they stand in relation to each other is largely a function of who is on the Court at a particular time. A justice who seems moderate at one time may look far more liberal (or conservative) later, not because he has changed his doctrinal outlook but because the justices who have come on the Court are more conservative (or liberal) than he.

As noted above, the process by which Supreme Court decisions are made is collegial. Although justices do much work on their own, in their own chambers, most important decisions are made in conference, and all opinions are circulated among all the justices before they are released. There may not be much explicit bargaining for votes among the justices, but a process of discussion and attempts at persuasion, either orally or in writing, goes on all the time and can affect the outcome of a case. If we define power as the opportunity to influence a decision, some justices even seem to seek power within the Court by becoming the key or "swing" vote. Because of the relevance of such matters for the Court's decisions, we need to look at the overall patterns of interaction among the justices and the degree to which they have voted together.

In this chapter, we turn first to the question of consensus and dissensus within the Court, followed by an exploration of patterns of interagreement among the justices; a note on justices' participation in cases is included. The chapter concludes with a look at opinion-assignment patterns and practices.

CONSENSUS AND DISSENSUS

Court-watchers have regularly noted the Court's votes in important cases, calling our attention to the unanimity of the 1954 school desegregation rulings and 5–4 votes in crminal procedure cases. For some time, people have criticized the frequency of open disagreement within the Court, feeling that it is used promiscuously rather than reserved for special occasions. Justices like Frankfurter, who often felt compelled to spell out his own particular view of a case in a concurring opinion, or Douglas, with his incessant dissents, have come in for special criticism. For some, the existence of separate opinions is merely disorderly; they expect the revered Supreme Court to speak with a single voice, perhaps out of the older view that the Court finds rather than makes the law. (After all, if the law is found, there can be only one discovery, not many.)

For others, the loss of the Court's institutional voice, which we see in the extreme in the *Pentagon Papers* and death penalty rulings, when each justice wrote a separate opinion, has possible policy implications. The norm that justices should not express themselves separately is supposed to be functional for the Court. Dissenting opinions, for example, are said to weaken the Court's authority and give those disagreeing with the ruling an excuse for noncompliance. A 5–4 ruling, it is said, will provide encouragement to wait for a change in personnel or a shift in the Court's alignment. Strength is seen in unanimity, weakness in division. On the other hand, there are those who say an occasional dissenting voice on the Court lets the losing side know it has been heard and its views considered. In addition, dissenting opinions often become the majority opinions of the future.

From the perspective of policy development, when the Court speaks with several voices, policy may often be less clear. Certainly when the Court can develop only a plurality or prevailing opinion (joined in by less than a majority) instead of an opinion of the Court, officially there is no Court doctrine or policy whatsoever. And if each justice feels compelled to express slight differences in approach, doctrine becomes difficult for lawyers or any other audiences of the Court to interpret. On the other hand, a statement in which all have joined may be so formless or ambiguous that it is almost useless as a statement of policy. Such policy implications, noted by many observers, require us to look further at division within the Court.

Certainly, there can be no doubt of the increased frequency of separate statements by the Court. For example, concurring opinions increased from 40 in the 1962 Term to 67 ten years later, and dissents rose from 76 to 178. The opinions of the Court, including *per curiam* rulings, also rose from 117 to 164 over the same period, so there were 409 opinions in 1972 compared to only 233 ten years before.[1] We can also see the increased division in the fact that in neither of the last two Warren Court years did the Court achieve unanimity in opinions or voting in half its cases; in 1967, the percentage of unanimous full opinion cases was 41.7, while the following year only one-third were unanimous.[2] However, relatively few of the last Warren Court cases were decided by close votes. Eighty percent of full opinion cases in the 1967 Term and just under 70 percent in the 1968 Term were decided by margins of at least four votes. The shift to the Burger Court brought a definite drop in consensus. In the new Chief Justice's first three terms, about one-third of the cases were unanimous, but the figure dropped to 25 percent in the 1972 Term, although it climbed back to almost a third in the 1973 Term.[3] Disagreement showed up more clearly in the size of majorities. In Burger's first term, 62 percent of the cases were decided by wide margins (four votes or more), but the following year less than half (48 percent) were, with over one-fourth of the signed full opinion cases decided by one-vote margins. In 1971 through 1973, with a more stable membership, the Court decided somewhat over 50 percent of its cases by wide margins, while 20 percent of the 1972 and 1973 cases were decided by a margin of only one vote; and many of the latter rulings involved major policy matters like newsmen's privilege or nonunanimous juries. Such figures support the proposition, largely confirmed for the Warren Court, that in decision-making bodies, decisions will be made by "minimum winning coalitions" (the smallest majority necessary). This is particularly true when the group is not under threat. Unlike the

Warren Court, which was threatened by Congress on several occasions,[4] the Burger Court has not been so threatened, although
it met President Nixon's advance hesitation about complying
with a judicial ruling on the subpoena for his tapes with unanimous judicial show of force.

The gross amount of opinion-writing is evidence of dissensus
within the Court. However, we must keep in mind that there is
considerable variation among the justices in their rate of dissents,
whether expressed only in dissenting votes or in the dissenting
opinions they write. It is usually the case that some justices have
few dissenting votes—or perhaps none—while others have quite
a few; who the justices are varies with the general pattern on the
Court. In the last two Warren Court terms (1967 and 1968), the
Chief Justice, Brennan, and Marshall seldom dissented—
something true of the Chief Justice during his entire career. The
overall rate of dissent was also low; in the last Warren term, four
justices had fewer than ten dissenting votes for the entire term
and only five justices cast any lone dissents. On the other hand,
Harlan was the most frequent dissenter and Douglas, Black,
White, and Stewart also dissented frequently. (Douglas and Black
were the most frequent solo dissenters.)

In Burger's first term, the number of dissents dipped only
slightly even with fewer cases decided, but now the Chief Justice
himself led the dissenters with 27; Black and Douglas had 24
each. By the following term, the discord was amazing. Some 200
dissenting votes were cast in the Court's signed full opinion cases,
although Burger's dissent frequency had dropped. That the liberals were now the most frequent dissenters was a clue to the direction of the Court's policy; even the previously nondissenting
Brennan had 28 dissenting votes. From then on, Brennan, Marshall, and Douglas were high-frequency dissenters, Douglas casting 57 dissenting votes in 1971, 15 of them alone, and 69 the
following year. Among the more conservative members of the
Court, the Chief Justice was the most frequent dissenter, although Rehnquist also appeared as a frequent nay-sayer. The
other three Nixon appointees and White, showing their majority
position, had relatively few dissents.

If we look at opinion-writing, we find an average of roughly
one concurring opinion in every other case, while each
nonunanimous case had an average of at least two dissenting
opinions. Here, too, the range of opinion-writing was great, just as
it had been for voting. Some justices, such as Chief Justice Warren, were generally infrequent writers of concurrences and dissents, but his predecessor was by no means as hesitant to write
opinions. Others, like Brennan or Harlan, were quiet in some

periods and prolific in others; Brennan's voice was heard more frequently as the liberals more frequently found themselves in the minority, while Harlan needed to speak out less as the transition to the Burger Court began to develop.

Dissensus is evident both in the frequency of opinion-writing and also in the justices' language. For example, the Court had to apply the "act-of-state" doctrine, in which courts of one country do not pass judgment on acts of another country within the latter's territory, to Cuba's seizure of banks.[5] The vote was 5–4; there was no opinion of the Court; Rehnquist wrote for himself, the Chief Justice, and White, while Douglas and Powell each wrote concurring opinions based on grounds different from the Court and each other. The dissenting justices, in particularly tart language, attacked Douglas for utilizing a case "not at all in point." They also charged Rehnquist with failing to read the Court's previous case on the subject carefully and for engaging in " 'an abdication of the judicial function to the Executive Branch.' " Later, a six-judge majority ruled that a car could be searched with the driver's consent even when he didn't know he could object. Here there were two concurring opinions and three separate dissents. An obviously furious Justice Brennan, indicating the dissenters' tone, said "It wholly escapes me how our citizens can meaningfully be said to have waived something as precious as a constitutional guarantee without ever being aware of its existence," and claimed the Court's conclusion wasn't even supported by common sense, while Justice Marshall called the majority view "narrow and inaccurate."[6]

PATTERNS OF AGREEMENT

Because pairs or larger combinations of justices vote together with some regularity, we need to examine not only their individual actions but the patterns of their interaction. Before we can say that a bloc exists, we must find a cohesive group voting together with some consistency, at least sometimes by itself. We must be careful not to overestimate the cohesion of the justices. Many times, when two or more justices vote together, they may do so for different reasons, and may even express these reasons in separate opinions. Thus, although we could call a grouping of justices a bloc simply on the basis of their voting together, we must be careful about doing so. We must also recognize that when we focus on particular pairs or triplets of justices, we often ignore whether those judges are voting together by themselves or whether somebody else has voted with them. We may find X and Y voting together much of the time, but if C is with them some of the time and C plus D join them on other occasions, it would be at least somewhat misleading to call X and Y a bloc. For example, Grossman found in the 1963–1965 Terms both that a bloc "voted together *alone* less than half the number of times it voted together" and that there were surprisingly large numbers of combinations of judges in dissent, making "the identity of the most persistent blocs ambiguous." His findings serve to remind us of "the tenuousness of the idea that there are stable, persistent and exclusive three- and four-judge dissenting blocs whose members interact substantially as a bloc."[7]

What picture can we obtain for the Warren and Burger Courts? Persistent groupings, like that of Burger, Blackmun, Powell, and Rehnquist, or Douglas, Marshall, and Brennan, appear, but patterns are extremely varied. If we use voting interagreement to array the justices along a general liberal-conservative dimension, for the 1962–1964 Terms it runs from left to right, from Douglas to Black, Warren, Brennan, Goldberg, Clark, White, and Stewart, to Harlan. The first five formed a liberal bloc; the other four, a conservative one.[8] In the 1965 and 1966 Terms, Fortas had replaced Goldberg in the liberal bloc but Black had left the liberal bloc and moved to the middle.

In 1967 and 1968, Douglas moved to isolation left of the liberal bloc, which now included Marshall, and Black remained in isolation from both them and the White-Stewart-Harlan conservative bloc. Indication of Black's movement away from the liberals is that he voted with Stewart as frequently as with Warren. In those two years, the highest voting interagreement was between Warren and Brennan, who joined in almost 90 percent of the nonunanimous decisions.[9] Among the liberals, the quartet of Warren, Black, Douglas, and Brennan were together in only a third of the cases, joined by both Fortas and Marshall in most of those. In almost three-quarters of the cases, two of the three joined the Chief Justice. Within the liberal side of the Court, there were also strong voting pairs, with Warren and Douglas, Black and Douglas, and Fortas and Marshall agreeing with each other in roughly half the cases. Among the more conservative justices, Harlan, Stewart, and White were frequent companions, with Harlan joining White more frequently in the majority and Stewart more frequently in dissent.

Patterns were in flux during the 1969 Term, but the threesome of Douglas, Brennan, and Marshall was forming, while Stewart, White, and Harlan continued to vote together often. Black, still staying away from the liberals, joined Chief Justice Burger far more often than he did Douglas. In the 1970 Term, the Douglas-Brennan-Marshall trio was even firmer, with the

Brennan-Marshall pair the strongest. As Kurland remarked, "If there are 'twins' on the Court, there is more than one set of them."[10] The most obvious new pair was Burger and Blackmun. The Minnesota Twins were together in 90 percent (66 of 74) of the nonunanimous cases, mostly in the majority, and there was only one criminal procedure case in which they did not vote together.

In the next term (1971), Blackmun and Burger, still together over 80 percent of the time, occasionally went separate ways, Blackmun departing from the Chief's company on such matters as durational residence requirements for voting and standing to bring environmental cases, as well as antitrust policy. It was during the 1971 Term that instead of a Warren-Brennan-Black-Douglas quartet, the new dominant force was Burger, Blackmun, Powell, and Rehnquist. The importance of Stewart and White, who paired in 70 percent of the nonunanimous cases, *never* in dissent, also became clear. Stewart and White clearly helped the Nixon appointees control the Court: the most frequent majority voting combinations were the Nixon Four plus White alone or Stewart and White.[11] The interagreement of liberals Brennan, Douglas, and Marshall continued, but their increased dissents indicated that "If we regard [them] . . . as the true heirs of the Warren Court philosophy, it can readily be seen that the Court is certainly no longer dominated by that jurisprudence."[12] A further indication of change in the Court is that in closely divided cases, Burger's highest rate of interagreement was with Rehnquist (95 percent), while it was an amazingly low *4.2 percent* with Douglas and only 10.9 percent with Brennan and 21 percent with Marshall.

In the 1972 Term, the Nixon Four were together in almost 60 percent of over 100 nonunanimous signed opinions; three of the four were together 85 percent of the time, and Burger and Blackmun voted together even more frequently than before (90 percent). Control of the Court by the Nixon appointees was clear, shown by the fact that in only one case (food stamps) were they together in dissent. They made a majority 14 times with White and another 25 times with White and Stewart. When only three of the Nixon Four voted together, Stewart and White created a majority on four occasions. This showed both that Stewart and White were crucial in the Court's alignment and that the Nixon appointees could lose one member and still control the Court. The next term one or the other joined the Nixon Four on 16 other occasions. Brennan, Douglas, and Marshall held together as often on their side of the Court, but they were in dissent in more than half of the cases where the Court was not unanimous.

In the 1972 Term, although the Nixon justices held together

best when criminal procedure was at issue, minor cracks appeared. Blackmun and Powell each departed once to become the fifth vote in a liberal criminal procedure majority. The Nixon appointees also split, 2-2, 16 times and the issues on which they divided were important—including Denver school desegregation, sex-related newspaper employment ads, and tuition grants for parochial education. (Here Blackmun and Powell took a more liberal position, while Burger and Rehnquist took a position closer to President Nixon's.)

In the 1973 Term, where the basic division in the Court remained sharply drawn, splits in the Nixon Four were somewhat more apparent, although they were together in three-fifths of the nonunanimous cases, *only once* in dissent, and three of the four voted together in another 30 percent of the cases. Thus at least three of the Nixon appointees voted together in a full 85 of 95 nonunanimous full opinion cases. The four, who split 2–2 in only eight cases, divided 3–1 twenty-five times, in eight of which the three were in the minority. For example, Powell's vote helped form a majority in cases on flag desecration, discrimination against women, and sentencing for contempt, while Blackmun helped form a majority in a major libel case and a case on welfare injunction procedure. Again, however, the four held firm on criminal procedure.

The information available from the initial transition years and the first three terms in which all four of President Nixon's appointees were seated makes clear the change in the composition and location of groupings in the Supreme Court. Where a liberal bloc of which Chief Justice Warren was a member was dominant during the last years of the Warren Court, a four-judge bloc of which Chief Justice Burger is a member now controls the actions of the Court in most cases, particularly because of the votes of either Justice White or Stewart or both. As we will see, the classic Burger Court voting alignment is a 6–3 ruling with Chief Justice Burger and Justices Blackmun, Powell, Rehnquist, White, and Stewart in the majority, and Justices Brennan, Marshall, and Douglas in dissent. However, this bloc is more evident in criminal procedure cases than in other areas of policy; a somewhat different majority, in which the Warren Court holdovers play a larger role, is more likely to predominate in cases on the First Amendment, school desegregation, and perhaps labor.

On the whole, the liberal bloc is rarely in charge, often in dissent. The bloc's dissent frequency makes clear that dissensus has increased from the last years of the Warren Court; there were fewer unanimous opinions, more decided by narrow margins. And the disagreement within the Court is not likely to decrease. Cohesion within both the bloc of four Nixon justices and the grouping of liberals is very high and not decreasing, although there are significant occasions on which the predominant grouping divides, sometimes even leaving the liberals in command. As one might expect for swing voters, Justices White and Stewart are less cohesive as a pair than are the other two groupings, and one often finds one with the majority and the other in dissent, a pattern also relatively clear.

A NOTE ON PARTICIPATION

In the foregoing, it was assumed that all the justices participate in all the cases. Although such participation is usually taken for granted, there are exceptions. From time to time there has been controversy over the propriety of the participation of certain justices in particular cases, and that controversy has again recently broken out.

Most justices never recuse (withdraw) from a case so much as once a term; usually illness that has caused a justice to miss oral argument or consideration of a case is the only factor that prevents participation. When justices do recuse, they do not give reasons. It may be because a justice knows one of the lawyers or has been associated with him in some way, or because the case comes from a state with which he was closely identified (Warren with California, White with Colorado). When, like White, Marshall, or Rehnquist, justices come to the Court from the government and may have had prior involvement in cases, they are more likely to withdraw frequently during their early time on the Court.

Recusancy became a major controversy in 1972 when Justice Rehnquist did not disqualify himself in several cases. There were three cases with which he arguably had been connected *and where his vote made the difference.* (While Rehnquist did recuse in other cases, including important ones on domestic surveillance and the scope of immunity as well as the later Nixon tapes case, in none of those situations was his vote necessary.[13]) The controversial cases were the 5–4 rulings in *Gravel* v. *United States* (interrogation of a senator's aide about publication of the Pentagon Papers); *Branzburg* v. *Hayes* (newsmen's privilege to protect confidential sources) and *Laird* v. *Tatum* (Army surveillance of civilians).[14] Rehnquist had helped prepare the government's case against the *New York Times* in the *Pentagon Papers* Case; he had been the Justice Department spokesman for the policy of subpoenaing newsmen during investigations of the Black Panthers; and he had been an administration witness on military surveillance before a congressional committee. He had specifically commented in that testimony that the already-commenced *Tatum* case was not justiciable. Indeed, that became the Court's position: no justiciable controversy existed because only a subjective chill to First Amendment rights, rather than objective harm, had been shown. Had Rehnquist not participated, the result would have been 4–4, affirming the lower court ruling in favor of hearing the case, and petitioners' claims could have been ruled on.[15]

Rehnquist's *Laird* v. *Tatum* participation brought not only a request that the case be reheard but also a specific request from the American Civil Liberties Union that he disqualify himself. The motion was based not only on the federal disqualification statute—used against Haynsworth in the nomination fight—but on the new and stiffer American Bar Association Code of Judicial Conduct, which required a judge to avoid both impropriety and the *appearance* of impropriety and called for disqualification when a judge's impartiality might reasonably be questioned. The Court refused to grant the rehearing, as it almost invariably does, but Rehnquist issued a long memorandum supporting his nondisqualification.[16] He relied on the statute rather than the ABA Code and "time after time . . . refused to deal with the ACLU charge that he had commented on the merits—or, as witness Rehnquist had testified, lack of merits—of the lawsuit itself."[17] He minimized his prior involvement not only with the case but with the policy issue as well, claiming he was merely the person chosen to present the administration's position before Congress. Looking to Supreme Court history, he said,

> My impression is that none of the former Justices of this Court since 1911 have followed a practice of disqualifying themselves in cases involving points of law with respect to which they had expressed an opinion or formulated policy prior to ascending to the bench.

Furthermore, he claimed, it would be unlikely for a justice, particularly if previously in government, not to have said something about many political matters, and even those who had not made public statements undoubtedly had opinions. None of that, however, required them to remove themselves from the cases: "Proof that a Justice's mind at the time he joined the Court was a complete *tabula rasa* in the area of constitutional abjudication would be evidence of lack of qualification, not lack of bias." Finally, he stressed a duty to *sit* rather than the ABA Code's preference for recusing, because an evenly divided Court was a distasteful occurrence, made worse "where companion cases reaching opposite results are heard together here."[18]

OPINION-WRITING

The Chief Justice's opinion-assignment function is one of the ways in which he can attempt to exercise his influence. Once the justices have voted on a case in conference, the Chief Justice assigns the writing of the Court's opinion to one of the majority. If he is not in the majority, the assignment is made by the majority's ranking justice. The initial assignment is particularly important, because the opinion might gain members for the majority or drive them away, and a justice's initial vote may later be changed.

It is through majority opinions that the Supreme Court's policy is most explicitly developed. Thus the Chief Justice's opinion assignments can affect that policy. They also affect the value of an opinion as precedent, because of the doctrinal bases the writer uses. The opinion's acceptability to those who watch the Court closely may also be affected by who writes for the Court. Such considerations constrain his choices when assigning opinions. Another restriction is that he must distribute the workload of writing opinions of the Court among all the justices. This is not easy if some justices are frequently not in the majority. Even if someone is frequently in dissent, that justice must share the Court's institutional work. The chief must also share in the work of writing opinions himself. There is also some expectation he will retain the "big" cases for himself. However, he cannot keep them all if he is to meet his administrative obligations as well as expectations imposed by the Court's internal social relations and created by professional observers of the Court.

The Chief Justice's assignment practices may also be affected by some strategies, related to the Court's internal politics, through which he might try to hold his majority together. Danelski suggested two:

> *Rule 1:* Assign the case to the Justice whose views are the closest to the dissenters on the ground that his opinion would take a middle approach upon which both majority and minority could agree.
>
> *Rule 2:* Where there are blocs on the Court and a bloc splits, assign the case to a majority member of the dissenters' bloc on the ground that he would take a middle approach upon which both majority and minority could agree and that the minority Justices would be more likely to agree with him because of general mutuality of agreement.[19]

Rohde recently found that assigning justices generally "favor those justices who are closest to them in the various issue areas."[20] However, workload considerations and the fact that some justices are never closest to the Chief Justice, made it impossible to do this all the time. McLauchlan found use of a tension-reduction strategy in which Chief Justice Warren overassigned to majority justices closest to the minority and to those joining the majority through votes inconsistent with their usual position in close political cases through 1962. In economic cases, opinions were assigned to maximize presentation of the liberal position.[21] The presence of large majorities—a situation in which it is "more likely . . . that a majority opinion can be created which is substantially different from the preferred position of the assigner"[22]—led to some overassignment to those in the mid-majority position, thus reducing *intra*majority tension. Chief Justice Warren, like Chief Justice Vinson before him, underassigned to himself.

Ulmer, going a step further, found that, in the early Warren Court, Warren assigned proportionately fewer cases to Frankfurter than to others, although he gave Frankfurter (and Black) proportionately more significant cases and Douglas and Clark proportionately fewer. The Chief Justice also assigned himself proportionately more significant cases, particularly on civil liberties. In close (5–4) cases, Warren substantially *under*assigned to himself, and overassigned to Frankfurter, Clark, and Douglas, the latter primarily in civil liberties cases. Danelski's rule about assignment to moderate justices seems supported when we find that Clark, who spoke for the Court in criminal procedure cases like *Mapp* v. *Ohio*, "received most of his assignments in cases that were liberally decided and in which Black or Douglas or both (along with Warren) were available for writing."[23]

At the end of the Warren Court, opinions of the Court were spread relatively evenly among the justices. Fortas and Brennan wrote disproportionate numbers of unanimous opinions in the 1967 Term, as did Warren in the 1968 Term. Warren seemed to save more major cases such as stop-and-frisk for himself than he had earlier, although major cases were also assigned to other justices.

Chief Justice Burger allegedly tried at first to control opinion-assignment even when in the minority. Initially, he was prevented from doing this by Black and Harlan. In the minority after initial argument of the abortion cases, he tried again, over Douglas's objection,[24] although he ultimately joined the majority in that case. More important, assignment patterns changed with Burger. Workload was not allocated as evenly as it had been earlier, perhaps because more cases were assigned by others as a result of the Chief Justice's propensity to dissent. Burger also seemed to keep more cases for himself than had Warren.

In Burger's first term, he gave himself mostly unanimous cases. He underassigned to both Brennan and Harlan and used Douglas regularly despite his frequent unavailability because of his dissents. White, assigned to write in eight split opinions, particularly on criminal procedure, also received four cases from the other assigners. Black and Douglas, now frequent assigners, primarily in the close case category, seemed not to favor anyone; however, they took several cases for themselves.

In the 1970 Term, some of the previous term's patterns continued. New colleague Blackmun wrote only eight opinions for the Court, but Burger relied heavily on Black and Stewart for opinions of the Court and wrote many himself, most notably the *Swann* busing cases. Douglas, Brennan, and Burger wrote primarily in unanimous cases, White and Black, primarily in close ones. (Black also assigned himself three 5–4 decisions.) Perhaps because of his increasing conservatism, Black fared *quite* well in assignment of key cases, such as the ruling on the 1970 Voting Rights Act and the crucial *Younger* v. *Harris* injunction cases.

After Powell and Rehnquist were seated in the middle of the 1971 Term, the *number* of opinions assigned to each judge then smoothed out and remained relatively smooth thereafter, although discrepancies in the *rate* at which judges received cases from the Chief Justice continued. Douglas, also an opinion-assigner, gave cases heavily to Brennan and himself during 1971 and 1972, but was more impartial in 1973.

The Chief Justice rewarded the other Nixon appointees as well as White and Stewart with opinions in major cases throughout the transition, although in 1973 he rewarded his own clique more fully than he did the "swing" justices, with White generally doing better than Stewart. Of some interest is the assignment of Rehnquist to criminal procedure cases, because such assignments contradict the strategy of centrist assignments in close cases—a strategy that would lead to the choice of someone like White (so used in other criminal procedure rulings). As might be expected, Brennan, Marshall, and Douglas received less major cases or wrote when the Court was unanimous, although Brennan did write in the Denver school case.

Despite the rewards given his colleagues, Burger's monopolizing of major cases and close cases (nine 5–4 opinions in the 1972 Term alone) was quite obvious and his self-assignment included plea-bargaining and Amish school attendance, key obscenity cases, and access to media. Most important, he wrote for the Court in the Nixon tapes case, decided unanimously, and in the 5–4 ruling in the Detroit cross-busing case. Thus, overall, we see the Chief Justice *not* underassigning himself as Warren had done and certainly not being hesitant to keep "good" cases for himself. However, after his first year, he did manage to allocate rewards more evenly, just as he also managed to smooth out the workload distribution.

CONCLUSION

In this chapter, we have seen how the patterns of interaction within the Supreme Court have reflected as well as caused the changes in the Court's direction. Even a relatively simple matter like participation in decisions has become related to the Court's direction as Justice Rehnquist, in situations when other justices might have recused, added his vote to provide conservative results. Patterns of dissent changed substantially during the transition: increased volume reflected increased dissensus, but also the dissenters changed over time as the liberals found themselves on the losing side more and more frequently instead of in charge of a predominantly liberal Court. While dissensus increased, evident in frequency of votes, frequency of concurring and dissenting opinions, and in the tone of the latter, cohesion within subgroups on the Court remained high. The dominant subgroup was the highly cohesive Nixon Four, which, despite the absence of absolutely monolithic voting, held together on criminal procedure— the issue area at the heart of President Nixon's campaign to change the Court. And, in Chief Justice Burger's opinion assignments, we see greater rewards for his own clique and for the White-Stewart swing pair, with the most conservative member of the Court, Justice Rehnquist, being a frequent spokesman in that policy area.

NOTES

1. Erwin Griswold, "The Supreme Court's Case Load: Civil Rights and Other Problems," *University of Illinois Law Forum* (1973), 624.

2. Figures from *Harvard Law Review* are somewhat understated, because concurring opinions and votes are counted as "breaking" unanimity. When a justice concurs in part and dissents in part, it is counted as a dissent.

3. Figures compiled by the author, based on nonunanimous signed full opinion cases. *Harvard Law Review*'s figures show an even sharper drop, to 28.7 percent in 1969, all the way to 18.9 percent in 1970, rising slightly to 22.5 percent

and 21.3 percent in 1971 and 1972. There was also considerable disagreement in the Court's actions summarily affirming or reversing lower court decisions.

4.   In nonthreat situations, 40 percent of the Warren Court's opinion coalitions are "minimum-winning"; in threat situations, while only 23 percent were minimum-winning, the most frequent size was a nine-member (unanimous) coalition (26 percent). With five- and six-member coalitions combined, 63 percent of the coalitions were minimum-winning size in nonthreat situations, while in threat situations only 43 percent were. David W. Rohde, "Policy Goals and Opinion Coalitions in the Supreme Court," *Midwest Journal of Political Science*, 16 (May 1972), 218–219.

5.   *First National City Bank* v. *Banco Nacional De Cuba*, 406 U.S. 759 (1972).

6.   *Schneckloth* v. *Bustamonte*, 412 U.S. 218 at 277, 290 (1973).

7.   Joel Grossman, "Dissenting Blocs on the Warren Court: A Study in Judicial Role Behavior," *Journal of Politics*, 30 (November 1968), 1083, 1080.

8.   Schubert's data on the earlier Warren Court is at Glendon Schubert, *The Quantitative Analysis of Judicial Behavior* (Glencoe, Ill.: Free Press, 1959), pp. 99–129.

9.   Data developed by the author based on nonunanimous signed full opinions.

10.   Philip B. Kurland, "1970 Term: Notes on the Emergence of the Burger Court," in Kurland, ed., *Supreme Court Review 1971* (Chicago: University of Chicago Press, 1971), p. 268.

11.   For an earlier study of two justices who voted together often and who were crucial to the Court's direction, see Schubert's "Hughberts" (Hughes and Roberts) analysis, *Quantitative Analysis*, pp. 192–210.

12.   Kurland, "1971 Term: The Year of the Stewart-White Court," in Kurland, ed., *Supreme Court Review 1972* (Chicago: University of Chicago Press, 1973), p. 163.

13.   *U.S.* v. *U.S. District Court*, 407 U.S. 297 (1972); *Kastigar* v. *U.S.*, 406 U.S. 441 (1972) and *Zicarelli* v. *New Jersey State Commission on Investigation*, 406 U.S. 472 (1972); *Nixon* v. *U.S.*, 418 U.S. 683 (1974). Less controversial was *S & E Contractors* v. *U.S.*, 406 U.S. 1 (1972), where he also recused.

14.   *Gravel* v. *U.S.*, 408 U.S. 606 (1972); *Branzburg* v. *Hayes*, 408 U.S. 665 (1972); *Laird* v. *Tatum*, 408 U.S. 1 (1972).

15.   An evenly divided Court would have *affirmed* the contempt convictions in two of three companion cases (*Branzburg* and *In Re Pappas*), but Rehnquist's participation was necessary to reverse the ruling in the third, *U.S.* v. *Caldwell*, and to allow an opinion to be written.

16.   409 U.S. 824 (1972).

17.   John MacKenzie, "The Rehnquist Recuse: Judging Your Own Case," *The Washington Monthly*, 6 (May 1974), 60. See also MacKenzie, *The Appearance of Justice* (New York: Charles Scribner's Sons, 1974).

18.   He added that to have an evenly divided court affirm both "would lay down 'one rule in Athens, and another rule in Rome' with a vengeance."

19.   David Danelski, "The Influence of the Chief Justice in the Decisional Process of the Supreme Court," in Walter Murphy and C. Herman Pritchett, eds., *Courts, Judges, and Politics* (New York: Random House, 1961), p. 503.

20.   Rohde, "Policy Goals, Strategic Choice and Majority Opinion Assignments in the U.S. Supreme Court," *Midwest Journal of Political Science*, 16 (November 1972), 667.

21.   William P. McLauchlan, "Research Note: Ideology and Conflict in Supreme Court Opinion Assignment, 1946–1962," *Western Political Quarterly*, 25 (March 1972), 16–27.

22.   Rohde, "Policy Goals, Strategic Choice and Majority Opinion Assignments," 673.

23.   S. Sidney Ulmer, "The Use of Power in the Supreme Court: The Opinion Assignments of Earl Warren 1953–1960," *Journal of Public Law*, 19 (1970), 65.

24.   "Burger Move May Shift Court's Abortion Stand," *Washington Post*, July 4, 1972, p. A1. The data below, developed by the author, assume, however, that the conventional assignment process was followed.

CHAPTER FOUR

The Transition: An Overview

The predominant view is that the Warren Court was uniformly liberal and activist. Yet if we are to have an accurate baseline or jumping-off point for understanding the changes that occurred during the transition from the Warren Court to the Burger Court, we need to see more clearly what the Warren Court did as well as what it did *not* do. We need to know questions the Court left unanswered, "oppressed peoples" the Court did not reach with its protections, and decisions that did not run in a liberal direction. If we are to estimate the amount of change that resulted from the transition along a liberal-conservative dimension, we must be careful not to overestimate the liberalism of the Warren Court. We must keep in mind that there was no simple shift from a liberal Supreme Court to a conservative one.

In this chapter, we will take a broad look at the Warren Court's general accomplishments, leaving details for our subsequent examination of specific policy areas. We then take a brief look at the content of the Court's docket, after which we present an overview of trends on the Burger Court. We end by discussing whether President Nixon got from the Court either the results he might have wanted or approaches to deciding cases that he would have found appropriate.

A LOOK BACK AT THE WARREN COURT

The tendency to exaggerate the Warren Court's liberalism through hindsight is not wholly unjustified. The Supreme Court before Earl Warren's time had not concentrated its effort on civil liberties and civil rights matters, and the Vinson Court's civil liberties record was not particularly distinguished.[1] For example, only 19 percent of the civil liberties cases during the 1946 Term were decided in favor of the claimant. If one were to compare the Burger Court with the Vinson Court, the Burger Court would look very good to liberals. But the Warren Court had decided in favor of the civil liberties claimant at a rate of over 76 percent after 1962 (when Frankfurter retired) and about 80 percent in its last two terms.[2] If we were also to take into account the intensity of the Court's feeling and the scope of the Court's concerns, the contrast would be even greater.

Even though the Supreme Court's attention to civil liberties had increased gradually through the twentieth century, the Warren Court "succeeded impressively in freeing itself from the self-doubts that deterred constitutional development during the 1940–1953 period,"[3] and was outstanding in its active acceptance of civil liberties claims:

> In relation to its predecessors, Warren's was the most activist court not only in America, but with a high degree of probability, also in world history, in regard alike to the number and the diversity of the civil libertarian causes that it sponsored, and the degree of favorable support that it gave to such causes.[4]

We tend to remember major decisions and the series of controversies in which the Warren Court became embattled. The growth in the civil liberties portion of the Warren Court's docket attracted most attention. The Court also handed down many rulings on economic matters, generally reaching liberal results through statutory interpretation or by eliminating state policy that conflicted with federal law. When the Court infrequently disapproved actions of federal regulatory agencies, the resulting rulings were also more economically liberal than the agencies' decisions.[5] One other type of case with which the Court dealt in the economic area involved workmen's compensation. These cases, arising under the Federal Employers Liability Act (FELA), had been a continuing source of friction among the justices because some felt they were not of sufficiently broad importance for the Court to be dealing with them. Because of the absence of workmen's compensation statutes like those in the states, the Supreme Court acted like a workmen's compensation commission when cases got to the high court. Here the justices tended to focus on the object (the physically injured employee) rather than his situation[6] and concentrated on dispensing justice rather than developing law.

If we turn to the Warren Court's rulings on civil liberties, the area in which it made its greatest mark, we see that the Court's first major ruling was the historic 1954 decision in the school desegregation case, *Brown* v. *Board of Education*,[7] that "separate but equal" had no place in education. Decided by a unanimous Court that the Chief Justice helped produce,[8] *Brown* signalled a difference in approach between the Warren Court and the Vinson Court. Along with the implementation ruling in the case the following year calling for "all deliberate speed" in achieving desegregation,[9] the decision was popular, at least outside the South.[10] However, the implementation ruling allowed Southern officials, including federal judges, to temporize. As a critic puts it, "Never in the history of the Supreme Court had the implementation of a constitutional right been so delayed or the creation of it put in such vague terms."[11]

Brown may have foretold great changes in the law of race relations, but the Court itself avoided further involvement in school desegregation questions for a decade. The one exception was in the Little Rock school controversy in 1958, where the Court repudiated and criticized efforts by Governor Faubus to block school desegregation. In 1964, the Court also invalidated efforts by officials in Prince Edward County, Virginia, to close the public schools rather than comply with a desegregation order.[12] While the Warren Court had made its name with school desegregation, it began to acquire new momentum in the area only in the late 1960s when it demanded results instead of promises to comply.[13] By this time, Congress and the executive branch had begun to dominate the field, and it was only through the fund cutoff provisions of the 1964 Civil Rights Act and the HEW desegregation guidelines[14] that substantial desegregation was accomplished.

The Warren Court had also "finished strong" in the areas of public accommodations and housing discrimination. However, while the Warren Court consistently reversed convictions of blacks for sitting in at restaurants, it *never* came to grips with the basic question of a proprietor's independent right to refuse service and to reinforce it by summoning the police to arrest for trespass.[15] When Congress passed the public accommodations section of the 1964 Civil Rights Act, the Court strongly affirmed this use of Congress' interstate commerce power.[16] The Court continued to interpret the 1964 Civil Rights Act broadly. The justices also read the 1965 Voting Rights Act broadly after upholding it as a proper exercise of Congressional power.[17] Similar action occurred in 1968 when the justices upheld an 1866 statute applied to housing, at the same time indirectly validating the 1968 Open Housing Act.[18]

The Court was relatively forceful in dealing with various attempts to force the NAACP to produce its membership lists or to apply the barratry ("ambulance-chasing") statutes to the organization.[19] When the rights of those engaged in demonstrations were at issue, the Court, while allowing a peaceful march to a state capitol, affirmed the power of the states to restrict picketing and demonstrations near courthouses and jails.[20]

If *Brown* v. *Board of Education* generated the first resistance to the Warren Court's civil rights policies, the Court's rulings in the field of internal security in the mid-1950s generated the next controversy, which enlisted conservatives from all over the nation. A series of decisions in 1956 and 1957 on the rights of those accused of being Communists brought sharp attacks from Congress, including nearly successful efforts to limit the Court's jurisdiction.[21] The Court responded in 1958 and 1959 by retreating from its earlier rulings.[22] However, the Court, recovering the initiative, later invalidated most state loyalty oath provisions when the steam had gone out of McCarthyism.[23] The inconstancy of the Warren Court's liberalism is shown by the finding that the volume of political liberalism decisions "doubled in 1956 and 1957 in comparison to 1954 and 1955, then dropped sharply during 1958 and 1959, and then rose sharply again in 1960."[24] Support of civil liberties claims even showed an unfavorable balance in 1958–1960.[25]

The early 1960s saw two additional controversies that brought efforts to amend the Constitution to reverse the Court. One was reapportionment of legislatures, where the Court first said, in *Baker* v. *Carr*, that the subject was justiciable, and then ruled in *Reynolds* v. *Sims* that both houses of all state legislatures had to be apportioned on the basis of population. The reapportionment ruling, considered by Chief Justice Warren to have been his most important, most clearly marked both the Warren Court's activism and the defeat of a position of judicial self-restraint identified particularly with Justice Frankfurter and stated in his *Baker* v. *Carr* dissent:

> Disregard of inherent limits in the effective exercise of the Court's "judicial power" . . . may well impair the Court's position as the ultimate organ of "the Supreme Law of the Land" in that vast range of legal problems . . . on which this Court must pronounce. [P]ublic confidence in its moral sanction . . . must be nourished by the Court's complete detachment, in fact and in appearance, from political entanglements and by abstention from injecting itself into the clash of political forces in political settlements. . . . [There should be] a frank acknowledgement that there is not under our Constitution a judicial remedy for every political mischief, for every undesirable exercise of legislative power.[26]

The other controversy was over prayer in the public schools. As part of its position that church and state should be clearly separated, the Court first invalidated a prayer *written by state officials* and then outlawed Bible-reading and recitation of the Lord's Prayer in school.[27] The ruling on reapportionment, although "virtually invisible to the general public,"[28] had been popular among those who knew of the decision.[29] By contrast, public opinion on school prayer, a decision of which many people were aware,[30] was clearly negative (30 percent for, 70 percent against the rulings in 1966). In addition to an unsuccessful constitutional amendment for voluntary prayer in public buildings, there was substantial noncompliance, particularly where school prayer had been most common, the South and Midwest.[31]

Also in the First Amendment area, the Court handed down rulings considerably changing the rules on libel and obscenity. The new policies eliminated many although not all restrictions on libelous and obscene speech. However, the rules for judging obscenity remained vague and murky, despite several attempts to clarify them. Considerable unhappiness about the obscenity rulings existed in conservative circles but was somewhat submerged by even greater displeasure with the Court's rulings in other areas.

Despite the activity over reapportionment and school prayer, dislike for decisions did not necessarily stir opponents to activity directed against the Court.[32] In fact, while specific decisions *had* produced considerable opposition, that did not necessarily mean an absence of general support for the Court. In the mid-1960s, "despite the unpopularity of its decisions, . . . the Court still retain[ed] a substantial reservoir of diffuse support," with "four times as many people lend[ing] the Court positive diffuse support as lend it positive specific support."[33]

In addition to race relations, we most often associate the Warren Court with the reform of criminal procedure; this was the policy area in which the Court's most controversial set of rulings was handed down. The Warren Court "criminal procedure revolution" began in 1961 when the Court excluded illegally seized evidence from state trials (*Mapp* v. *Ohio*).[34] That ruling was followed by the decision granting right to counsel at trial to indigents (*Gideon* v. *Wainwright*).[35] The two rulings that most rankled the police granted access to counsel at the stationhouse (*Escobedo* v. *Illinois*)[36] and required that people be warned of their rights if their confessions were to be used (*Miranda* v. *Arizona*).[37] This last case produced a 35 percent–65 percent negative evaluation in a 1966 public opinion poll. As a result of these rulings, criminal procedure decisions became far more visible between late 1964 and late 1966, replacing civil rights and school prayer in people's minds. The cases also show the Court's preference for broad rules rather than judging individual cases on the basis of the "totality of circumstances" involved. The Warren Court continued to deal separately with each portion of the Bill of Rights, using the idea of "selective incorporation," which meant that only *portions* of the Bill of Rights were intended to be included (incorporated) in the Fourteenth Amendment Due Process Clause as prohibitions against the states; "full incorporation"— including the entire Bill of Rights at once—was not supported. However, by the end of the Warren Court, almost all the criminal procedure provisions of the Bill of Rights had been incorporated into the Fourteenth Amendment Due Process Clause as restrictions against the states. The Court had also extended some protections into new areas like the juvenile court, and had dealt with complicated problems like the conflict between free press and fair trial rights.[38]

Yet the Warren Court was not uniformly pro-defendant. The same Court that had increased the rights of criminal defendants also approved police "stop-and-frisk" of suspicious individuals, increased the types of material that could be taken in a search, approved the government's use of informants, and provided the basis for electronic surveillance with a warrant. The Court also refused to apply most of its new criminal procedure rules to those already in prison, perhaps responding to negative feedback over the rulings themselves.

Much—in fact, a great deal—that the Warren Court did was liberal; much was ground-breaking. Yet the Court that had handed down the major ruling in school desegregation almost totally avoided the area for close to fifteen years. The justices never reached the major constitutional question involved in the sit-ins, although they saved those sitting-in from convictions and later upheld Congress' power to act on the subject. The Court, although casting down a lightning bolt on reapportionment, never specified acceptable redistricting standards. Although voiding loyalty oaths, the justices pursued an uneven course in the 1950s on internal security in responding to congressional attacks; they were also hesitant to extend rights to demonstrators protesting in front of public buildings. The Court was extremely clear in adopting new and liberal libel law standards and movie censorship procedures. However, although trying hard, the Court was never able to articulate a clear standard for obscenity, although a more liberal set of rules was produced. While search-and-seizure, right-to-counsel, and other criminal procedure protections were adopted, the Court also upheld basic tools of law enforcement and seldom would apply its ground-breaking rules to past cases. Thus we see a Court that advanced much, much farther down the road on civil rights and civil liberties matters than its predecessor, but that at the same time was neither consistently liberal nor consistently activist.

In large measure, because it was a court, the Warren Court also did *not* reach all problem areas and only began to reach some toward the very end. Welfare was one example; here the Court's liberalism was restrained. While durational residence requirements for welfare recipients were eliminated, little was done to affect benefit levels. While the justices had invalidated school prayer, they did not deal with aid to parochial schools. Rights of prisoners and women were hardly touched, and Indians' rights were considered on only a haphazard basis. In all these areas, which were presented to the Court principally by poverty lawyers, the justices seemed to lag behind at least some segments of society. While the issues were new and the Court was dependent on what was presented to it, the Court could have done more with what was offered. Yet, despite these omissions, Chief Justice Warren left a massive legacy of judicial liberalism.

DOCKET CONTENT

The earlier transition between the Vinson and Warren Courts had produced great changes in docket composition. Economic and civil liberties cases averaged 58 percent of all cases decided on the merits during the Vinson Court and the Warren Court's first two terms, but the figure rose to 81 percent in the remaining Warren Court years, most of the increase coming from civil liberties matters.[39]

Changes in docket composition from the Warren Court to the Burger Court have also occurred but have not been great. From 1967 through 1973, the number of federal and state criminal cases taken by the Supreme Court for full disposition remained roughly the same, although the number of appeals from federal habeas corpus cases taken by the justices increased. Civil cases taken from the state courts did not increase, but those accepted from the lower federal courts increased, most of that increase being cases involving state or local governments. In 1972, the Court also accepted more federal government litigation resulting from direct enforcement of federal statutes.[40]

Much of the Supreme Court's caseload remained in the area of civil liberties and criminal procedure. According to Griswold, the number of civil rights cases increased from one-third of those with written opinion in the 1962 Term to close to two-thirds ten years later.[41] More than 50 percent of all the Court's cases in the 1972 Term involved criminal law issues; over half were petitions from prisoners saying they were too poor to file the regular papers. These *in forma pauperis* petitions are said to have deluged the Court. Although Judge Friendly pointed out that they increased only in about the same proportion as other cases taken to the Court in the 1960s, that still meant a large increase in their numbers.[42] However, on the basis of filings in the lower courts, petitions challenging convictions are likely to decrease and to be replaced to some extent by challenges to the conditions of prisoners' confinement.

With the coming of the Burger Court, some observers expected business and commercial cases to receive greater emphasis and criminal procedure cases less.[43] Confirming this expectation, Howard has noted a substantial drop from 1968 through 1973 in the granting of certiorari petitions from the Courts of Appeals in criminal cases; at the same time, private civil actions increased from 34 percent in 1968 to 50 percent of the Court's docket in 1973–1974. In addition, "dispositions with full opinions in economic matters rose from 39 percent in the 1968 Term to 55 percent in the 1972 Term, while the proportion of criminal and habeas corpus cases fell from 42 percent to 32 percent."[44] The civil liberties-criminal law portion of the docket has remained high but has been partly displaced.

The majority of the Court's cases involve constitutional issues; the other cases involve such matters as interpretation of federal statutes and conflicts between lower courts. Thus the volume of criminal and noncriminal constitutional cases is substantial, but there are still many cases in traditional fields of jurisdiction such as admiralty, bankruptcy, civil procedure, taxation, patents, and antitrust, many of which have far-reaching policy implications. For example, the ultimate fate of our system of railroad transportation is substantially affected, if not fully controlled, by the rulings in complex merger cases involving economically distressed railroad corporations.[45] The growth of Community Antenna Television (CATV) systems is vitally affected by rulings like those handed down by both the Warren and Burger Courts, that CATV retransmission of programs does *not* constitute "performance" under the Copyright Act.[46]

Similarly, rulings in the area of labor-management relations may have an effect on labor peace (or unrest). Although Congress has made many statements about labor policy, the Court is still left with the task of interpreting the statutes and determining who—the courts, administrative agencies, or workers and management—should make basic labor policy. Thus the Court has had to decide cases on the enforcement of agreements between union and management for arbitration combined with "no-strike" clauses and has enforced them against both company and union.[47] Still other cases involve the relationship between the government and its contractors on such matters as defaults on payments and renegotiation of contract terms. Others raise the issue of the relationship between federal law and state law and the degree to which the supremacy of federal law should be enforced.

POLICY DIRECTIONS: GENERAL TRENDS

The Supreme Court's docket may be diverse, and some shifts in its content may have taken place. Of greater importance are the policy changes that occurred during the transition. Before turning to particular policy areas, we need to stress that the general consensus is that no great across-the-board change in policy occurred, although some areas, such as criminal procedure, were affected more than others. There was some limited retreat, but there were no initial sharp departures from the Warren Court's work. The Burger Court's work was characterized by a limitation on expansion of Warren Court doctrine, marginal change, and a generally unsettled Court, the last only partly a result of the Nixon appointees coming to the Court over several years. Because most government policy-making occurs incrementally, this should not surprise us. Changes in personnel stimulate changes in policy, but the changes are unlikely to be radical. Institutional factors such as precedent, the flow of cases to the Court, and its collegial nature, as well as a Supreme Court justice's role expectations, serve as constraints. Even someone with an already well developed role as an appellate judge, like Chief Justice Burger, is affected by the Supreme Court's earlier work, and a judge coming to the Court with the intent and commitment to bring about great change would have to spend considerable time persuading his colleagues against the background of precedent and their consistency of attitudes.[48]

    Little change was noticeable in the first term after Earl Warren's departure. One reason was that the docket contained many cases to which the Court had already granted hearing before Chief Justice Burger came to the Court. That first term produced a noticeably less assertive tone. There were no sharp departures from the past, no expected "first strides to the rear" but instead "sidesteps and refusals to step forward."[49] The 1970 Term showed somewhat more change, but again it was easier to see that forward movement had been halted than to identify the contours of new doctrines. The Burger Court did not yet have its own directions. Later impressions were not radically different; observers found the Burger Court unpredictable, with no clear decisional pattern, or, as one observer stated, "divided, uncertain, and adrift."[50]

Within this broad picture of limited change, there is also evidence of considerable retrogression from the Warren Court's rulings. Schubert found that, for the period since the mid-1930s, the last Warren Court ranked first on political (civil liberties) liberalism, with the middle Warren and Roosevelt Courts next, *followed by the Nixon Court*. Nixon, he says, "Clearly has succeeded . . . in turning the Supreme Court ideological clock backward, by almost a generation to about the point where it was when he became vice-president and Earl Warren was in his first term or two. . . ."[51] Change in even greater degree is evident on economic policy. While the late Warren Court ranked most liberal, the Nixon Court ranked just above the Hughes Court of the mid-1930s against which FDR did battle. "Clearly," says Schubert, "we must concede that the President has been even more successful in reshaping the economic orientation of the court than he has been in stamping out Warren Court libertarianism."[52]

DID NIXON GET WHAT HE WANTED?

What happened to the wishes President Nixon had expressed for the Court and tried to implement? At a 1972 press conference, President Nixon said he thought he had achieved as balanced a Court as possible, given his opportunities to name members of the Court. Whether the public would agree with his assessment is unclear. In 1973, a Gallup Poll showed the public giving the Court a rating higher, but only slightly higher, than four years earlier (and well lower than in the mid-1960s): 37 percent rated it good or excellent, as against 33 percent in 1969, but only 6 percent rated it excellent, down from 8 percent; 35 percent thought the Court too liberal, 26 percent, too conservative.[53] A 58 percent majority favored the Court's recent obscenity ruling, and a 57 percent majority, siding with the Nixon appointees, disapproved of the invalidation of the death penalty. However, a similar

majority (57 percent) opposed the ruling that the First Amendment did not give newsmen a right to protect confidential sources,
and 53 percent, siding with the President, disagreed with the
Court's parochial school aid decisions. Thus, at least as far as
public opinion was concerned, the Court had still not moved as far
from the Warren Court's rulings as it could have done. Over a
year later, a Harris survey did show that the Supreme Court was
receiving increased public respect. Forty percent of those responding said they had a great deal of confidence in the Court, as
compared with 23 percent in 1971.[54] Yet some of that respect may
have come from the Court's ruling against Mr. Nixon in the tapes
case.

Elite opinion about the quality of the Court's work has, however, not changed much, although Howard has said the Court has
adopted a "new temper" which "improved [its] standing among
former critics and reduced its political risks."[55] Yet the new Court
seems to be criticized for the quality of its work much as was the
Warren Court. The Warren Court was said not to be providing
adequate reasons for its decisions and to be using "tortured evasive judicial response to basic constitutional issues."[56] One critic
even suggested that the Court had "failed abysmally to persuade
the people that its judgments had been made for sound reasons,"
leaving to its successor the task of restoring "the confidence of the
American public in the rule of law."[57] (While President Nixon did
not promise a more competent Court, and Senator Hruska had
justified mediocrity during the Carswell nomination, concern for
improved analysis in the Court's rulings could easily be inferred
from such criticisms.)

The greatest loss in quality came from the departures of Justices Black and Harlan; for the latter, "the obligation of a high
court judge was to resolve the issues brought to him only after
recognizing and dealing with the complexities of the problems
and not by ignoring them."[58] While the skills of Potter Stewart
and Lewis Powell are now being appreciated, one can often hear
criticism of the Court's handling of particular cases, for example,
Justice Blackmun's abortion opinion, Chief Justice Burger's
opinion in the Nixon tapes case, or Burger's opinion in *Harris* v.
New York, the ruling limiting *Miranda*. Law professors have said
the latter showed "a total absence of analysis and provides no
support for its result," failing to discuss adequately the case's
important policy considerations or to resolve the problems they
raised.[59] Thus the Burger Court reached a result appreciated by
the law-enforcement community, but without telling us *how* it did
so, thus opening it to the same criticism as the Warren Court.
This case is only one example of the broader pattern in which the

new justices seem not to have worked out a way of confronting the underpinnings of Warren Court opinions they dislike, leaving "the most crabbed handling of precedents and the most inarticulate reasoning."[60]

The clearest indication of President Nixon's success was the Court's record. In the Warren Court's last term, the claim had been upheld in 81 percent of the relevant cases involving a civil liberties claim. With Warren and Fortas gone and the new Chief Justice on the bench, only 55 percent of the 1969 Term cases were so decided. In the 1972 Term, the figure was down to 43.5 percent, the lowest since 1957.[61] In the last term of the Warren Court,

> the Court majority had favored the government in criminal prosecutions in only eight of twenty-six cases; in the Burger Court's first term, the majority sided with the government prosecutor eighteen of twenty-nine times.[62]

In the 1972 Term, criminal justice rulings were 2–1 *un*favorable to the civil liberties claim, and there was also a 13 favorable –21 unfavorable record in free speech. The Court's 1972 Term record on the rights of blacks, women, and the poor was 11–6 favorable to the claimed rights, but this was well below past 4–1 favorable ratios. The Burger Court was unwilling to go as far in some areas of race relations law as the Warren Court had; was more willing to allow restrictions on freedom of speech, particlarly on obscene materials; showed increased resistance to granting rights to welfare recipients; and issued search-and-seizure rulings more in line with the views of law-enforcement officers.

However, the President did not get all he might have wanted in crucial policy areas, and, to quote a newspaper headline, "President Nixon hasn't turned Supreme Court into Rubber Stamp."[63] Certainly one would have been hard put to call the Burger Court conservative on the basis of the last day of the 1972 Term (June 25, 1973), when the Court upheld the rights of aliens, invalidated aid to parochial schools, struck down restrictive food stamp amendments, and outlawed textbooks for private schools that discriminated in admissions. That Mr. Nixon's appointees did not join in all of these rulings does not diminish the point that the President had not fully turned the Court around.

As we have seen, the justices appointed by the President were not totally cohesive, leading to some defeats for the administration's position. For example, the Court rejected an effort to reach labor union violence through the Hobbs (extortion) Act when Justice Blackmun joined the majority. (In this case, Justice Douglas, joining the other Nixon appointees in dissent, took a shot at the majority for "judicial legislation."[64]) But it was not only such instances that led to discomfort for Mr. Nixon. When the Court invalidated restrictive state abortion statutes, only Justice Rehnquist (joined by Justice White) voted the President's position, and Justice Blackmun wrote the Court's opinion.

In the church-state area, where the President had promised Catholics aid to parochial schools when consistent with the Constitution, the Court invalidated virtually every state plan for aid to lower education on which it ruled. In one of the first cases over which Chief Justice Burger presided, the Court, in a unanimous *per curiam* ruling, refused to allow further administration-requested delay in desegregation, and put "all deliberate speed" to death. Burger later wrote for a unanimous Court upholding massive cross-busing as a remedy for previously segregated schools although the remedy was limited to *de jure* segregation. Other efforts to evade desegregation in the South met with near-unanimous resistance from the Court. The Court even extended the march of desegregation to the North, although it did finally draw the line in 1974 in refusing to uphold busing across school district lines. As Howard observed, "For all the talk of a Southern strategy to be worked through judicial action, the Burger Court has fulfilled the President's pledges on race relations far less in the South than in the North."[65]

In the criminal procedure area, the justices extended right to counsel at trial, and said that criminal charges had to be dismissed when a speedy trial was not provided. More important, the Court unanimously invalidated domestic security electronic surveillance without a warrant, with Powell writing, and threw out many surveillance orders as not authorized by the proper officials, a ruling the Court topped off by rejection of the President's executive privilege claim in the tapes case, although the Court did recognize executive privilege as a concept.

If we turn from *policy results* to the new justices' *approaches*, the President should have been more pleased. The justices did exercise more restraint, indicating that changes in the laws had to come from elsewhere. The Chief Justice said that the Court's task was not to correct all state laws or "cure every disadvantage human beings can experience."[66] Justice Powell also clearly showed this position when the Court rejected the challenge to financing education through the property tax, which was said to deprive those living in tax-poor districts of equal educational services:

> The consideration and initiation of fundamental reforms with respect to state taxation and education are matters reserved for the

legislative processes of the various States and we do not do violence to the values of federalism and separation of powers by staying our hand. . . . The ultimate solutions must come from the lawmakers and from the democratic pressures of those who elect them.[67]

In taking this stance, the justices often used a distinction between what they would do if they were members of the other branches of government and what they could do as judges, already noted in connection with Justice Blackmun's death-penalty dissent.

This new-found restraint was applauded by conservatives. Columnist James Kilpatrick found in 1973 that in cases "that offered opportunities either to exercise judicial restraint or to leap into judicial innovation" that the Court came out on the side of restraint in fully eighteen of twenty-four, and "In at least a dozen cases . . . , the Court upheld the doctrine that used to be known, in my own magnolia day, as the Doctrine of States Rights."[68] However, the Court was not always restrained even with the Nixon appointees present. Kilpatrick has said that the abortion decisions had "not even a colorable hint of restraint" and were "judicial legislation, judicial activism, judicial usurpation."[69]

The Nixon appointees also gave greater weight to the government when the interests of the individual citizen and those of the government conflicted. The government's good intentions had never been taken for granted during the Warren Court; intentions of government officials were given greater weight during the Burger Court. In examining state regulations, the Warren Court had indicated that laws based on categories like race and poverty were suspect. The justices had also used a "strict scrutiny" test under which a regulation was set aside if the protected interest was thought "fundamental," unless the state interest was "compelling." Although not every right claimed was found to be fundamental, "the Warren Court never found a state measure sufficiently compelling to override anything it deemed fundamental";[70] many state regulations were invalidated even when the states' interest was recognized and considered legitimate. Indicating that the test used is at least partly a function of the justices' values, the new appointees applied a looser test; when a state regulated some activity, its means had only to be "rationally related" to its goals and the state did not have to adopt the least burdensome alternative. Yet this shift did not mean that citizens' claims would be rejected out-of-hand. In the 1971 Term, of fifteen cases involving equal protection claims, in only four was the state's action sustained without intensive examination. In seven of the cases, the claims were either sustained or sent back to lower courts; included were cases on the rights of unwed fathers and illegitimates, anticontraception laws, and preference to men as administrators of estates.[71]

In criminal procedure cases, new broad rules, such as extending right to counsel for indigents at trial to any situation where jailing would occur,[72] were still to appear. However, the new justices generally moved away from adoption of broad rules and decided cases on the basis of "totality of circumstances" in the case. When a violation of Warren Court criminal procedure precedents was shown, the justices often said it was "harmless error." Such devices produced fewer overturned state convictions but meant potentially *more* detailed scrutiny of state cases than broad rules would require.

Outside the criminal procedure area, there was less consensus on the Court about using a case-by-case or individualizing approach. Considering an alien's right to practice law, Justice Powell stressed the need for individual determinations, while Rehnquist, dissenting, talked in terms applicable across the board. But Rehnquist also objected that if the Court kept striking down broad rules adopted by the states, it or the states would be forced into many more individualizing determinations.[73]

The new judges also showed deference to the lower courts, but the deference had limits, particularly when they wanted to establish conservative criminal procedure policy. Thus, despite the general rule that findings of fact by two lower federal courts (the district court affirmed by the Court of Appeals) will not be reversed, the four Nixon appointees jointed White to uphold the reliability of the identification of a defendant despite lower federal court rulings that a lineup would be more appropriate than the suggestive showup that had taken place.[74] That restraint could be overcome by ideology appeared in other areas as well, but it was not always in the conservative direction. When the Court held the Sierra Club did not have standing to raise environmental claims because it had not alleged injury to itself or its members, Justice Blackmun asked in dissent: "Must our law be so rigid and our procedural concepts so inflexible that we render ourselves helpless when the existing methods and the traditional concepts do not quite fit and do not prove to be entirely adequate for new issues?"[75] Similarly, in ruling that abortion cases were not moot even though pregnancy might already be terminated, because of the possibility of repetition, he stressed that "Our law should not be that rigid" as to prevent a ruling.[76]

Just as "liberalism" and "conservatism" are terms with an uncertain content, so "restraint" and "activism" provide an uneasy dichotomy. However, the two pairs of terms are related through the justices' values. When conservative justices find that

deference to legislative or executive policy will produce conservative results, they remain restrained; when activism is necessary
to defeat or restrain liberal policy, the same justices can become
active, just as they can set precedent aside (also a nonrestrained
stance) when it is helpful to their values. And the liberal justices
who had adopted a more activist or interventionist posture to
achieve their values can quite comfortably utilize restraint when
they think it will produce favorable results. Such changes produce some seeming inconsistencies in posture, as when the liberal
justices remaining on the Burger Court began to argue for positions associated with the conservative members of the Warren
Court. This simply reminds us of the Holmesian aphorism that
the life of the law has been not logic but experience.

CONCLUSION

The Warren Court left behind numerous major decisions, many of
which had provoked considerable controversy because of the
strongly liberal stance the Court had adopted. Included were rulings on race relations, internal security, reapportionment, school
prayer, obscenity, and criminal procedure, the last receiving the
most attention as the Warren Court came to an end. Although the
Warren Court was not fully consistent in its liberalism and dealt
with matters in addition to civil liberties, we remember it for the
substantial attention it gave to that broad policy area. The transition produced some change in docket content, but the bulk of the
Burger Court's rulings remained in the constitutional area. The
policy changes from the Warren Court to the Burger Court were
more substantial. Here we have noted mixed policy results stemming from a posture of not expanding Warren Court doctrine;
retrogression from the earlier Court has also been noted. When
we look at the Burger Court from the perspective of the person
who appointed the new justices, we find that, despite defeats for
the administration's policy, President Nixon seemed to come off
reasonably well in terms of the approaches his nominees adopted.
They were restrained when it was helpful, and reached out when
it proved useful to obtain other ends. As Kilpatrick put it,

> . . . this is a good court; and if one can overlook a few appallingly
> bad decisions, the Court is providing a large measure of stability
> and solid progress in the law. As conservatives gaze upon the ruins
> of much of the Nixon Administration, we can look to the Court, and
> be thankful.[77]

NOTES

1. C. Herman Pritchett, *The Vinson Court and Civil Liberties* (Chicago: University of Chicago Press, 1954).

2. Glendon Schubert, *The Constitutional Polity* (Boston: Boston University Press, 1970), p. 50. There was a regression in 1964, and the percentage of full opinion cases decided against the government dropped noticeably in that year.

3. Robert G. McCloskey, "Reflections on the Warren Court," *Virginia Law Review*, 51 (November 1965), 1234. McCloskey calls the 1940–1953 period "a period of irresolution marked by the alternate flowing and ebbing of judicial self-confidence."

4. Schubert, p. 71.

5. Schubert, pp. 47–48. For another study showing support of the agencies, see Joseph Tanenhaus, "Supreme Court Attitudes toward Federal Administrative Agencies," *Vanderbilt Law Review*, 14 (1960–1961), 473–502.

6. Harold Spaeth et al., "Is Justice Blind?" *Law & Society Review*, 7 (Fall 1972), 131. See also Schubert's work on strategy in granting certiorari in FELA cases, "The Certiorari Game," in *The Quantitative Analysis of Judicial Behavior* (Glencoe, Ill.: Free Press, 1959), pp. 210–254.

7. 347 U.S. 483 (1954).

8. S. Sidney Ulmer, "Earl Warren and the Brown Decision," *Journal of Politics*, 33 (August 1971), 689–702.

9. *Brown* v. *Board of Education*, 349 U.S. 294 (1955).

10. Along with school prayer, the civil rights decisions of the Court accounted for more than 68 percent of the likes and dislikes with respect to the Court stated in a Survey Research Center 1964 post-election survey. See Walter F. Murphy and Joseph Tanenhaus, "Public Opinion and the United States Supreme Court: Mapping of Some Prerequisites for Court Legitimation of Regime Changes," *Law & Society Review*, 2 (May 1968), 362. Also in Joel Grossman and Joseph Tanenhaus, eds., *Frontiers of Judicial Research* (New York: John Wiley, 1969), pp. 273–303.

11. Lewis M. Steel, "Nine Men in Black Who Think White," *New York Times Magazine*, October 13, 1968, p. 57. Steel, a white NAACP attorney, lost his job over this article.

12. *Cooper* v. *Aaron*, 358 U.S. 1 (1958); *Griffin* v. *Board of Education of Prince Edward County*, 377 U.S. 218 (1963).

13. *Green* v. *County School Board of New Kent County*, 391 U.S. 430 (1968).

14. See Gary Orfield, *The Reconstruction of Southern Education* (New York: John Wiley, 1969).

15. For a study of these cases from a policy perspective, see Grossman, "A Model for Judicial Policy Analysis: The Supreme Court and the Sit-in Cases," in Grossman and Tanenhaus, eds., *Frontiers of Judicial Research* (New York: John Wiley, 1969), pp. 405–460.

16. *Heart of Atlanta Motel* v. *U.S.*, 371 U.S. 241 (1964); *Katzenbach* v. *McClung*, 379 U.S. 294 (1964). The Court also abated still-pending pre–Civil Rights Act sit-in convictions, further avoiding the basic constitutional issue from the sit-ins. *Hamm* v. *City of Rock Hill*, 379 U.S. 306 (1964).

17. *South Carolina* v. *Katzenbach*, 383 U.S. 301 (1965). After use of the poll tax had been invalidated in federal elections by the Twenty-Fourth Amendment, the Court struck it down in state elections. *Harper* v. *Virginia State Board of Elections*, 383 U.S. 663 (1966).

18. *Jones* v. *Mayer*, 392 U.S. 409 (1968).

19. *Bates* v. *Little Rock*, 361 U.S. 516 (1960); the almost continuous *NAACP* v. *Alabama* litigation, see 357 U.S. 449 (1958); and *Gibson* v. *Florida Legislative Investigation Committee*, 372 U.S. 539 (1963). On the latter, *NAACP* v. *Button*, 371 U.S. 415 (1963).

20. *Edwards* v. *South Carolina*, 372 U.S. 229 (1963); *Cox* v. *Louisiana*, 379 U.S. 536 and 599 (1965), convictions reversed on technical grounds (courthouses); *Adderly* v. *Florida*, 385 U.S. 39 (1966) (jails).

21. See Walter Murphy, *Court and Congress* (Chicago: University of Chicago Press, 1962).

22. Compare *Pennsylvania* v. *Nelson*, 350 U.S. 497 (1956), with *Uphaus* v. *Wyman*, 360 U.S. 72 (1959); *Watkins* v. *U.S.*, 354 U.S. 178 (1957), with *Barenblatt* v. *U.S.*, 360 U.S. 109 (1959); *Slochower* v. *Board of Higher Education*, 357 U.S. 468 (1958), with *Lerner* v. *Casey*, 357 U.S. 468, and *Beilan* v. *Board of Education*, 357 U.S. 399 (1958).

23. See *Baggett* v. *Bullitt*, 377 U.S. 360 (1964), and *Whitehill* v. *Elkins*, 389 U.S. 54 (1967).

24. Schubert, *The Judicial Mind* (Evanston, Ill.: Northwestern University Press, 1965), p. 278.

25. Partly because Frankfurter shifted position. Schubert, *Constitutional Polity*, p. 112.

26. *Baker* v. *Carr*, 369 U.S. 186 at 267–270 (1962).

27. *Engel* v. *Vitale*, 370 U.S. 421 (1963); *Abington School District* v. *Schempp/Murray* v. *Curlett*, 374 U.S. 203 (1963).

28. Murphy and Tanenhaus, 363. They used 1964 and 1966 post-election surveys involving a national sample. They also caution against results derived from "forced choice questions of the variety so typical in commercially conducted public opinion polls," which they say "strenuously overestimate the Court's visibility because they solicit responses from people who may possess no meaningful information." 360. In Wisconsin, where redistricting had taken place, there were "remarkably low levels of knowledge" about reapportionment in 1966. Kenneth M. Dolbeare, "The Public Views the Supreme Court," in Herbert Jacob, ed., *Law, Politics, and the Federal Courts* (Boston: Little, Brown, 1967), p. 199. However, in another study, redistricting was one of the four areas of Court activity or decisions to which respondents referred. (The others were civil rights, prayers in school, and Communists.) John Kessel, "Public Perceptions of the Supreme Court," *Midwest Journal of Political Science*, 10 (May 1966), 175, using a 1965 Seattle sample.

29. It received a 76–24 favorable rating in a 1966 Harris Poll, suggesting that "Conservative opposition to the Court is less widespread in the general public than the outcries of proponents would suggest." Dolbeare, p. 207. Perhaps this is also an example of the point that "Congruence between respondents' political outlooks and the jurisprudence of the Warren Court meant . . . increased support for the Court." Walter F. Murphy, Joseph Tanenhaus, and Daniel L. Kastner, "Public Evaluation of Constitutional Courts: Alternative Explanations," Sage Professional Papers, 01–045 (Beverly Hills, Cal.: Sage Publications, 1973), p. 49.

30. "The prayer decisions have apparently been one of the most salient actions of the Court, being unknown only to the same seemingly irreducible number of persons who have managed to remain unaware of the segregation decisions." Dolbeare, p. 199. Among the politically more active, "Political views—not knowledge—were dominant in determining support for the Court." Murphy, Tanenhaus, and Kastner, p. 54.

31. See Stephen L. Wasby, *The Impact of the United States Supreme Court: Some Perspectives* (Homewood, Ill.: Dorsey Press, 1970), pp. 126–135, as well as Richard Johnson, *The Dynamics of Compliance* (Evanston, Ill.: Northwestern University Press, 1967); William Muir, *Prayer in the Public Schools* (Chicago:

University of Chicago Press, 1967); and Kenneth Dolbeare and Philip Hammond, *The School Prayer Decisions: From Court Policy to Local Practice* (Chicago: University of Chicago Press, 1971).

32.   When asked whether they would do anything to change a Court decision they disliked, 36 percent of a Wisconsin sample said they would; while half would contact their congressmen, only "about a quarter would act within the established legal processes, and . . . a scattered few would have recourse of agitation with the general public to develop opposition to the Court." Dolbeare, p. 208. "This is quiescence indeed," he observed. See also Kessel, 191.

33.   Murphy and Tanenhaus, 374. On the other hand, "Almost nobody who liked the Court's particular decisions was critical of it as an institution." Ibid., 376. Murphy and his colleagues found that "attitudes toward public policy as measured by the scale of liberalism/conservatism" was the single item with the best power to explain support or opposition to the Court. Murphy, Tanenhaus, and Kastner, p. 50.

34.   367 U.S. 643 (1961).

35.   372 U.S. 375 (1963).

36.   378 U.S. 478 (1964).

37.   384 U.S. 436 (1966).

38.   *In Re Gault*, 387 U.S. 1 (1967); *Sheppard* v. *Maxwell*, 394 U.S. 333 (1966).

39.   Schubert, *Constitutional Polity*, p. 50.

40.   For greater detail, see *Harvard Law Review* tables.

41.   Erwin Griswold, "The Supreme Court's Case Load: Civil Rights and Other Problems," *University of Illinois Law Forum*, 1973, 619.

42.   Henry Friendly, *Federal Jurisdiction: A General View* (New York: Columbia University Press, 1973), pp. 47–48.

43.   See Ulmer, "Supreme Court Justices as Strict and Not-So-Strict Constructionists: Some Implications," *Law & Society Review*, 8 (Fall 1973), 27–28.

44.   J. Woodford Howard, Jr., "Is the Burger Court a Nixon Court?" *Emory Law Journal*, 23 (Summer 1974), 757.

45.   See the *New Haven Inclusion Cases*, 399 U.S. 392 (1970), a continuation of the *Penn-Central Merger Cases*, 389 U.S. 498 (1967).

46.   *Fortnightly Corp.* v. *United Artists TV Corp.*, 392 U.S. 390 (1970); *Teleprompter Corp.* v. *C.B.S.*, 415 U.S. 394 (1974).

47.   *Boys Markets, Inc.* v. *Retail Clerks Union*, 398 U.S. 235 (1970), overruling *Sinclair Refining Co.* v. *Atkinson*, 370 U.S. 195 (1962); *Chicago & Northwestern Railway* v. *United Transportation Union*, 402 U.S. 571 at 597–598 (1971).

48.   Murphy deals with such a goal-oriented judge. *The Elements of Judicial Strategy* (Chicago: University of Chicago Press, 1964).

49.   Gerald Gunther, "The Supreme Court, 1971 Term: Foreword: In Search of Evolving Doctrine in a Changing Court," *Harvard Law Review*, 86 (November 1972), 2.

50.   Ibid., 1.

51.   Glendon Schubert, "The Future of the Nixon Court," University Lecture, University of Hawaii, May 9, 1972, p. 12. He used 1972 as his baseline year for the Burger Court.

52.   Ibid., p. 13.

53.   "Public Rates Burger Court Higher Than Warren's," *Milwaukee Journal*, July 29, 1973.

54.   "Public's Respect for Institutions Continues Dwindling," *Southern Illinoisan* (Carbondale), September 30, 1974.

55.   Howard, 763.

56. Gunther, 3–4.

57. Philip Kurland, "Toward a Political Supreme Court," *University of Chicago Law Review*, 37 (1969), 45–46.

58. Kurland, "1970 Term: Notes on the Emergence of the Burger Court," in Kurland, ed., *The Supreme Court Review 1971* (Chicago: University of Chicago Press, 1971), p. 320. For Kurland's examination of other terms of the Burger Court, see the appropriate volumes of *The Supreme Court Review*.

59. Alan Dershowitz and John Hart Ely, "Harris v. New York: Some Anxious Observations on the Candor and Logic of the Emerging Nixon Majority," *Yale Law Journal*, 80 (1971), 1189 ff., quoted at James Simon, *In His Own Image: The Supreme Court in Richard Nixon's America* (New York: David McKay, 1973), p. 159.

60. Gunther, 6.

61. The statistics are those of the American Jewish Congress, reported by Simon, pp. 110–131, and Norman Dorsen, "The Court of Some Resort," *Civil Liberties Review*, 1 (Winter–Spring 1974), 82–104.

62. Simon, p. 111.

63. *Southern Illinoisan* (Carbondale), October 3, 1973, p. 4.

64. *U.S.* v. *Enmons*, 410 U.S. 396 (1972).

65. Howard, 749. Others have noted that there was little negative Congressional response to the Burger Court, except for school busing. Justin J. Green, John R. Schmidhauser, and Larry L. Berg, "Variations in Congressional Responses to the Warren and Burger Courts," *Emory Law Journal*, 23 (Summer 1974), 725–743.

66. *Vlandis* v. *Kline*, 414 U.S. 441 at 460, 463 (1973).

67. *San Antonio School District* v. *Rodriguez*, 411 U.S. 1 at 58, 59 (1973).

68. James L. Kilpatrick, "This Much, At Least: The Court," *National Review*, 25 (37, September 28, 1973), 1050. See also his newspaper columns, "At Long Last, A Little Restraint," *Milwaukee Journal*, April 18, 1973, p. 23, on the school property tax decision, and "The Supreme Court: Stability, Solid Law," *Milwaukee Journal*, July 7, 1973, p. 25, mostly about reapportionment.

69. Kilpatrick, "This Much, At Least . . . ," 1051.

70. Wallace Mendelson, "From Warren to Burger: The Rise and Decline of Substantive Equal Protection," *American Political Science Review*, 66 (December 1972), 1227; in italics in original.

71. Gunther, 25–26.

72. *Argersinger* v. *Hamlin*, 407 U.S. 25 (1972).

73. See his dissent in *LaFleur* v. *Cleveland Board of Education*, 414 U.S. 632 (1974), on mandatory fixed-date maternity leaves for school teachers.

74. *Neil, Warden* v. *Biggers*, 409 U.S. 189 at 193, note.

75. *Sierra Club* v. *Morton*, 405 U.S. 727 at 755–756.

76. *Roe* v. *Wade*, 410 U.S. 113 at 125 (1973).

77. Kilpatrick, "This Much, At Least . . . ," 1052.

CHAPTER FIVE

Policy During the Transition: Judicial Review

The Supreme Court's power comes largely from its exercise of judicial review, the ability to declare unconstitutional the acts of other branches of the government. To some extent, the Supreme Court's activism is determined by how it exercises this power. Certainly the Supreme Court in the early days of the New Deal used judicial review fully to invalidate most of President Franklin D. Roosevelt's economic program. After 1937, however, use of judicial review of *national* legislation subsided substantially, although the Court has continued to exercise its power to invalidate state laws inconsistent with the Constitution, particularly where individual rights are involved. In this chapter, we focus on how the Court, in using its power of judicial review, has treated the other branches of government during the transition. In so doing, we see the range of non–civil liberties issues with which the Court had to deal and the way in which civil liberties questions became intertwined with other issues.

INVALIDATING ACTS OF CONGRESS

The Warren Court exercised its power of judicial review most frequently and fully on constitutional questions involving action by the states contravening the Fourteenth Amendment's Equal Protection and Due Process Clauses. Such rulings constituted a major part of the Court's effort to achieve equality for blacks, greater freedom of speech, and expanded criminal procedure rights. The Court exercised its judicial review power less vigorously when federal statutes were before it than when state rules were contested, just as it more vigorously defended civil liberties against state than against federal encroachment. The justices upheld 85 of 115 civil liberties claims (65 percent) against the states during the 1960–1964 Terms of the Court. At the same time, such claims against the national government were upheld at a lower rate, in 44 of 81 cases (54 percent). There was no wholesale invalidation of congressional statutes by the Court to achieve its liberal position,[1] and the Court specifically upheld all the civil rights legislation to come before it. However, in rulings virtually all of which had civil liberties implications, at least twenty federal statutes (or parts of statutes) were struck down by the Warren Court. As these invalidations were in aid of liberal policy, liberals had to change their views because "The historic position of liberalism toward judicial review has been that the judicial function is a limited one."[2]

The Warren Court exercised its power of judicial review frequently in the field of internal security; here it encountered its greatest resistance. Regulations restricting Communist Party members' right to travel, their employment in defense plants, and their right to be labor union officers were invalidated.[3] Enforcement of the Internal Security Act's compulsory registration provisions was struck down because the provisions forced self-incrimination under the Smith Act.[4] The Court also used the Fifth Amendment to invalidate provisions in the federal gambling tax stamp, firearms, and marijuana tax laws. The laws created a double bind for the individual by subjecting him to prosecution if he did not comply with federal registration requirements, and additional state or federal prosecution when he did comply.[5]

Most of the Court's exercise of judicial review dealt with citizenship and courts-martial. Using the prohibition on bills of attainder and the Eighth Amendment's ban on cruel and unusual punishment, the Court said citizenship could not be taken away for desertion from the military, remaining abroad to avoid military service, or voting in a foreign election.[6] The Court also severely limited use of courts-martial. Trying civilians (the wife of a serviceman stationed overseas; ex-servicemen, for offenses committed while in the service; civilian employees of the military) by court-martial was banned, as was court-martialing servicemen for non-service-connected offenses committed outside a war zone.[7] Also related to due process was the invalidation of the Lindbergh Kidnapping Act death-penalty provisions, which allowed imposition of capital punishment by the jury but not the judge.[8] A major act of judicial review having nothing to do with these areas was the invalidation of Social Security Act durational residence requirements for receiving welfare benefits as an interference with the right to travel.[9]

The Burger Court also invalidated a number of federal statutes, some of which involved First Amendment questions like the right to hold demonstrations on the grounds of the U.S. Capitol or to wear military uniform in a play if the armed services might be discredited.[10] Due process issues were behind the invalidation of several other laws, such as the one that discriminated between male and female members of the armed services as to requirements for payment of dependents' benefits or food stamp legislation aimed at communes and college students.[11]

One constitutional ruling that quickly produced a new constitutional amendment was the Court's decision on the eighteen-year-old vote. The justices said that Congress, in passing the Voting Rights Act of 1970, could validly provide for the eighteen-year-old vote in national elections, but could *not* do so in state and local elections.[12] This 5–4 ruling led directly to submission and ratification of the Twenty-Sixth Amendment, providing the eighteen-year-old vote in all elections.

ECONOMIC POLICY

In the area of economic policy, the Burger Court fairly consistently upheld Congress' power to act and interpreted congressional statutes broadly. This was the case even when civil liberties questions were connected with the economic issues. For example, Justice Douglas, apparently letting his economic liberalism override his liberal free speech position, wrote for a unanimous Court that First Amendment rights were not immune from regulation when used as part of an antitrust violation, although Justice Stewart pointed out that the Court was retreating from a Warren Court ruling.[13]

Another example of the mixture of economic regulation and civil liberties policy was the Court's initial ruling on the so-called Bank Secrecy Act, which required that banks *record* checks and foreign and domestic transactions, and the Secretary of the Treasury's regulations, under which only a relatively narrow set of transactions were to be *reported*. The majority upheld some parts of the act, saying the record-keeping requirements were reasonable and within Congress' commerce power, because financial transactions would help reveal patterns of criminal activity.[14] Other claims, based on the Fourth and Fifth Amendments, were deferred as premature, primarily because the reports had not yet been required on all transactions. The dissenters, arguing that bank customers had a "constitutionally justifiable expectation of privacy" in the contents of their bank accounts, thought the statute a "sledge hammer approach to a problem that only a delicate scalpel can manage." Brennan and Marshall also objected that the majority was engaging "in a hollow charade whereby Fourth Amendment claims are to be labelled premature until such time as they can be deemed too late."

The Court's rulings interpreting the antitrust statutes, providing a large part of the Burger Court's commercial diet, show a mixed response to government antitrust efforts. On one side, for example, the justices upheld an order to Ford to divest itself of Autolite (spark plugs); affirmed a lower court ruling ordering Phillips Petroleum to sell California oil refining and marketing operations acquired with the Tidewater Oil Company facilities; and found a marketing cooperative's marketing restrictions a violation of the Sherman Act.[15] The Court also said the Federal Power Commission had an obligation to check for anticompetitive effects before permitting certain activities by utilities.[16] However, on the other side, the Court refused to approve the government's effort to have a deep-shaft mining corporation divest itself of a strip-mining corporation[17] and decided against the government in two bank cases under Section 7 of the Clayton Act, involving mergers that may substantially lessen competition or create a monopoly.[18] In one of its antitrust cases, the Court also showed its attitude toward its own precedent. Ruling on Curt Flood's attack on the baseball reserve clause, the justices refused to remove the anomaly of having only baseball—of all the major sports—not subject to the antitrust rules. This would have required overruling precedent, and the justices said changing the law was for Congress, not the Court.[19]

The Burger Court also upheld Congress' authority to make certain activity illegal because of its connections with commerce, thus following the Warren Court's strong affirmance of such use of the interstate commerce power to deal with public accommodations. Congress' interstate commerce power and customs and postal authority over obscene material were affirmed, and congressional legislation on "loan-sharking" was also sustained.[20] At times, however, the Court was unwilling to interpret commerce broadly, for example, being unwilling to consider gambling covered under the Travel Act simply because out-of-state people used the gambling facilities.[21] In a conservative ruling involving commerce, the justices held that union picketing of foreign ships, not to organize their workers but to protest substandard wages paid their seamen, did not affect commerce under the Labor-Management Relations Act.[22]

Judicial review in the economic area also entailed considerable attention to state legislation. The Court, just as it had to determine the reach of Congress' commerce power, also had to determine whether state law interfered with ("burdened") interstate commerce. The Burger Court, following Supreme Court practice since 1937, generally treated the states gently, upholding a head tax, a use tax applied to aviation fuel stored in a state and loaded there aboard airplanes for interstate flights,[23] and a personal property tax assessed on cash registers sitting in a warehouse for shipment abroad to foreign buyers.[24] The Court was even faced with a case involving the *reasonableness* of state economic regulations, used by judges to invalidate such laws during the pre-1937 controversy over substantive due process. As it had done for years, the Court restrained itself and upheld the state rules.[25]

There were, however, limits on the Court's restraint. When an Arizona official ordered a cantaloupe grower, who grew in Arizona and packed nearby in California, to ship to California in specific types of containers, the Court overturned the order.[26] Mississippi's attempt to recover the wholesale markup from out-of-state liquor dealers selling to military bases in the state was also invalidated on the basis of the Twenty-First Amendment. Here Justices Douglas and Rehnquist, an unusual combination, dissented, claiming "irreparable harm to the cause of States' rights."[27]

Another aspect of judicial review of state statutes was whether federal rules gave the national government exclusive control, thus ousting state legislation. The Warren Court had used this pre-emption doctrine in the area of internal security as well as in the economic realm. The Burger Court, however, seemed disinclined to use the doctrine in the same way. For example, a Florida oil spills law imposing no-fault liability on waterfront oil-handling facilities and ships and allowing the state its share of cleanup costs was challenged for being in conflict with the Water Quality Improvement Act. The Court, giving environmentalists a victory, upheld the law. (However, a noise pollution ordinance imposing a nighttime curfew on jet flights was later invalidated because it conflicted with the Noise Control Act of 1972.)[28]

The supremacy issue was also involved in copyright cases, where the Court upheld, 5–4, California's statute prohibiting the pirating of recordings, saying Congress' power to issue copyrights was not exclusive.[29] This ruling, apparently a sharp departure from prior thinking on the subject, opened up the possibility for state protection for many items (including computer programs, performers' rights, choreographic works, and printed forms) not covered by federal law.[30] The Court extended this policy by allowing states to deal with industrial espionage through their trade secret laws. Douglas, dissenting and arguing for openness and against protection, thought Congress intended that an item should be in the public domain, with free competition prevailing, where no patent existed.[31]

This question of pre-emption also arises frequently in labor law. Here the Court has generally favored national policy. In reinforcing Congress' economic policy, the Court has allowed injunctions against strikes, saying that the legislative policy of promoting labor peace and industrial self-government overrides the terms of the federal anti-injunction laws.[32] Such rulings have, however, provoked some justices to claim that the idea of voluntary settlements (backed up by the strike) is being damaged. The justices also have consistently ruled in favor of broad coverage for arbitration agreements, even on such subjects as safety problems in the mines,[33] thus supporting the idea that Congress intended that labor and management should solve problems by themselves by entering into arbitration agreements.

SEPARATION OF POWERS

In a sense, all the Court's cases dealing with national statutes and regulations involve the authority of the other branches to pass a law or issue a regulation, at least in a particular form or with a specific meaning. However, most rulings deal only with the scope and content of policies, not with the operation of the Congress or the presidency as institutions. Having looked at the former type of judicial review, we now turn to the latter. Here we find that the Warren Court started a practice of looking at the inner workings of the legislature. Having accepted reapportionment cases (see Chapter Six), saying the subject was no longer a political question, the Court found it easier to deal with questions like refusals by legislative bodies to seat duly elected members. Once the Warren Court had taken this step, the Burger Court found little difficulty in dealing with other internal legislative matters.

Traditionally the Supreme Court has been reluctant to intervene in the workings of the other branches of the national government. The Vinson Court had overturned President Truman's 1952 seizure of the steel mills. But the Court, particularly in time of war, had been hesitant to challenge exercises of presidential power. The Court had also been chary of disturbing the procedures by which Congress carries out its work, although it has done so from time to time, necessarily in determining the validity of contempt citations voted by investigating committees. For example, the Warren Court set aside the contempt conviction of a labor leader who had refused to answer House Un-American Activities Committee (HUAC) questions, on the ground that the pertinency of the questions had not been made clear. In that case, Chief Justice Warren severely lectured the House of Representatives for approving a vague committee charter and for not adequately overseeing its activities, and reprimanded the committee itself for its fishing expedition into political beliefs. However, in a subsequent case, the same Court backed off; the justices, saying there was no First Amendment right to silence, upheld the contempt conviction of a professor who had refused to answer pertinent HUAC questions.[34]

In 1969, the Court intervened more directly in congressional affairs, ruling on the House of Representatives' refusal to seat Congressman Adam Clayton Powell. This case was, in a way, a follow-up to the Court's ruling that the Georgia legislature could not refuse to seat Julian Bond because of his statements on the draft and Vietnam.[35] In the Powell case, Chief Justice Warren said the issue of the House's refusal to seat a duly elected Congressman was *not* a political question to be avoided and was not mooted by Powell's having been seated in the next Congress. The Court, ruling that Congress' power to judge its members' qualifications extended only to qualifications stated in the Constitution, then invalidated the House's action, but stopped short of issuing coercive relief against the House.[36] While the Burger Court did not have to deal with anything like the Powell issue, it did rule that a state recount would not interfere with the congressional prerogative of judging its members' qualifications, because the Senate or House would still have to make its own determination.[37] President Nixon's resignation eliminated the possibility of the Court's having to decide whether to rule on an appeal from an impeachment trial.[38]

In *Powell*, the Court had said that members of Congress themselves were immune from suit because of the Constitution's Speech and Debate Clause, but the activities of Congress' employees, carrying out Congress' work, could be reached through litigation. Important Burger Court cases revolved around this issue. The bribery prosecution of Senator Daniel Brewster of Maryland was upheld when the majority narrowly defined legislative activity.[39] Although the majority said activity "related" to legislative acts, such as a promise to carry out a bribe, was not immunized, the dissenters felt the majority was ignoring a six-year-old Warren Court precedent, in which a bribery prosecution of a Congressman was invalidated because it was based on a speech he made.[40]

When Senator Mike Gravel (D–Alaska) read large portions of the Pentagon Papers at a subcommittee session and helped to arrange with Beacon Press for publication of the Papers, his legislative assistant was subpoenaed to testify before a grand jury on both matters. Here the four Nixon appointees and Justice White said that arranging for publication of the Pentagon Papers was not "legislative activity"; thus the aide (and presumably the senator himself) could be questioned about it. However, the Court did say the aide was immune from questioning about his legislative activities because his assistance to a senator or representative was an essential part of the legislative process.[41] Justice Douglas, dissenting, would have barred questioning of the senator, his assistant, *and* the Beacon Press on the ground that publication arrangements were necessary to inform the public concerning the war.[42]

A suit to stop circulation of a House committee report on the District of Columbia schools that named specific school children produced an interesting about-face when the Nixon appointees found their limiting of legislative activity used against them. The liberals plus White and Powell ruled that the distribution of defamatory materials outside Congress was not part of the legislative process. Thus congressional employees, plus the Public Printer and the Superintendent of Documents, were not immune from suit, although committee members, staff consultants, and investigators were immune from action for compiling and publishing the report or securing votes for its publication.[43] The Chief Justice, dissenting, thought the majority was engaged in "a continuing surveillance" of Congress' reports on subjects "plainly within the legislative powers conferred on Congress by the Constitution." Justice Blackmun, sounding like Douglas in the *Gravel* case, thought the publication and dissemination of the report an essential part of the information-gathering function of the legislature, although he thought it unfortunate that some people's reputations would be damaged by the publication.

The Court's position as judge of separation of powers led to its being faced with questions of the President's war-making authority. That authority was challenged during the Vietnam war on the ground that Congress had the sole authority to declare war. The Supreme Court consistently refused to review lower court rulings that the issue was nonjusticiable as a political question or that Congress had acquiesced in the war by passing appropriations for it.[44] Justice Douglas, occasionally joined by Justice Stewart and once by Justice Harlan, dissented consistently, objecting to the Court's refusal to deal with important, precisely framed issues dealing with "executive war-making," which posed "an ominous threat to our republican institutions."[45]

In 1973, the Court had to use particularly fancy footwork to avoid the challenge to the Cambodian bombing brought by Congresswoman Elisabeth Holtzman (D–N.Y.). The process illustrates both deference to the executive branch, shown through refusal to accept the case, and the Court's internal tensions. A trial judge had granted an injunction against the bombing, which he said lacked congressional authorization.[46] The Court of Appeals then stayed the injunction, and when the plaintiffs appealed to Justice Marshall as Circuit Justice, he ruled that the appeals court had not exceeded its authority but that he would exceed *his* authority if he were to vacate the stay. However, he said that there was an increasing number of lower court rulings providing standards that would make challenges to presidential war-making justiciable. He also suggested that "as a matter of substantive constitutional law, it seems likely that the President may not wage war without some form of congressional approval except in extreme emergencies." Clearly showing his position on the merits, he added: "When the final history of the Cambodian war is written, it is unlikely to make pleasant reading," with the war possibly to be "adjudged to have not only been unwise but also unlawful."[47]

Unsuccessful with Marshall, the plaintiffs then persuaded Justice Douglas to vacate the stay.[48] Douglas said the case was like any capital punishment case, and his action was taken to avoid having someone die unnecessarily. *On the very same day*, Marshall overruled Douglas after communicating with every other member of the Court. Douglas dissented bitterly: "The telephonic disposition of this grave and crucial constitutional issue is not permissible. . . . A Gallup Poll of inquiry of widely scattered justices is, I think, a subversion of the regime under which I thought we lived."[49]

President Nixon did not escape as easily when he resisted a subpoena for tapes and related documents for the Watergate cover-up trial. In an earlier ruling, District Judge John Sirica had recognized executive privilege. He insisted, however, that a *judge*, not the executive, must make the decision on the validity of an executive privilege claim.[50] The Court of Appeals upheld the order, rejecting the President's claim that it threatened the "continued existence of the presidency as a continuing institution."[51] The President did not appeal this ruling further, perhaps because he learned he would win at most two votes for his position.[52] Instead, we got the "Saturday-night massacre" of the Cox, Richardson, and Ruckleshaus, followed by presidential compliance with the subpoena.

When Judge Sirica issued a new order for production of a much larger number of tapes in the Watergate cover-up case, the ruling *was* appealed. The President's lawyer claimed that a President defines his own powers and should decide whether or not to withhold evidence, saying that he could be reached only through impeachment. Special Prosecutor Jaworski argued that the Constitution did not speak of executive privilege and that the President could not conceal evidence for a criminal trial. In its unanimous ruling, the Supreme Court rejected the President's claims.[53] (The issue of the grand jury's naming the President as an unindicted co-conspirator in the cover-up was not decided, being dismissed on the ground that the Court had "improvidently granted" the President's request to hear that matter.)

To make its decision on the tapes subpoena, the Court had to cut through several obstacles. There had been rulings, including one by the Burger Court itself,[54] that an order denying a motion to quash a subpoena was *not* appealable. However, Chief Justice Burger, noting exceptions, said it would be "unseemly" to force a President to disobey a court order to get review of the subpoena and difficult for a federal judge to hold a President in contempt for disobeying. The Court then rejected the argument that the case was an unreviewable in-house dispute between President and the special prosecutor. The executive, said Burger, citing several Warren Court rulings,[55] was bound by the Attorney-General's regulations giving the special prosecutor specific power "to contest the invocation of executive privilege in the process of seeking evidence deemed relevant to the performance of these specially delegated duties."[56]

Arriving at the substance of the President's executive privilege claim, the Chief Justice recognized and supported the "President's need for complete candor and objectivity from advisers." However, he said a generalized claim of executive privilege not involving protection of special types of secrets would interfere with the judiciary's ability to handle criminal cases properly and would "upset the constitutional balance of 'a workable government.' " The courts, said Burger, needed the subpoena power to carry out their work, and a "full disclosure of all the facts" was necessary in criminal cases. Thus "the generalized assertion of privilege must yield to the demonstrated, specific need for evidence in a pending criminal trial." Burger then approved Judge Sirica's procedure for *in camera* inspection of claims of privilege, in which only appropriate materials would be turned over to the parties in the case. Stressing the need to protect against the "leaking" of material, Burger said all material that did not meet tests of admissibility and relevance would have to be removed and returned to the President.

In this ruling, the justices reasserted their power to decide claims involving the other branches of government, reaffirming Chief Justice John Marshall's *Marbury* v. *Madison* language that it is "emphatically the province and the duty" of the Court "to say what the law is." However, while they rejected the President's specific claim of executive privilege in the case—and, by extension, in other cases where information was necessary for criminal trials—the justices had for the first time legitimated the concept of executive privilege. This left results perhaps more far-reaching than the resounding personal defeat for President Nixon, which led directly to his departure from office.

REVIEW OF AGENCY DETERMINATIONS

In addition to reviewing the operations of the presidency and the Congress and their policies, the Supreme Court is also called upon to review decisions made by the federal regulatory commissions and numerous agencies in the executive branch. These cases involve challenges to both agency policies and agency procedures. Because of the broad range of economic matters regulated by the agencies, the Supreme Court's decisions affirming or overturning agency rulings clearly have implications for the direction of national policy.

Supreme Court support for the agencies has varied over time and between agencies, but overall it has been high. During the Warren Court, the justices supported the agencies at rates exceeding 70 percent in cases reviewed; the rates are even higher if denials of certiorari are included. The Burger Court has continued with a high rate of support. One way to provide that support is to affirm an agency's "primary jurisdiction" over a subject, for example, the Food and Drug Administration's authority over the effectiveness of new drugs.[57] Here Justice Douglas, who wrote for the Court, allowed the FDA to use summary procedures rather than full hearings in some situations, something he would have been quite likely to reject for criminal trials. Showing his economic liberalism and stressing public health and the need for quick effective relief from unsafe or ineffective drugs, he ruled that a single hearing at which all manufacturers could be heard, rather than a separate hearing for each, would comport with due

process. He also said that "administrative controls over drugs
. . . must be exercised with dispatch," to avoid the paralysis that
case-by-case battles in the courts would produce.

The Court also may sustain the exclusive nature of the agency's proceeding. When management, upon the union's request,
had discharged an employee who had failed to pay his union dues,
the employee, instead of filing an unfair labor practice charge
with the National Labor Relations Board, sued the union for violating its constitution and by-laws. Here the Supreme Court said
the case was exclusively within the NLRB's jurisdiction.[58] As this
suggests, the Supreme Court must deal often with the overlap
between the actions of the agencies and those of the courts, as
well as the question of whether a person must first go to the
agency (or perhaps his union) before going to court, and whether
he can get to court at all.[59]

Another way of supporting agencies is to protect their information. The Freedom of Information Act of 1965 had been
enacted to provide increased public access to agency documents.
However, when the act's exceptions were used to deny requests
for information, the Court sustained the agencies in rulings that
were clearly conservative in their protection of the bureaucracy
at the expense of the public's "right to know." For example, several members of Congress tried to get information from the Environmental Protection Agency (EPA) about an underground
nuclear test, but the Court upheld the agency's refusal to provide
the information because the documents, classified Secret or Top
Secret, were entitled to protection under the statute.[60] (Justice
Stewart, however, did protest Congress' "unquestioning deference
to the Executive's use of the 'secret' stamp.")

Still another way to support the agencies is to limit complainants' ability to obtain review of agency rulings. For example,
the Internal Revenue Service revoked the tax-exempt status of
two groups because of lobbying and a racially discriminatory admissions policy said to be dictated by the group's religious beliefs.
Here the Court said that only an action for refund of taxes could
be used to litigate the agency's action.[61] Only Justice Blackmun
dissented, launching a substantial attack on the IRS Commissioner's "virtual plenipotentiary power over philanthropic organizations" based on no clear standards with "little to circumscribe
the almost unfettered power of the Commissioner" with "the
means to challenge that power . . . unfavorable and unsatisfactory at best."

A limited standard of review is also used to support the agencies. This was clear, for example, when the Court unanimously
rejected a challenge to the ICC's car service rules on the return of

empties in the direction of the owning railroad. Justice Rehnquist pointed out that under the well-established standard for reviewing ICC actions, the Court does not weigh evidence before the commission; the commission's regulations were not judged for their wisdom; "and we inquire into the soundness of the reasoning by which the Commission reaches its conclusions only to ascertain that the latter are rationally supported."[62] Similar support for determinations of the executive branch departments has also been shown by the Court, even when some judges think the result is to make administrative action virtually unreviewable. In one case Justice Stewart argued that his colleagues were "serv[ing] notice upon the federal judiciary to be wary indeed of venturing to correct administrative arbitrariness." He thought this particularly unfortunate "at a time when serious concern is being expressed about the fairness of agency justice."[63]

The Court remains at least partly deferential to the agencies even when it is demanding that they take certain action. For example, in ordering the FPC to consider the anticompetitive effects of a utility's security issue and saying an adequate explanation for any summary action would have to be provided by the commission, the Court also reinforced the commission's broad policy-making power and ruled as well that the commission did not have to hold hearings in every case or investigate every allegation made to it.[64] In an environment case involving the legislative provision that construction of a highway through a park was prohibited if a "feasible and prudent" alternate route existed, the Court said that the Secretary of Transportation had to follow necessary procedural requirements in making his determination, but was not required to make formal findings.[65]

As these examples suggest, the justices have generally— albeit not with total consistency—supported the agencies, if the agencies clearly set out the basis for their decisions and support them by some evidence. However, the Court has not ceased careful scrutiny or criticism of the regulatory commissions' work and at times does subject agency actions to an independent fine-tooth-comb review. Agency orders have been set aside when the agency has not developed or presented standards for its action and has failed to connect its findings and conclusions, or has not sufficiently justified departures from past practice.[66]

The agency shown the least deference is the National Labor Relations Board, perhaps because of the highly controversial policy area with which it deals. At times, the Court has narrowly interpreted the agency's jurisdiction; at others, the agency's judgment within the scope of its acknowledged jurisdiction has been revised. For example, in holding that Congress intended to exclude from the coverage of the National Labor Relations Act *all* managerial employees, not just those supervising a company's labor relations,[67] the justices overruled a new NLRB interpretation although the dissenters thought the agency was closer to congressional policy. Similarly, after the board ruled that a bargaining unit *and* contract carried over from one employer to another, the Court also held to the contrary.[68] However, the Court later did uphold the board's action in directing a successor company, which knew of the existence of unfair labor proceedings when it purchased, to reinstate a worker and give him back pay.[69]

Deference to agencies became mixed with free speech policy in both the Warren and Burger Courts. The Warren Court had upheld the Federal Communications Commission's personal attack and political editorial rules, which required a station to provide to the person it had attacked a tape or transcript and an opportunity to reply, whether or not the person could afford to pay. The Supreme Court said the commission had properly exercised authority validly delegated by Congress and had not misapplied the standard of operating in the public interest.[70] (The FCC's authority was also upheld after the commission issued rules to Community Antenna Television Systems (CATV) requiring those covering more than 3,500 subscribers to have independent originating facilities.[71])

The FCC later determined that stations did not have to accept paid political editorial advertisements. Hearing challenges from an anti-Vietnam war businessmen's group and the Democratic National Committee, the Court upheld the commission's determination as reasonable; furthermore, the Court allowed the FCC the latitude to change its mind later.[72] Chief Justice Burger said the stations, not the potential speakers, ought to be able to decide what went on the air, subject to the FCC's review of their operation at the time of renewal of their licenses. This ruling was a clear defeat for the disaffected groups' freedom of speech and reinforcement for the stations' discretionary authority to limit what was to be available to the public, as Douglas and the dissenters made clear. In this case, their free speech ideology was more important than deference to the agency. Douglas thought the Fairness Doctrine "sanctions a federal saddle on broadcast licensees that is agreeable to the traditions of nations that never have known freedom of the press"; however, he concurred because he thought radio and television were entitled to be treated the same as newspapers, with no government interference. Brennan, dissenting, criticized the broadcasters' unwillingness to give the public controversial subjects, which would be relegated "to formats such as documentaries, the news, or panel shows . . . tightly controlled and edited" by broadcasters who rejected material as "scandalous," "crackpot," "insignificant," "trivial," and "beyond the bounds of normally accepted taste."

Individual rights were also involved in other agency cases, particularly in the labor relations area, where the question was often that of the individual's rights against the union. A majority of the Court upheld the NLRB in saying a union could not waive its members' rights to on-premises distribution of literature,[73] although the Court sustained the NLRB's decision that it could not determine the reasonableness of fines imposed on some union members who had resigned from a union during a strike and had continued to work.[74] Justice Douglas, dissenting, thought the board clearly had more expertise in labor matters than did the state courts, but he was also extremely critical of the union, whose fine—greater than the pay the worker had earned during the strike—"reflect[ed] the raw power exercised by a union in its hunger for all-pervasive authority over members." In a related case where a union, whose constitution and by-laws were silent on resignation, had attempted court enforcement of fines against resigned employees for prohibited strikebreaking, the Court, upholding the NLRB, said the union had committed an unfair labor practice.[75] The Court also upheld a Court of Appeals ruling that had reversed the NLRB on the question of a union's right to fine supervisory personnel who were union members for performing the work of rank-and-file workers on strike. The Court said that a company could refuse to hire union members as supervisors, but if it allowed supervisors to join unions, they were properly subject to union discipline.[76]

CONCLUSION

Looking at the Burger Court's overall treatment of the Congress, the President, and the administrative agencies, we find a Court *generally* although not fully self-restrained. The Court's decisions on questions involving Congress' inner workings and its strong rebuke of the President in the tapes case show its willingness to become involved in controversial issues. Yet much deference is paid to officials of executive branch agencies and regulatory commissions, both in rhetoric and in the Court's decisions. Deference to the agencies is to some extent independent of agency policy but also masks feelings about that policy; the justices' ideologies affect their willingness to support or reject agency decisions.

Because of the Court's overall deference to the agencies and the relatively small proportion of their cases that come to the

Court, the individual citizen will remain largely dependent on the agencies, not the Court, for decisions to meet his needs and interests. Similarly, he will be dependent on Congress and the state legislatures for economic and social legislation because of the Court's continuing deference to legislative bodies. This can be seen in its reinforcement of Congress' use of the commerce power, which the Court has now supported for several decades. The present Court is, if anything, somewhat more deferential than its predecessor, by not being as predisposed to use the doctrine of federal pre-emption to strike down state laws in areas where the Congress also legislates.

For all its restraint, the Burger Court has certainly not turned to the sort of position for which Justice Frankfurter or Justice Harlan argued. The pattern is clear not only in the few cases at which we have already looked but also in other areas to be examined in subsequent chapters. The justices allow the other branches of the national government and the states more flexibility than did the Warren Court, but the Burger Court is hardly unwilling to deal with important issues through which the justices might hope to implement their political and social ideologies.

NOTES

1. See Robert B. McKay, "The Supreme Court as an Instrument of Law Reform," *St. Louis University Law Journal*, 13 (Spring 1969), 387–402.

2. C. Herman Pritchett, *The Roosevelt Court: A Study in Judicial Politics and Values, 1937–1947* (New York: Macmillan, 1948), p. 71.

3. *Aptheker* v. *Secretary of State*, 378 U.S. 500 (1964); *U.S.* v. *Robel*, 389 U.S. 258 (1967); *U.S.* v. *Brown*, 381 U.S. 437 (1965). Spaeth tells us that the Court's rulings here were more a function of the object (the security risk) than the situation. The exercise of judicial review was thus apparently in aid of those "who are victims of lawlessness," so that the Court would not "legitimate the activity of those who would punish 'political offenders.'" Harold Spaeth et al., "Is Justice Blind?" *Law & Society Review*, 7 (Fall 1972), 134.

4. *Albertson* v. *Subversive Activities Control Board*, 382 U.S. 70 (1965).

5. *Marchetti* v. *U.S.*, 390 U.S. 39 (1968), gambling; *Haynes* v. *U.S.*, 390 U.S. 85 (1968), firearms; *Leary* v. *U.S.*, 395 U.S. 6 (1969), marijuana. In *Leary*, the Court also invalidated the presumption that if one had "pot" in one's possession, one knew it was imported, although the Court later upheld a comparable presumption with respect to heroin. (What about those domestic poppies?) When Congress revised the firearms laws, the Burger Court upheld it because it protected the transferee of a gun against the use of information he filed. *Mackey* v. *U.S.*, 401 U.S. 667 (1971). However, the Court struck down tax law provisions for forfeiture of property (money) used in violating tax laws. *U.S.* v. *U.S. Coin & Currency*, 401 U.S. 715 (1971).

6. *Trop* v. *Dulles*, 356 U.S. 86 (1958), loss of citizenship through a court-martial for wartime desertion; *Kennedy* v. *Mendoza-Martinez*, 372 U.S. 144

(1963), remaining abroad to avoid military service; *Afroyim* v. *Rusk*, 387 U.S. 253 (1967), voting in foreign election, overruling *Perez* v. *Brownell*, 356 U.S. 44 (1958), affirming loss of citizenship for avoiding military service by remaining abroad and voting in foreign election, in which Warren dissented.

7.   Respectively, *Reid* v. *Covert*, 354 U.S. 1 (1957); *Toth* v. *Quarles,* 350 U.S. 11 (1955); *McElroy* v. *Guagliardo*, 361 U.S. 281 (1960); and *O'Callaghan* v. *Parker*, 395 U.S. 258 (1969).

8.   *U.S.* v. *Jackson*, 390 U.S. 570 (1968).

9.   *Shapiro* v. *Thompson*, 394 U.S. 618 (1969).

10.   *Chief of Capitol Police* v. *Jeanette Rankin Brigade*, 409 U.S. 972 (1972); *Schacht* v. *U.S.*, 398 U.S. 58 (1970).

11.   *Frontiero* v. *Richardson*, 411 U.S. 676 (1973); *U.S. Department of Agriculture* v. *Moreno*, 413 U.S. 529 (1973); *U.S.D.A.* v. *Murry*, 413 U.S. 508 (1973).

12.   *Oregon* v. *Mitchell*, 400 U.S. 112 (1970).

13.   *California Motor Transport Co.* v. *Trucking Unlimited*, 404 U.S. 508 (1972). The earlier case is *Eastern Railroad Conference* v. *Noerr Motor Freight*, 365 U.S. 127 (1961). For a story of the situation resulting in that litigation, see Andrew Hacker, "Pressure Politics in Pennsylvania: The Truckers vs. The Railroads," in Alan Westin, ed., *The Uses of Power* (New York: Harcourt, Brace and World, 1962), pp. 323–376. The Warren Court had also been willing to sustain government action with First Amendment implications, in 1969 upholding antitrust action against agreements by which two newspapers in the same city were operated with combined printing, circulation, and advertising functions. *Citizens Publishing Co.* v. *U.S.*, 394 U.S. 131 (1969). The Court said that only business restraints were involved in the case, not restraints on newsgathering or publishing. The ruling was overturned by Congress the following year through passage of the Newspaper Preservation Act.

14.   *California Bankers Association* v. *Schulz*, 416 U.S. 21 (1974).

15.   *Ford Motor Co.* v. *U.S.*, 405 U.S. 562 (1972); *Tidewater Oil* v. *U.S.*, 409 U.S. 151 (1972); *U.S.* v. *Topco Associates*, 405 U.S. 596 (1972).

16.   *Gulf States Utilities* v. *Federal Power Commission*, 411 U.S. 747 (1973).

17.   *U.S.* v. *General Dynamics Corp.*, 415 U.S. 486 (1974).

18.   *U.S.* v. *Marine Bancorporation*, 418 U.S. 602 (1974); *U.S.* v. *Connecticut National Bank*, 418 U.S. 656 (1974).

19.   *Flood* v. *Kuhn*, 407 U.S. 258 (1972). Justice Blackmun's opinion for the Court is filled with baseball information and "Casey at Bat," as well as a list of stars; Part II begins with Flood's batting averages. After Blackmun's opinion appears this note: "The Chief Justice and Mr. Justice White join in the judgment of the Court, and in all but Part I of the Court's opinion." 407 U.S. at 285. Perhaps Burger and ex–football player White had a different "All-Star Team" or perhaps no sense of humor.

20.   *U.S.* v. *Orito*, 413 U.S. 139 (1973); *U.S.* v. *12 200-Ft. Reels of Super 8MM. Film,* 413 U.S. 123 (1973); and *U.S.* v. *Reidel*, 402 U.S. 351 (1971); *Perez* v. *U.S.*, 402 U.S. 146 (1971).

21.   *Rewis* v. *U.S.*, 401 U.S. 808 (1971).

22.   *Windward Shipping Ltd.* v. *American Radio Association, AFL-CIO*, 415 U.S. 104 (1974).

23.   *Evansville-Vanderburg Airport Authority District* v. *Delta Airlines,* 405 U.S. 707 (1972); *United Air Lines* v. *Mahin*, 410 U.S. 623 (1973).

24.   *Kosydar* v. *National Cash Register,* 417 U.S. 62 (1974).

25.   *North Dakota State Board of Pharmacy* v. *Snyder's Drug Stores*, 414 U.S. 156 (1973), statute requiring pharmacy to be owned by pharmacist or by corporation with majority of stockholders registered pharmacists.

26.   *Pike* v. *Bruce Church, Inc.*, 397 U.S. 137 (1970).

27. *U.S.* v. *State Tax Commission of Mississippi*, 412 U.S. 363 at 381 (1973).

28. *Askew, Governor* v. *American Waterways Operators*, 411 U.S. 315 (1973); *City of Burbank* v. *Lockheed Air Terminal*, 411 U.S. 624 (1973).

29. *Goldstein* v. *California*, 412 U.S. 546 (1973).

30. Donald A. Kaul, "And Now, State Protection of Intellectual Property?" *American Bar Association Journal*, 60 (February 1974), 198–202.

31. *Kewanee Oil Co.* v. *Bicron Corp.*, 416 U.S. 470 at 480 (1974).

32. See Chapter Four, note 47. *William Arnold Co.* v. *Carpenters District Council*, 417 U.S. 12 (1974).

33. *Gateway Coal Co.* v. *U.M.W.*, 414 U.S. 368 (1974).

34. *Watkins* v. *U.S.*, 354 U.S. 178 (1956); *Barenblatt* v. *U.S.*, 360 U.S. 109 (1959).

35. *Bond* v. *Floyd*, 385 U.S. 116 (1966).

36. *Powell* v. *MacCormack*, 395 U.S. 386 (1969).

37. *Roudebush* v. *Hartke*, 405 U.S. 15 (1972).

38. Raoul Berger says the *Powell* abandonment of the political question doctrine would allow the Court to take such a case. *Impeachment* (Cambridge, Mass.: Harvard University Press, 1972), p. 108.

39. *U.S.* v. *Brewster*, 408 U.S. 501 (1972).

40. *U.S.* v. *Johnson*, 383 U.S. 169 (1965).

41. *Gravel* v. *U.S.*, 408 U.S. 606 (1972). Material on *Gravel*, Cambodia, and the Nixon tapes case is drawn from "The Presidency Before the Courts," in Stephen L. Wasby, ed., *The Contemporary Presidency* (Corte Madera, Calif.: Chandler and Sharp, forthcoming 1976).

42. Douglas also took a swipe at the press, saying that government officials' deception of the public was "successful not because they were astute but because the press had become a frightened, regimented, submissive instrument, fattening on favors from those in power and forgetting the great tradition of reporting."

43. *Doe* v. *McMillan*, 412 U.S. 306 (1973).

44. See *Mitchell* v. *U.S.*, 386 U.S. 972 (1967); *Mora* v. *McNamara*, 389 U.S. 934 (1967); *Holmes* v. *U.S.*, 391 U.S. 936 (1968); *Hart* v. *U.S.*, 391 U.S. 956 (1968). See also Anthony A. D'Amato and Robert M. O'Neil, *The Judiciary and Vietnam* (New York: St. Martin's Press, 1972).

45. *McArthur* v. *Clifford*, 393 U.S. 1002 (1968).

46. *Holtzman* v. *Richardson*, 361 F. Supp. 553 (E.D.N.Y., 1973).

47. *Holtzman* v. *Schlesinger*, 414 U.S. 1304 at 1311 (1973).

48. *Holtzman* v. *Schlesinger*, 414 U.S. 1316 (1973).

49. *Schlesinger* v. *Holtzman*, 414 U.S. 1321 at 1324 (1973). Subsequently the Court of Appeals reversed the district court order and remanded with instructions to dismiss. 484 F. 2d 1307 (C.A. 2, 1973).

50. *In Re Subpoena to Nixon*, 360 F. Supp. 1 (D.D.C., 1973).

51. 487 F. 2d 700 (C.A.D.C., 1973).

52. Louis Kohlmeier, "Supreme Court Insiders Say Nixon Would Have Lost Appeal, 8–1 or 7–2," *Boston Globe*, October 29, 1973, p. 15.

53. *U.S.* v. *Nixon*, 418 U.S. 683 (1974).

54. *U.S.* v. *Ryan*, 402 U.S. 530 (1971).

55. *Accardi* v. *Shaughnessy*, 347 U.S. 260 (1953); *Service* v. *Dulles*, 354 U.S. 363 (1957); *Vitarelli* v. *Seaton*, 359 U.S. 535 (1959).

56. See 38 F.R. 30789. The regulations had earlier been the basis of a lower court ruling that Cox was improperly dismissed. *Nader* v. *Bork*, 366 F. Supp. 104 (D.D.C., 1973).

57. *Weinberger* v. *Hynson, Westcott & Dunning*, 412 U.S. 609 (1973).

58. *Motor Coach Employees* v. *Lockridge*, 403 U.S. 274 (1971). The earlier case is *San Diego Building Trades Council* v. *Garmon*, 359 U.S. 256 (1956).

59. See *Vaca* v. *Sipes*, 386 U.S. 171 (1967).

60. *Environmental Protection Agency* v. *Mink*, 410 U.S. 73 (1973).

61. *Bob Jones University* v. *Simon*, 416 U.S. 725 (1974); *Alexander* v. *"Americans United,"* 416 U.S. 752 (1974).

62. *U.S.* v. *Allegheny-Ludlum Steel Corp.*, 406 U.S. 742 at 749 (1972). When rule-making rather than application of the rules in an adjudicative proceeding was involved, the standards of judging were to be even less strict. The Court similarly upheld Federal Power Commission orders, overruling a Court of Appeals decision and saying the lower court should have deferred to the FPC's findings as there was substantial evidence to support them. *Gainesville Utilities Department* v. *Florida Power Corp.*, 402 U.S. 515 (1971). See also *Mobil Oil Corp.* v. *F.P.C.*, 417 U.S. 283 (1974), where the commission had reopened and amended an order after Court of Appeals approval of its initial determination.

63. *Butz* v. *Glover Livestock Commission*, 411 U.S. 182 at 191 (1973).

64. *Gulf States Utilities Co.* v. *F.P.C.*, 411 U.S. 747 (1973). Justice Powell, dissenting, was even more supportive of the agency and the utilities industry, stressing the industry's need to obtain money "upon the most favorable terms" as a justification for the commission's limited inquiry.

65. *Citizens to Preserve Overton Park* v. *Volpe*, 401 U.S. 402 (1971).

66. See *F.T.C.* v. *Sperry* & *Hutchinson Co.*, 405 U.S. 233 (1972); *Santa Fe Railroad* v. *Wichita Board of Trade*, 412 U.S. 800 (1973).

67. *N.L.R.B.* v. *Bell Aerospace Co. Division of Textron*, 416 U.S. 267 (1974).

68. *N.L.R.B.* v. *Burns Security Services*, 406 U.S. 272 (1972). The dissenters would not even have carried over recognition of the union, saying the wishes of the majority of employees were being ignored.

69. *Golden States Bottling Co.* v. *N.L.R.B.*, 414 U.S. 168 (1973).

70. *Red Lion Broadcasting Corp.* v. *F.C.C.*, 395 U.S. 369 (1969).

71. *U.S.* v. *Midwest Video Corp.*, 406 U.S. 649 (1972).

72. *Columbia Broadcasting System* v. *Democratic National Committee*, 412 U.S. 94 (1973). Deference to the FCC can also be seen in the Court's rejection of an appeal challenging the commission's policy with respect to "drug-oriented" songs. *Yale Broadcasting Co.* v. *F.C.C.*, 414 U.S. 914 (1973).

73. *N.L.R.B.* v. *Magnavox*, 415 U.S. 322 (1974). Burger and Blackmun were in the majority; Powell and Rehnquist, along with Stewart, dissented.

74. *N.L.R.B.* v. *Boeing*, 412 U.S. 67 (1973).

75. *Machinists* & *Aerospace Workers* v. *N.L.R.B.*, 412 U.S. 84 (1973).

76. *Florida Power and Light Co.* v. *I.B.E.W.*, 417 U.S. 790 (1974).

CHAPTER SIX

Policies During the Transition: Equality

How to deal with discrimination against minorities in this country has created both political and constitutional difficulties for the Supreme Court. The political problem involves not getting too far out of line with public opinion. The constitutional problem is finding ways to achieve the goals the Court establishes for itself, through the less than clear language of the Thirteenth, Fourteenth, and Fifteenth Amendments. Until the Court breathed life into the Thirteenth Amendment in 1968 in connection with housing, it seemed restricted to the question of slavery itself, and the Fifteenth Amendment applies only to voting. That left the Fourteenth Amendment, particularly the provision requiring "equal protection of the laws," as the Court's primary vehicle for dealing with discrimination. But what is "equal protection"? Equal with respect to what? The language does not by itself bestow any rights, for example, to education or to welfare benefits. All it does is provide a handle (or bootstrap) by which judges can extend certain benefits already provided to some to others who have been excluded. The Court can try in this way to see that they are treated equally, or at least not discriminatorily on the basis of race—and, more recently, poverty. That appears to be the most the Court can do where Congress has not acted. If Congress, using the enforcement power granted by the amendment, has provided for greater protection of rights, the Court can do more by sustaining Congress' action. In such situations, its task is somewhat easier, as it usually is when the justices can act out of deference to their congressional brethren. But even when Congress has appeared to expand rights, the justices still must determine whether Congress acted within the scope of its constitutional authority.

The most difficult constitutional problem connected with the Fourteenth Amendment—one of the most intractable problems in constitutional law—is that the amendment bans only discriminatory action by the *states*, not by private individuals. That position was reinforced by the Court's post–Civil War emasculation of Congress' enactment of a public accommodations law on the ground that only private action was involved in such discrimination. In recent years, the justices have changed their position, at times stretching considerably to show state action. They have found state action in judicial enforcement of private agreements; when the state has encouraged (not required) discrimination; and when private individuals are interacting with or tied to state authority. Through such interpretation, the Court has been able to develop important policies supporting equality. Yet we must not forget that the "state action" requirement does create a constitutional problem. The provision can also be used as the basis for *not* extending rights, more easily than it can be used to further those rights. Those resistant to equal treatment for racial and other minorities have been able to limit the meaning of state action, for example, saying that granting a club a state liquor license still leaves it a private club, and to limit as well the meaning of equality in the Equal Protection Clause of the amendment. These problems mean it takes serious commitment by the justices to forge and implement policies to bring about equality. Perhaps the lesson of the Warren Court is that such commitment was indeed possible and that the constitutional problems, while extremely difficult, were not insuperable.

Many observers have noted that a principal, perhaps *the* principal, theme of the Warren Court's liberalism was its stress on equality. That concept received special and immediate prominence through the decision in *Brown* v. *Board of Education*, and was implemented throughout the period of the Warren Court. For the Warren Court, equality meant primarily racial equality, but it also came to mean equality without regard to economic position, reflected in poll tax and welfare decisions. Equality also meant voting equality, both equal access to the ballot regardless of one's economic position or the color of one's skin and equal representation through proper apportionment of legislatures. Equality was given greatest effect in these fields, although it was also used in other areas, for example, criminal procedure, and as a general standard for judging state legislation.

In this chapter, we look first at school desegregation, then we turn our attention to other aspects of racial equality—housing, parks, public accommodations, and employment. Some attention is then devoted to the Court's treatment of other minorities and women. This is followed by an examination of voting rights, including reapportionment. The chapter concludes with a look at the Court's work on welfare policy and consumer issues.

TREATMENT OF MINORITIES

In the area of race relations, we find that where formal school segregation had occurred, the Supreme Court still insisted that desegregation be carried out and not evaded, but the justices were unwilling to apply remedies across school district boundaries, thus marking the end of the road for extending the desegregation battle. Those trying to attack discrimination in privately owned housing and in employment found a favorable pattern of Supreme Court rulings, but decisions with respect to use of parks and eating and drinking facilities had mixed outcomes.

Education

The Warren Court, as we noted earlier, had started off with a flourish in school desegregation and then, with a few exceptions, retreated from considering the subject. The justices returned to the question in 1968 to demand that the school officials *do* something. Resistant Southern school districts had finally adopted "freedom of choice" plans as a minimal way of meeting Department of Health, Education and Welfare demands to take action or have federal funds cut off. The Court would not rule such plans *per se* invalid, but made clear they were not proper if they did not produce *results*.[1] This demand for positive school board action was reinforced when the Court upheld the power of judges who were trying to obtain effective desegregation to impose broad remedies. For example, requiring faculty desegregation on a ratio basis, that is, the same proportion of white and black teachers in each school, was allowed.[2]

Just as school desegregation had been one of the first matters to confront Earl Warren, so it was for Warren Burger. The Nixon administration had requested delay in desegregating holdout Mississippi school districts, but the Court unanimously ruled, in a short *per curiam* opinion at the end of October 1969, fifteen years after the ruling in *Brown* v. *Board of Education*, that "all deliberate speed" was no longer the law and that no further delays should be allowed.[3]

Shortly after that decision, disagreement arose over the rule's application, and the Chief Justice asked openly for consideration of the issues of busing and the drawing of school district lines.[4] Faced with judge-ordered desegregation of the large Charlotte, North Carolina, school district in the *Swann* case, the Court unanimously said that school officials could not use school construction to perpetuate or re-establish segregation. Not every school had to reflect the community's overall racial composition, but the burden was on school officials to explain continuation of one-race schools. This case also involved the district judge's requirement of massive cross-busing. Here the Court unanimously upheld him, although Chief Justice Burger tried to make clear that the ruling applied only where formal segregation had existed.[5] This ruling on busing was reinforced after Congress suggested delay in busing "for racial balance" while appeals were processed. Justice Powell, in an in-chambers opinion, rejected this infringement on judicial authority and disemboweled the statute by suggesting most busing was ordered not for that purpose but to dismantle constitutionally improper dual school systems.[6] (However, Powell was later to call busing a "disruption of public education" likely to divert attention from providing quality education for all.)

Because of the Chief Justice's care in limiting the *Swann* ruling to situations where *de jure* segregation had occurred, perceived to be primarily a Southern problem, *Swann* was perhaps at first most important for its reinforcement of the discretion of lower court judges in bringing about desegregation. Busing was one of those remedies, but not the only one. However, the Supreme Court, following the lead of some lower court judges, began to treat Northern school desegregation in the same way it had treated desegregation in the South, as produced by the actions of school officials. This made the busing remedy of *Swann* —and all the other remedies for formal segregation—immediately applicable to the North, increasing the temperature of the already-heated busing controversy and substantially increasing *Swann*'s significance.

The Court continued its Southern desegregation work by invalidating the separate city school districts created within countywide districts when whites saw that their children would have to be educated alongside blacks.[7] However, the Nixon Four were not happy about this ruling. The Chief Justice, who would accept a school district's plan if it effectively eliminated segregation rather than seeking the best plan, complained about reliance on numbers and said consistent racial ratios could be pursued as a matter of *policy* but were not constitutionally mandated. The goal was to dismantle dual school systems "rather than to reproduce in each classroom a microcosmic reflection of the racial proportions of a given geographical area," he argued.

The Court also rejected indirect schemes for evading desegregation. First, following Warren Court rulings enjoining tuition grants to students attending racially discriminatory schools, the justices threw out Mississippi's policy of loaning textbooks to private schools without regard to whether they discriminated.[8] A virtually unanimous Court also ruled that all-white private schools in Montgomery, Alabama (which had a history of avoiding school desegregation), could not be given exclusive use of park facilities; such use made the segregated schools more attractive and helped them financially.[9] However, the majority sent back to the lower courts the question of whether the schools could use the facilities on a nonexclusive basis.

Then the Court had to deal with Northern school segregation. Some had hoped the ruling in a case from Denver would deal with *de facto* segregation, that is, segregation alleged to be the result of housing patterns rather than official action. Both Justices Douglas and Powell did urge the Court to discard the *de facto–de jure* distinction. Powell said the Court's rulings based on *Brown* v. *Board of Education* now meant that there were remedies for segregated schools, regardless of what caused them and regardless of their location. However, the majority did not accept these arguments. Instead, the Court expanded the scope of what would be considered *de jure* segregation and ruled that the Denver school board had segregated by manipulating attendance zones and by selecting school sites and using the "neighborhood school" policy to achieve segregated schools.[10] The Court also ruled that Chicanos should be counted along with—rather than separately from—blacks in looking at school district treatment of minorities, thus further restricting the school board. (Later the Court also recognized the rights of Chinese children, finding a violation of federal law where they had not been provided education in the English language so they could take advantage of educational opportunities.[11]) In another important ruling in the Denver case, the Court also helped minority parents by shifting some of the burden of proof involved in desegregation cases from them to the school board; when intentional segregation was shown in *one part* of a school district, school authorities now had to show that patterns elsewhere in the district were *not* the result of discrimination.

The Denver case had involved only a single district, and left open the extremely touchy question whether a judge, by ordering busing *across district lines*, could follow the whites who had fled to the suburbs. In 1974, the Court was faced with just such a case from one of the nation's more racially troubled metropolitan areas, Detroit. There a federal judge, dealing with a suit to desegregate the schools in Detroit itself, had decided to deal with the central city problem by including in the desegregation plan 53 of the 85 outlying schools in a three-county metropolitan area; he also ordered the purchase of *at least* 295 school buses to carry out the busing required under his plan. Part of the problem in the case was that the judge had included the other districts without giving them an adequate opportunity to be heard, but the Supreme Court did not stop with that aspect of his ruling.

On the very last day of the 1973 Term, the Court ruled 5–4 that interdistrict remedies would not be allowed unless the other districts contributed to the segregation, for example, by keeping blacks out, or unless district lines were drawn to segregate. Otherwise, said Chief Justice Burger, desegregation remedies would have to be carried out within the single central city school district. School district lines, said Burger, could not be "casually ignored or treated as a mere administrative convenience"; local control over operation of schools, a strong tradition, could not easily be set aside.[12] Burger's ruling had technically not fore-closed interdistrict busing, but it had obviously closed off most busing outside central cities, and at least created stormy weather for proponents of busing. Even though the ruling did not restrict judges' ability to order busing within a single city—as in the Boston controversy—the political signal of the case ("Go Slow!") was perhaps more conservative than the legal meaning of the majority's words.

That broader meaning was certainly understood by the dis-senters. They said the Court had severely hindered judges' ability to correct segregation. Douglas said that blacks were being hemmed into segregated and inferior schools, because of this rul-ing and the Court's refusal to give relief from property tax financ-ing of schools. For him, the Court had retreated beyond the *Plessy* doctrine of "separate but equal," because *Plessy* at least required equal facilities. White criticized the majority's substitution of its views for that of judges who knew the situation better; he also felt that the judiciary's ability to remedy segregation had been crip-pled and that deliberate acts of segregation performed by local government units would go unremedied. Marshall thought the ruling "a giant step backwards" and said no hope could be found in a desegregation plan involving only the central city. The state, which had kept whites and blacks purposely apart "so that they could not become accustomed to learning together," should be blamed for the flight of whites to the suburbs. He felt fundamen-tal rights were being abridged on superficial grounds and because of public opposition, which should not be allowed to interfere with enforcing the Constitution. He also felt the ruling would ill serve the nation, arguing with considerable emotion that "unless our children begin to learn together, there is little hope that our people will ever learn to live together."

The Court had not retreated from *Brown* on the need for re-moving segregation in education. However, in a ruling that served as a practical judgment on how far school desegregation could be pushed in the North, the Court had clearly taken a position on desegregation remedies that would *not* produce more than partial integration of the schools, at least where residential segregation had left a school district with a largely black population. And it thus reinforced the national pattern of desegregation, with more now accomplished in the South than in the North—at least as measured by percentage of black students in previously all-white schools or in desegregated schools. Were we to look at other aspects of school desegregation such as concealed segregation within nominally desegregated schools[13] or separation of students into separate educational "tracks," we would find even less progress.

Almost as much awaited as the Detroit case was a ruling on "affirmative action" programs for correcting discriminatory practices, which either gave or seemed to give preference to minorities. Despite the intense interest shown in the case of a rejected white law school applicant who had claimed that less qualified blacks had been admitted, the Court at least temporarily avoided the issue. The student had been admitted under a protective order while the case was pending and was only a few weeks from graduation when the Supreme Court was ready to rule. This allowed the Court to dismiss the case as moot,[14] although the majority suggested the Court would deal with the issue when another case was presented. Justice Brennan said the Court had strained not to decide the case and had "disserved the public interest" by doing so. Douglas, also dissenting, felt that reserving part of an entering class for minorities created serious problems, although applications from members of minority groups could be given separate consideration if the Law School Admissions Test (LSAT) were culture-biased. He also felt an applicant "had a constitutional right to have his application considered on its individual merits in a racially neutral manner" and decried the "dimensions and orientation of the Organization Man" reflected in the admissions tests.

Housing

Because school desegregation in the North is alleged to stem from housing patterns, discrimination in the sale or rental of housing has particular importance, even beyond the basic question of a person's right to choose where to live without regard to the color of his or her skin. The Warren Court did not reach questions of racial discrimination in housing until the late 1960s, although it had numerous earlier opportunities. Then in 1967, the Court dealt with a voter-adopted California constitutional amendment

(Proposition 14) that had repealed the state's open housing laws and forbidden enactment of any law that would interfere with an individual's disposition of his property. Invalidating the provision, the Court said it was state *encouragement* of discrimination.[15] The ruling was one of the most expansive readings of the Fourteenth Amendment state action requirement, because the state provision here clearly had not *compelled* discrimination— the sort of action usually covered by the amendment.

Having thus bolstered the Fourth Amendment, the following year, 1968, the Warren Court in its major open housing ruling resurrected and extended the Thirteenth Amendment. A couple (one white, one black), turned down because of race when they tried to buy a house in a St. Louis area subdivision, sued the developer under a statute enacted in 1866 to enforce the Constitution's new antislavery provision.[16] Because to be unable to buy property on the same basis as whites would be a "badge of slavery," the Court sustained the suit. Immediately before the Court ruled, Congress had passed the broader 1968 Open Housing Act, and the justices spoke directly of the need for both laws because their coverage was different; thus they implicitly approved the new statute at the same time they utilized the older one.

The Burger Court's action with respect to the open housing area was to reinforce what the Warren Court had done. Coverage of the new law was read broadly, and the Court allowed suits for damages as well as for injunctions against discriminatory practices under the old law.[17] However, in the area of public housing, the Burger Court handed down a decision that clearly limited desegregation. The Warren Court had prohibited referenda on open housing laws when those were the only laws needing the voters' approval, because of the obvious obstacle to equal treatment such requirements provided.[18] The Burger Court, faced with referenda on low-cost housing, upheld their validity, despite the clear but implicit presence of the underlying racial issue, which led the dissenters to complain that communities were being allowed to fence out minorities.[19] The Court also gave its approval to snob zoning, in upholding zoning regulations that prohibited more than two unrelated people from living together. The regulations were said to bear a rational relationship to the government's goal and to be a valid land-use regulation addressed to family needs.[20]

Racial Discrimination in Other Areas

The Warren Court had sustained Congress' power to enact the public accommodations provisions of the 1964 Civil Rights Act, and the Burger Court continued to extend the act's coverage. For example, when an amusement place, charging a nominal membership fee to white members and denying blacks admission, claimed to be a private club, the Court held it was covered by the act in view of its clear purpose and its widespread advertising.[21] However, just as the Warren Court had had trouble deciding questions of a proprietor's rights to exclude potential customers, the Burger Court was also troubled by a case in which a private proprietor called a policeman to enforce a trespass law. A white school teacher, accompanying black students, was arrested for vagrancy as she left a Kress store where the students (but not the teacher) had been served lunch. When she sued for violation of her civil rights, the Court, showing its continuing reluctance to include private action under the civil rights statutes, said that to recover damages she had to show she was denied service through state-enforced custom, that is, persistent practices by state officials having the force of law.[22]

Later the Court was faced with the question of discrimination by a purely private club holding a state liquor license. The majority said that having the liquor license did not bring the club's discrimination under the Fourteenth Amendment's ban. Receiving some state benefit, like the license, or being subject to government regulation was not enough to make the actions of "an otherwise private entity" equivalent to state action.[23] However, the Court did invalidate the state's requirement that the organization enforce its own by-laws, which discriminated against blacks, because that would put the state in the position of enforcing discrimination. This case clearly marked the limit of the Court's willingness to interpret the state action doctrine broadly so as to include private activity in which the state was involved or entangled. As the Warren Court probably would have decided the case the other way, one can even see in it a Burger Court withdrawal from the Warren Court's direction.

Several cases involving parks also were before the Court. In one difficult case, land had been given to Macon, Georgia, for use by whites only. The city had desegregated the park, but later appointed private trustees to operate the park on a segregated basis. In the suit that resulted, the Supreme Court first held, 5–4, that the public character of the park was not changed by the city's attempted withdrawal and it must be desegregated.[24] On remand, the Georgia courts said that because the purpose of the donor in giving the park could not be carried out, a clause in the will reverting the property to his heirs should be enforced. When the Burger Court received the follow-up appeal in 1970, the Court upheld, 5–2, what the Georgia courts had done.[25] Justice Black said the earlier ruling required only that the park be desegregated *if* it were to be operated as a park. Stressing the weight our society gives to allowing people to determine the disposition of their property at death, he said terminating the park would be a loss to both races but was not discriminatory. The racial restrictions in the will were not state-assisted but were "solely the product of the testator's own full-blown social philosophy." The dissenters claimed, however, that Black ignored state laws allowing the will's discriminatory provisions, as well as government involvement in the park's development, which they said required its desegregation.

The following year, the Court ruled that Jackson, Mississippi, claiming financial problems, could close all its swimming pools.[26] Although the dissenters said the closing came only in the face of a desegregation order, the majority, including Black, refused to look at motive. White, exhibiting his liberal position in race relations cases, thought the city's action "an expression of official policy that Negroes are unfit to associate with whites." Justice Marshall, in language like his later Detroit school dissent, harked back to *Brown* and said the Court "turned the clock back 17 years." Coupled with the Court's later action banning a city's grant of exclusive use of its parks to all-white schools, the cases apparently meant that the Court's policy was to be that a city did not have to operate parks and could close them to all, but must operate them nondiscriminatorily as long as they were open.

Employment was one subject not really touched by the Warren Court, making it the first race relations area to be dealt with by the Burger Court alone. Just as the Warren Court had upheld Congress' work in the fields of voting, public accommodations, and housing, the Burger Court reinforced the thrust of the 1964 Civil Rights Act equal employment opportunities provisions. The Court did this by holding that non-job-related employment tests, even if impartially administered, could not be used if the *result* was discrimination,[27] and by deciding cases dealing with the act's procedures in the employees' favor, shifting some of the burden to the company to prove nondiscrimination,[28] and giving an employee a wide range of options to pursue in pressing claims of racial discrimination.[29]

In the area of racial equality, the Burger Court did essentially what it might have been expected to do. Broad policy on race relations had already been decided by the Warren Court, through the constitutional doctrine of *Brown* and support for congressional initiatives. As a result, there was not much policy to develop. For the Burger Court, there remained mostly the task of applying the policy and extending it in some areas. Although the justices did resist busing across school district lines, they generally carried forward the Warren Court's work.

Women's Rights

We tend to see women's rights (or what is coming to be called "gender discrimination") as a contemporary subject that has only recently come to the Supreme Court. However, much earlier in the century the Court had indicated that women were not going to receive equal treatment under the Fourteenth Amendment. Those earlier rulings were both restrictive (preventing women from entering professions like law because they were unfit for many occupations) and solicitous (upholding minimum wage and maximum hours laws passed to protect them); in either event, they reinforced a subordinate status for women, with the justices talking of women as tender and delicate.

When the Women's Liberation Movement began to produce new women's rights issues for the Court to decide, the most obvious claims were of sex discrimination in employment. Here the Court upheld claims under both the 1963 Equal Pay Act and the 1964 Civil Rights Act, for example, ruling that refusing to hire women with preschool children while hiring men with such children was a violation of the latter statute.[30] Other rulings by the Burger Court were made under the Fourteenth Amendment and fed the discussion of whether equal rights for women could be obtained without the Equal Rights Amendment (ERA). The Court might have made some decisions in anticipation of ERA, but the pattern of rulings was sufficiently mixed as probably not to have been so motivated. In any event, where the Court had earlier not accorded women protection under the Fourteenth Amendment, the modern Court now seemed willing to do so.

The Burger Court's first women's rights ruling had been the decision to strike down Idaho's automatic preference to men to administer estates.[31] Then came the already-mentioned *Frontiero* ruling (see p. 93) on benefits to spouses of those in the armed forces, particularly important for Justice Brennan's plurality statement that sex was a "suspect category." This statement did not, however, mean that every sex-based discrimination would be found invalid. This soon became evident when the Court upheld Florida's $500 property tax exemption for widows, because the state could reasonably decide that financial difficulties facing lone women were greater than those facing lone men.[32] Brennan dissented, saying the statute, under which well-to-do widows qualified, could be more narrowly drawn.

The Court did invalidate school board requirements that pregnant teachers go on leave at a fixed time, because the rules established irrebutable presumptions as to when women could not perform their tasks and forced educationally counterproductive mid-school year departures.[33] However, faced with the complaint that normal pregnancies were being excluded from disability benefit coverage, the Court held the exclusion not discriminatory.[34] The majority, deferring to the state's wishes in setting up a social welfare program, said there was no requirement that all employment risks be covered: "So long as the line drawn by the State is rationally supportable, the courts will not interpose their judgment as to the appropriate stopping point." However, Justice Brennan disliked the state's double standard created when less favorable treatment was given to a gender-linked disability that only women could incur, while men were compensated for disabilities affecting only or primarily them.

Closely related to women's rights were the contraception and abortion cases. The Warren Court had broken new ground by invalidating a Connecticut birth control statute that penalized the use of contraceptives, even by married couples, where Justice Douglas had spoken of the right to privacy as the basis for the ruling.[35] When Massachusetts rewrote its statute so that use was not penalized but only married people could get material to prevent conception, the Burger Court invalidated the law because "the rights of the individual to access to contraceptives . . . must be the same for the unmarried and the married alike." Justice Brennan also suggested that the right of privacy meant the right of the individual, "married or single, to be free from unwarranted governmental intrusion into matters so fundamentally affecting a person as the decision whether to bear or beget a child."[36] Chief Justice Burger, dissenting, felt that the state could subject the choice of birth control methods to medical supervision as a health matter.

The abortion ruling stimulated controversy that has yet to end. After multiple rounds of argument, the Court, by a 7–2 vote, struck down most state abortion statutes.[37] The state had an interest in the woman's health, said the majority, but because of the extremely low danger to health from an abortion during the first trimester of pregnancy, that interest was subordinate to the woman's right to determine whether or not to have the abortion. (The woman would, however, have to be acting in consultation with her physician; as Chief Justice Burger pointed out, the Court was not providing "abortion on demand.") After the first trimester, the state could prescribe the conditions under which abortions could take place, and in the last trimester could even pro-

hibit them. This action by the Court limiting the states' authority
was called an "extravagant exercise" of "raw judicial power" by
Justice White, dissenting.

Aliens and Indians

The Burger Court also paid new heed to the rights of aliens. The
question of removing citizenship, a concern of the early Warren
Court, was revived after a long period in which most citizenship
cases were related to deportation procedure. The Warren Court
had consistently invalidated the government's efforts to expatri-
ate citizens for various reasons, but the new Court denied citizenship to a person, born abroad of one American citizen parent,
who had not fulfilled the requirement of five years residence in
the United States between the ages of fourteen and twenty-
eight.[38] Where an alien had given up his right to become a citizen
in exchange for exemption from military service, the Court did
say he could be held to his agreement only where the exemption
was complete and permanent.[39] The Court then revealed its conservative stance in the area by upholding the government's refusal to accept a belated citizenship petition from a Filipino who
had served in our armed forces during World War II, even though
the government had failed to publicize the rights of such nonciti-
zens to obtain citizenship. Justice Douglas complained that the
majority was ignoring "the deliberate—and successful—effort on
the part of agents of the Executive Branch to frustrate the congressional purpose and to deny substantive rights . . . by administrative fiat."[40]

Aliens were also the subject of welfare (p. 129) and employment cases. With only Douglas dissenting, the Court said that
employment discrimination on the basis of citizenship was not the
discrimination on the basis of national origins forbidden by the
1964 Civil Rights Act.[41] However, the Court upheld the rights of
resident aliens to enter regulated professions (law) and to obtain
government employment, over Burger and Rehnquist dissents.[42]

Questions concerning Indians also began to come before the
Court. Generally, they were decided on the basis of particular
treaties and statutes applying to specific tribes, resulting in shifting and inconsistent policy that at times limited the tribes' power
rather than establishing broad doctrine.[43] Through such interpretations, the Warren Court upheld certain Indian fishing rights
but also held that fishing by Indians could be regulated along
with fishing by others.[44] Following up the latter case, the Burger
Court, holding that a state's bar against net fishing of steelhead
trout discriminated against Indians, required the state to come to

an accommodation between sportsmen's rights and the Indians' rights.[45] Other clashes between Indians and the states involved taxes and title to land. Also litigated were Indians' rights under the Major Crimes Act, which provided for trial of Indians for major offenses in regular federal courts instead of on the reservation; the secretary of the interior's authority to set aside an Indian's will; and general assistance benefits for certain Indians. In these cases, the Court generally held for the Indians.[46] In a case of broader symbolic as well as considerable practical importance, the Court in 1974 unanimously upheld the long-standing Bureau of Indian Affairs hiring and promotion preference for Indians. It was not racial discrimination but was "reasonably designed to further the cause of Indian self-government and to make the BIA more responsive to the needs of its constituent groups." This decision reinforced Congress' "plenary power . . . to legislate on behalf of federally recognized Indian tribes" as well as "the unique legal status of Indian tribes under federal law."[47]

VOTING

Voting Rights

One of the great battles of the 1960s had been to assure voting rights for blacks. In the late 1960s and 1970s, the voting rights of other groups also came before the Court. The Burger Court continued the Warren Court's broad reading of the 1965 Voting Rights Act, which had eliminated all "tests and devices" in areas with low voting turnout, felt by Congress to be the result of discrimination. The justices said consistently that a wide variety of changes in voting arrangements could not be made without the prior approval required by the law or a showing that they were not discriminatory.[48] The Court similarly upheld Congress' action, in the 1970 Voting Rights Act, eliminating literacy tests throughout the country.[49]

The 1970 law's short and uniform residence requirements for presidential elections, intended to prevent people from being disfranchised because of their geographical mobility, were also upheld, 8–1.[50] The Court initially struck down long durational residence requirements for eligibility to vote in state and local elections, saying a thirty-day period would be acceptable for administrative reasons, but later, accepting the state's explanation for the needed time, approved a fifty-day period.[51] As we have already noted, the eighteen-year-old vote provisions in the 1970 statute produced conflicting rulings, because Justice Black said

Congress could give the vote to eighteen-year-olds in *national* elections but *not* state and local elections.

Some voting cases involved prisoners and ex-prisoners; their claims did not fare well. The Warren Court had said that the state did not have to provide absentee ballots to unconvicted persons in jail.[52] The Burger Court, over Justice Blackmun's objection that the Court was unnecessarily interfering with legitimate state policy, first blocked New York's denial of the vote to pre-trial detainees unable to make bail and convicted misdemeanants not stripped of their rights by conviction, but only because the law did not operate evenly.[53] Then the Court said that even after sentence and parole were completed, states were not required to allow convicted felons to vote, because of the Fourteenth Amendment's provision allowing disfranchisement for crime.[54] This ruling was quite serious because its policy ran directly counter to prevailing ideas about rehabilitation, in which continuing disabilities were not to be imposed on those who had paid their debt to society.

The economic status of our citizens remained a factor affecting voting and political participation. In addition to invalidating the poll tax, the Warren Court swept away most remaining property-holding or tax-paying requirements for voting in local elections.[55] The Burger Court, definitely not of the same mind, gave greater weight to property-holders' interests. First the justices helped protect the taxpayers' pocket by approving use of a 60 percent special majority rule in bond referendum elections. Then it approved an arrangement in which only land*owners*, but not tenants, voted for a water district board of directors, with votes apportioned according to assessed land value.[56] The result was to give control of many districts to single companies and to disfranchise and disadvantage those not owning land but living in the district and thus subject to floods supposed to be controlled by the district.

The poor did, however, find the Court sympathetic to complaints about high filing fees for candidates. Here the justices uncharacteristically looked quite critically at state enactments and partly continued the Warren Court's policy that economic status and the right to participate were not rationally related. Although the Court would allow fees to cover filing costs, Texas' filing fees of up to $8,900 for primary candidates were thrown out as "patently exclusionary."[57] Two years later, the Court said that, despite an interest in deterring frivolous candidacies, the state could not require filing fees from an indigent when he could not pay them, unless a reasonable alternative means of access to the ballot were available.[58]

When minor parties rather than poor candidates sought access to the ballot, the new Court did give the states much leeway and did not follow the Warren Court's decision invalidating the complicated Ohio structure, which had initially kept George Wallace off the ballot there.[59] In 1974, the Court, saying the states had a valid interest in preventing fractionation of parties, affirmed state rules placing considerable burdens on minor party candidates.[60] Comparable deference was also shown to some state rules for voters wishing to change parties. New York rules requiring a voter to enroll in the party of his choice at least thirty days before the *general election* to be able to vote in the next party *primary* (that is, as much as *eleven months* before the primary) were upheld as a protection against opposition party raiding. However, the vote was only 5–4, and dissenting Justice Powell criticized the rules' severity and charged that the right to vote and to associate with others in the party of one's choice was being infringed. A voter having to make such an early choice had to do so before candidates and issues responsive to his concerns would be known.[61] Despite this ruling, later in the year the Court did invalidate an Illinois rule prohibiting changes in party primary voting for twenty-three months from the date of participation in one primary; it did so because the law interfered with the right of association and because less drastic means to avoid raiding were available.[62]

At about the time when concern about election financing and campaign practices was building, the Court ruled on the federal laws that prohibited labor organizations and corporations from making contributions or expenditures in federal elections. With Powell and Burger dissenting, the Court held that the law did *not* prevent contributions from voluntarily financed separate political funds, even if union officials administered them, because Congress had not intended to prevent expenditures of funds union members had given "of their own free and knowing choice."[63] Powell thought the decision "opens the way for major participation in politics by the largest aggregations of economic power, the great unions and corporations."

Reapportionment

The Warren Court, after rulings that courts could hear reapportionment controversies, had held that congressional districts within a state must be equal.[64] This was quickly followed by the landmark ruling that *both* houses of all state legislatures must be reapportioned on the basis of population at least every ten years.

Chief Justice Warren asserted, in what he later said was his most important ruling, "Legislators represent people, not trees or acres. Legislators are elected by voters, not farms or cities or economic interests. . . . The right to elect legislators in a free and unimpaired fashion is a bedrock of our political system."[65] However, the Warren Court, beyond saying that legislative districts were to be "as nearly of equal population as is practicable," did not create a standard by which to judge the validity of apportionments. Even when Missouri congressional districts with an average variance from the ideal of 1.6 percent and a ratio of largest to smallest districts of 1.06:1 were rejected, the Court refused to specify what was required, for fear of discouraging legislators from trying to achieve equality of representation.[66] Although redistricting produced some important political effects in the states, expected major effects on substantive policy seldom materialized.[67]

The Warren Court also extended the one man–one vote rule to local governments.[68] The Burger Court initially reinforced this extension,[69] but soon allowed an 11.9 percent variance in districts used for choosing local government positions.[70] This ruling, while applicable only to local governments, foreshadowed the Burger Court's new general direction on reapportionment. In its major decision on this subject, the Burger Court in 1973 upheld a Virginia reapportionment with a ±3.8 percent average variance and a 16.4 percent maximum variance between districts, in which more than one-fourth of the legislators would be elected from districts 5 percent or more from the ideal size and in which one part of the state was systematically overrepresented at the expense of another.[71] Justice Rehnquist, stressing that more flexibility would be allowed for state than for congressional districting and suggesting that use of political subdivisions as dividing lines for districts might be feasible in the states, said that to apply absolute equality to state reapportionment could impair the operations of state and local governments.

The Court then reinforced the distinction between state and congressional districting. They unanimously invalidated a congressional apportionment with a variance of less than 1 percent where the differences were not unavoidable.[72] The Nixon appointees are clearly restive with the strict congressional districting standard, and Justices Powell, Rehnquist, and the Chief Justice indicated their agreement with the dissent in the Warren Court's last congressional districting case; in effect they invited their colleagues to overrule that decision. Then the Court upheld state legislative apportionments with greater variations, which they said did not establish a *prima facie* malapportionment claim.[73]

Thus apparently variations of roughly ±2 percent and a maximum deviation between districts of almost 8 percent were to be treated as *de minimis*. Here Justice White stressed the need for flexibility so legislatures rather than courts could reapportion. White felt too much weight was being given to population figures, which could "furnish a ready tool for ignoring facts that in day-to-day operation are important to an acceptable representation and apportionment arrangement." These shifts in the Court's position did not go unchallenged as Justice Brennan noted the Court's "substantial and unfortunate retreat from the principles established in our earlier cases." He felt the changes undermined the efforts to carry out the one man–one vote principle and jeopardized the gains recently achieved, which he thought substantial.

The Supreme Court has not yet ruled on the validity of the intentional drawing of legislative district lines to benefit the majority party, at least where race has not been involved. However, it has implicitly indicated it would not interfere with such gerrymandering by approving an apportionment embodying a "political fairness" principle intended to approximate the strengths of the two major parties. Faced with metropolitan-area multi-member legislative districts (in Indianapolis) challenged because they produced fewer black legislators than did single-member districts, the Court also ruled that multi-member districts were not inherently unconstitutional,[74] thus showing the justices' reluctance to interfere. Such districting was acceptable, said the Court, even if the effect was to reduce the percentage of black representatives, as long as blacks' access to the political system was not hindered. Where minorities' access had been limited, as in certain Texas counties, the Court would not allow the multi-member districts.[75] If the Warren Court had used its reapportionment rulings as an indirect way to help blacks achieve progress by improving their opportunities for political involvement, the Burger Court seemed disinclined to follow.

WELFARE AND THE POOR

Cases involving the poor, particularly those on welfare, finally began to reach the Court in some numbers in the late 1960s, as a result of the work of Office of Economic Opportunity poverty lawyers and the National Welfare Rights Organization (NWRO). We have already noted cases on the relation between poverty and voting or running for office. Far more cases dealt specifically with welfare problems. In one case, Justice Brennan did talk of the important rights involved in removing welfare benefits to which

a person was statutorily entitled, and in a footnote suggested
that such benefits might be seen as a form of property rather than
as charity. However, there was not much follow-through on the
idea of a *right* to welfare, a view clearly distasteful to the Nixon
appointees. Thus, despite an occasional major ruling, the justices
did not do very much for the welfare recipient.[76] The Court was
willing, on the whole, to make state legislators follow the Social
Security Act, to make them calculate benefits openly, and to enforce certain due process requirements. However, when the issue
was forcing legislatures to spend money to raise the level of welfare benefits, the Court generally supported the states, not the
welfare clients. The states were allowed much freedom to determine both *how much* money should be spent and *how* to spend it,
even when it meant exclusion of some potential beneficiaries. Although it was the *agencies'* failures that led to the court cases, the
Court seemed not very well suited for the supervisory task of
making welfare bureaucracies perform their assigned task.

The Burger Court's welfare case most indicative of its position involved the cutting off of benefits to welfare recipients who
refused to allow a social worker without a warrant to examine
their homes during a visit to the recipient's home. Labelling the
visit a "gentle means, of limited extent and of practical and con-
siderate application" to assure that the public's money was properly spent, Justice Blackmun said the social worker's search was
not unreasonable.[77] Justice Marshall, speaking for the welfare
recipient and complaining of the Court's "departure from princi-
pled adjudication," pointed out that the Court had protected a
businessman's refusal of a warrantless search of his warehouse,[78]
where he received only a $100 suspended fine. Here, "for protect-
ing the privacy of her home, Mrs. James lost the sole means of
support for herself and her infant son." Marshall also rejected the
idea that the government could provide welfare to rehabilitate
people at the cost of their constitutional rights.

Policy questions considered by the Court in the welfare area
included exclusion from welfare of those eligible under the federal
statutes, due process in denying benefits, and the amount and distribution of welfare funds, as well as the rights of illegitimates
and consumer protection matters. In looking at the Court's rulings on the welfare policy questions, we find that most involved
not constitutional questions but interpretation of statutes and
regulations. Typical of the Court's involvement with the Social
Security Act and its mass of implementing regulations were the
"man-in-the-house" cases, which the Court handled on the basis
of the act's definition of "parent." The justices did this when
Alabama denied AFDC (Aid to Families with Dependent Chil-

dren) benefits to welfare mothers cohabitating with able-bodied
men (in *or* out of the home) even when the man had no obligation
to contribute to the children, and when California presumed that
the income of nonadoptive stepfathers was available for AFDC
benefit calculations.[79] The latter ruling came from the earlier
Burger Court, although with the new Chief Justice and Justice
Black dissenting. These rulings seemed to make clear that unless
Congress specifically said so, a state could not establish a nar-
rower basis for eligibility than that provided by the federal statute.[80] Similarly, when a state delayed payment of unemploy-
ment compensation benefits while employers appealed initial determinations that a worker was eligible, the Court said the statute's requirement that the payment be made "when due" meant
when the agency first determined eligibility after a hearing, *not*
after the employer's appeal.[81] (However, the Court later allowed
the states to place somewhat more burden on the worker if benefits were to be continued.[82])

The Warren Court's major decision favorable to welfare recipients, a ruling of constitutional dimensions, was to invalidate
durational residence requirements for receiving benefits.[83] However, both Chief Justice Warren and Justice Black dissented because they were afraid the ruling would lead to invalidation of
residence requirements in other situations. The Burger Court
showed no sign of retreating from this decision. Thus, questioning
classifications based on noncitizenship, it struck down a *fifteen-
year* residence period before aliens could get categorical aid and a
one-year residence requirement for indigents for nonemergency
hospitalization or medical care at a county hospital.[84] Douglas,
agreeing with the latter decision, wondered whether the Court's
constitutional rulings were sufficient to protect indigents' health.
With atypical judicial restraint but obvious liberal political ideology, he argued that "The political processes rather than equal
protection litigation are the ultimate solvent of the present problem" of the enormous economic and legal aspects of medical care.

Another major, constitutional question in the welfare area
involved due process in termination of welfare benefits. Here,
coming closest to the position of welfare as a right, the justices
held that a *pre*-termination evidentiary hearing was essential,
because HEW's post-termination "fair hearing" did not come soon
enough.[85] However, Justice Black, who called the payments
"gratuities," complained that the government was being prevented from stopping payments to those not entitled to receive
them. The Court later did not demand highly formalized procedure at these and comparable hearings. In one case, Justice
Blackmun said that procedure "should not necessarily be stiff and

comfortable only for the trained attorney, and should be liberal and not strict in tone and operation," while Douglas objected that the government was cutting corners.[86]

Procedural difficulties encounted by welfare recipients and other poor people were further increased by rulings on access to the courts. Of particular relevance to welfare was the decision upholding as reasonable a $25 state filing fee for court review of agency determinations on the ground there had already been an agency review.[87] More broadly affecting the poor was the earlier ruling that access to bankruptcy proceedings was not available without payment of the required filing fee.[88] Effectively undercutting the principle of its own ruling that the state could not require indigents seeking divorces to pay court fees, because of the state's monopoly over the marriage relationship and its termination,[89] the Court said there was "no constitutional right to obtain a discharge of one's debts in bankruptcy"; furthermore, other methods for resolving one's debts were available. However, Justice Stewart said the government kept the debtor indebted by allowing courts to enforce his contracts and that a really destitute person had no viable alternative to bankruptcy proceedings; he objected, "The Court today holds that Congress may say that some of the poor are too poor even to go bankrupt."

When questions arose about legislative allocations of money for welfare benefits, the Court's stance was both very restrained and conservative. For example, the Court held, 4–3, that the Social Security Act's reduction in Social Security benefits to reflect workmen's compensation payments was acceptable, despite the fact that people receiving other types of payments did not have their Social Security payments lowered. Here the Court also rejected the claim that Social Security payments, because financed in part by the worker's contributions, could not be reduced; the majority said there was no contractual right in such benefits,[90] a statement that flew in the face of the expectations of many Americans that they were *entitled* to the Social Security benefits to which they had made contributions.

Another important case involved the congressional requirement that amounts used to determine welfare needs be recalculated to show cost-of-living increases. Adopting what amounted to a policy of full disclosure but not full payment, the Court turned aside a challenge to New York's changes that had resulted in some families receiving less money.[91] To comply, the state had only to *show* the true standard of need, although only a percentage of that amount might be *paid*. Chief Justice Burger and Justice Black would not go even this far, taking the position that welfare recipients should have taken their case to HEW before coming to the courts. At the same time, in a case that made clear that there was no chance the Burger Court would say there was a *right* to welfare, the Court also upheld a state-imposed maximum on the welfare grant any family could receive, even though each child in large families received less than those in small families.[92] Justice Marshall, who argued that children cannot control the size of the family into which they are born, expressed the view that the Equal Protection Clause had been emasculated in the welfare area.

The majority's policy of leaving money decisions on welfare largely to the states was further reinforced in 1972. The policy of paying a lower percentage of needs for AFDC beneficiaries than for those in other aid categories was sustained, as were certain methods for calculating outside income even though they made many people ineligible for basic benefits or supplemental services like Medicaid.[93] We can also see deference to the states in some of the cases involving the constitutional question of the supremacy of federal laws. For example, the Court held that state work rules for AFDC recipients were not pre-empted by federal law[94] and praised the regulations as an "attempt to promote self-reliance and civic responsibility." The Court's position on flexibility for the states was also clear from its statement that the rules were necessary to meet the state's desire that "limited state welfare funds be spent on behalf of those genuinely incapacitated and most in need."

Because of the number of illegitimate children supported through AFDC programs, the Court's rulings on the rights of illegitimates are clearly related to the welfare policy issues we have been discussing. Protecting the rights of illegitimate children, the justices invalidated statutes that said they could not sue in court or obtain benefits as a result of injuries to their fathers, or that denied them welfare benefits.[95] (Justice Rehnquist, however, thought that state legislatures, in order to protect the family, could give the family unit aid not given to others.) The Court even invalidated a portion of the Social Security Act that kept disability insurance benefits from certain illegitimate children unless they had been supported by the disabled wage-earner before the disability, because there was no opportunity for an ineligible illegitimate to prove dependency.[96]

. However, the Court also showed great deference to the states. In one case, it did so by upholding Louisiana laws that prevented acknowledged (but not legitimated or adopted) illegitimate children from inheriting when the father died without a will;[97] here the stress was on power to make rules concerning disposition of property, power held dear by the justices. Another case in which the Court's ruling disadvantaged illegitimates occurred when a mother of an illegitimate child sought to prosecute the father for nonsupport. The majority said she had no interest in seeing another person jailed.[98] This ruling led Justice White, adopting a liberal and sympathetic position, to say the Court was making nonpersons of the mother and illegitimate children, because the state *did* prosecute fathers of legitimate children for nonsupport on the mother's complaint.

The Court also spoke to the question of the rights of unwed fathers, ruling in a liberal direction. Illinois had presumed such men unfit to care for their children upon the death of the children's mother. Because the state made no such presumption about unwed mothers, a majority of the justices struck down the rule over the Chief Justice's objection that the state need recognize only those father-child relationships arising within legal marriage.[99] Certainly not hiding distaste for unwed fathers, Burger said that "the biological role of the mother in carrying and nursing an infant creates stronger bonds between her and the child than the bonds resulting from the male's often casual encounter," particularly where the unwed father might be more interested in welfare payments than in taking care of his children.

Also closely related to the welfare decisions is the Court's policy on the rights of consumers, because the poor are the hardest hit by shady consumer practices. Here the Burger Court, with much deference to Congress and the Federal Reserve Board, upheld the board's installment purchase regulations under the Truth-in-Lending Act.[100] The Warren Court had said that wage garnishment could not take place without notice to the debtor and a hearing.[101] The Burger Court also extended this requirement of notice and hearing to several other situations, including "confession of judgment" provisions in contracts, in which a person agreed that if he defaulted on his payments, the other party could have judgment entered in court without notice or hearing. The Court said such provisions were not *per se* unconstitutional, as someone signing them could waive his rights. However, consumers who signed such provisions without being fully aware of what was involved could not be held to have properly waived those rights.[102]

Notice and hearing requirements were also initially extended to summary repossession of consumer goods, so that the consumer would have an opportunity to assert he had paid the debt.[103] Later the Court undercut this ruling by allowing a creditor to repossess goods to protect them, without an adversary hearing, because the debtor had an opportunity to go to court to get his goods back.[104] Here the majority, accepting the argument that if the creditor could not seize the property, the debtor might damage or sell it, held that the state had achieved a proper accomodation of the interests of the buyer and the seller. The Court's withdrawal from its earlier position was shown by Justice Stewart's objection that the Court was ignoring precedent and by Justice Powell's comment that the Court had overruled its "broad and inflexible" earlier rule, which had "considerably altered settled law with respect to commercial transactions and basic creditor-debtor understandings."

While the Court seemed at least partly willing to help consumers, it was not so disposed with tenants. As we have seen, the Court aided communities in fencing out public housing. Where individual tenants were concerned, the Court was also unhelpful. Tenants tried to defend against an eviction for refusal to pay rent while living in substandard conditions, by saying the landlord had a duty to maintain the premises. The Supreme Court decided against them, saying the state could require tenants to sue the landlord separately for damages, something difficult to do once they had to move out.[105]

CONCLUSION

Equality had been a primary theme of the Warren Court, particularly in the area of race relations. However, it was certainly not as central to the work of the Burger Court, in race relations or other areas. The Burger Court continued the Warren Court's work in school desegregation, particularly where formal *de jure* segregation had existed, whether in the South or in the North, and the Court even increased the scope of actions it would include within *de jure* segregation. The breadth of remedies for segregation allowed in the South was substantial, but remedies were limited in the North by the Court's ruling that cross-busing could not include suburbs not themselves guilty of discriminatory practices. In other areas of race relations—public accommodations, employment, housing—where Congress had acted, the Court sustained broad applications of the legislation. In an area like parks, in the absence of such legislation, the picture was mixed—broad rulings in aid of school desegregation but not necessarily otherwise. When voting rights issues shifted from blacks, the poor received good treatment in terms of ability to become candidates, but property interests were given noticeable weight in certain voting arrangements. In addition, minority parties and voters wishing to change parties found themselves subordinated to the continued predominance of the two major parties.

While the Burger Court continued to deal with problems of blacks, it also dealt with cases brought by women, Indians, and aliens. Despite some landmark language on women's rights, the results were mixed, with some victories for women's interests—most notably in the area of abortion—but some defeats as well, for example, exclusion of pregnancy as a disability. The rights of aliens to become or remain citizens were not sustained by the new Court. However, resident aliens found at least some, although not all, job discrimination held invalid by the Court; here some of Mr. Nixon's appointees disagreed with the alien's right to practice professions. Indians tended to be treated on a tribe-by-tribe, treaty-by-treaty basis. This approach produced little consistent doctrine, although a number of decisions favored Indians' fishing and employment rights.

On the subject of reapportionment, a major area in which the Warren Court stressed equality, the Burger Court's retreat was evident, as it approved state and local apportionment schemes with wider variances than those previously allowed. Indicating not merely differences in result but also substantial differences in approach and judicial ideology, the new Court showed its distaste for the Warren Court's active involvement in correcting state districting efforts.

With respect to welfare and related matters, neither the Warren Court, which entered the policy area only in the late 1960s, nor the Burger Court was particularly generous or liberal. However, the Warren Court handed down a major ruling on durational residence requirements; the Burger Court seemed quite willing to follow it. On matters of procedure, and particularly on the crucial matter of expenditures for welfare benefits, welfare recipients could expect little help—and a sour attitude—from the new members of the Court. The new Court's view of procedure also seemed to indicate that the consumer could count on a decreasing amount of help and that the tenant interested in asserting his rights against his landlord would also not find much assistance.

NOTES

1. *Green* v. *School Board of New Kent County,* 391 U.S. 430 (1968); *Raney* v. *Gould School District,* 391 U.S. 443 (1968); *Monroe* v. *Commissioners of City of Jackson,* 391 U.S. 450 (1968).
2. *U.S.* v. *Montgomery Board of Education,* 395 U.S. 225 (1969).
3. *Alexander* v. *Holmes County,* 396 U.S. 19 (1969).
4. *Carter* v. *West Feliciana School Board,* 396 U.S. 290 (1969); *Northcross* v. *Memphis Board of Education,* 397 U.S. 232 (1969).

5. *Swann* v. *Charlotte-Mecklenberg Board of Education*, 402 U.S. 1. The Chief Justice was concerned about overbroad readings of his opinion. See *Winston-Salem/Forsyth County Board of Education* v. *Scott*, 404 U.S. 1221 (1971).

6. *Drummond* v. *Acree,* 409 U.S. 1228 (1972).

7. *Wright* v. *City of Emporia,* 407 U.S. 451 (1972); *U.S.* v. *Scotland Neck Board of Education*, 407 U.S. 484 (1972).

8. *Norwood* v. *Harrison*, 413 U.S. 455 (1973).

9. *Gilmore* v. *City of Montgomery,* 417 U.S. 556 (1974).

10. *Keyes* v. *Denver School District*, 413 U.S. 189 (1973).

11. *Lau* v. *Nichols,* 414 U.S. 567 (1974).

12. *Milliken* v. *Bradley*, 418 U.S. 717 (1974). The Court had earlier divided 4–4 in a Richmond case on the question, because of Justice Powell's recusance. *School Board of Richmond* v. *State Board of Education*, 412 U.S. 92 (1973).

13. On this issue in higher education, see *McLaurin* v. *Board of Regents,* 339 U.S. 637 (1950).

14. *DeFunis* v. *Odegaard*, 416 U.S. 312 (1974).

15. *Reitman* v. *Mulkey*, 387 U.S. 369 (1967).

16. *Jones* v. *Mayer*, 392 U.S. 409 (1968).

17. *Sullivan* v. *Little Hunting Park*, 396 U.S. 229 (1969).

18. *Hunter* v. *Erickson*, 393 U.S. 385 (1969).

19. *James* v. *Valtierra*, 402 U.S. 137 (1971). See Inez Smith Reid, "The Burger Court and the Civil Rights Movement: The Supreme Court Giveth and the Supreme Court Taketh Away," *Rutgers-Camden Law Review*, 3 (Spring 1972), 410–440. Another evaluation is by Lucius J. Barker, "Black Americans and the Burger Court: Implications for the Political System," *Washington University Law Quarterly*, 1973, 747–777.

20. *Village of Belle Terre* v. *Boraas*, 416 U.S. 1 (1974).

21. *Daniel* v. *Paul*, 395 U.S. 298 (1969).

22. *Adickes* v. *Kress*, 398 U.S. 144 (1970).

23. *Moose Lodge* v. *Irvis*, 407 U.S. 163 (1972).

24. *Evans* v. *Newton*, 382 U.S. 296 (1966).

25. *Evans* v. *Abney*, 396 U.S. 435 (1970).

26. *Palmer* v. *Thompson*, 403 U.S. 217 (1971).

27. *Griggs* v. *Duke Power Co.*, 401 U.S. 424 (1971).

28. *McDonnell-Douglas* v. *Green*, 411 U.S. 792 (1973).

29. *Alexander* v. *Gardner-Denver,* 415 U.S. 36 (1974). In an earlier ruling on remedies, the Warren Court had held that, with a race relations complaint, when the reactions of union officials indicated that grievance-processing in the union would be futile, an individual need not exhaust internal union remedies before suing. *Glover* v. *St. Louis-San Francisco Railway*, 393 U.S. 324 (1969).

30. *Phillips* v. *Martin Marietta*, 400 U.S. 544 (1971); see also *Corning Glass Works* v. *Brennan*, 417 U.S. 188 (1974).

31. *Reed* v. *Reed*, 404 U.S. 71 (1971).

32. *Kahn* v. *Shevin*, 416 U.S. 351 (1974).

33. *Cleveland Board of Education* v. *LaFleur*, 414 U.S. 632 (1974).

34. *Geduldig* v. *Aiello*, 417 U.S. 484 (1974).

35. *Griswold* v. *Connecticut*, 381 U.S. 579 (1965).

36. *Eisenstadt* v. *Baird*, 405 U.S. 438 at 453 (1972).

37. *Roe* v. *Wade*, 410 U.S. 113 (1973); *Doe* v. *Bolton*, 410 U.S. 179 (1973).

38. *Rogers* v. *Bellei,* 401 U.S. 815 (1971).

39. *Astrup* v. *I.N.S.*, 402 U.S. 509 (1971).

40. *Immigration and Naturalization Service* v. *Hibi*, 414 U.S. 5 at 11 (1973).

41. *Espinoza* v. *Farah Manufacturing Co.*, 414 U.S. 86 (1973).

42. *In Re Griffiths*, 413 U.S. 717 (1973); *Sugarman* v. *Dougall*, 413 U.S. 634 (1973).

43. J. Youngblood Henderson and Russel L. Barsh, "Oyate Kin hoye keyuga u pe" ("The Tribe sends a voice as they come"), *Harvard Law School Bulletin*, 25 (April 1974), 10–15; (June 1974), 10–15; and 26 (Fall 1974), 17–20.

44. *Puyallup Tribe* v. *Department of Game of Washington*, 391 U.S. 329 (1968); *Menominee Tribe* v. *U.S.*, 391 U.S. 404 (1968).

45. *Department of Game of Washington* v. *Puyallup Tribe*, 414 U.S. 44 (1973). See also *Mattz* v. *Arnett*, 412 U.S. 481 (1973), fishing rights related to termination of reservation.

46. *Keeble* v. *U.S.*, 412 U.S. 205 (1973); *Tooahnippah* v. *Hickel*, 397 U.S. 598 (1970); *Morton* v. *Ruiz*, 415 U.S. 199 (1974).

47. *Morton* v. *Mancari*, 417 U.S. 535 (1974).

48. For example, *Perkins* v. *Matthews*, 400 U.S. 379 (1971); *Georgia* v. *U.S.*, 411 U.S. 526 (1973). An example from the Warren Court is *Allen* v. *Board of Elections*, 393 U.S. 544 (1969). The act had been upheld in *South Carolina* v. *Katzenbach*, 383 U.S. 301 (1965).

49. *Oregon* v. *Mitchell*, 400 U.S. 112 (1970).

50. Also in *Oregon* v. *Mitchell*, 400 U.S. 112 (1970).

51. *Dunn* v. *Blumstein*, 405 U.S. 330 (1972); *Marston* v. *Lewis*, 410 U.S. 679 (1973).

52. *McDonald* v. *Board of Election Commissioners*, 394 U.S. 802 (1969).

53. *O'Brien* v. *Skinner*, 414 U.S. 524 (1974).

54. *Richardson* v. *Ramirez*, 418 U.S. 24 (1974).

55. *Kramer* v. *Union Free School District*, 395 U.S. 621 (1969), voting in school district elections only if one owned/leased taxable real property or had children in school; *Cipriano* v. *City of Houma*, 395 U.S. 701 (1969), property taxpaying requirement for voting in municipal revenue bond elections.

56. *Gordon* v. *Lance*, 403 U.S. 1 (1971); *Salyer Land Co.* v. *Tulare Lake Basin Water Storage District*, 410 U.S. 419 (1973); and *Associated Enterprises* v. *Toltec Watershed Improvement District*, 410 U.S. 743 (1973).

57. *Bullock* v. *Carter*, 405 U.S. 134 (1972).

58. *Lubin* v. *Panish*, 415 U.S. 709 (1974).

59. *Williams* v. *Rhodes*, 393 U.S. 23 (1968).

60. *Storer* v. *Brown/Frommhagen* v. *Brown*, 415 U.S. 724 (1974); *American Party of Texas* v. *White/Hainsworth* v. *White*, 415 U.S. 767 (1974).

61. *Rosario* v. *Rockefeller*, 410 U.S. 752 at 763 (1973). Powell enunciated some cogent political science in support of his position:

> Partisan political activities do not constantly engage the attention of large numbers of Americans, especially as party labels and loyalties tend to be less persuasive than issues and the qualities of individual candidates. The crossover in registration from one party to another is most often impelled by motives quite unrelated to a desire to raid or distort a party's primary. To the extent that deliberate raiding occurs, it is usually the result of organized effort which depends for its success upon some relatively immediate concern or interest of the voters. (410 U.S. at 771.)

62. *Kusper* v. *Pontikes*, 414 U.S. 51 (1973).

63. *Pipefitters* v. *U.S.*, 405 U.S. 385 at 416 (1972).

64. *Wesberry* v. *Sanders*, 376 U.S. 1 (1963).

65. *Reynolds* v. *Sims*, 377 U.S. 533 (1964).

66. *Kirkpatrick* v. *Preisler*, 394 U.S. 526 (1969).

67. Early studies showed little relationship between degree of malappor-

tionment and policy outcomes. See, for example, Thomas R. Dye, "Malapportionment and Public Policy in the States," *Journal of Politics,* 27 (August 1965), 586–601; Richard I. Hofferbert, "The Relation Between Public Policy and Some Structural and Environmental Variables in the American States," *American Political Science Review,* 60 (March 1966), 73–82. For a discussion of the effect of redistricting, see Robert Dixon, *Democratic Representation* (New York: Oxford University Press, 1968), and also Robert S. Erickson, "The Partisan Impact of State Legislative Reapportionment," *Midwest Journal of Political Science,* 15 (February 1971), 51–71.

68. *Avery* v. *Midland County,* 390 U.S. 474 (1968).

69. *Hadley* v. *Junior College District of Metropolitan Kansas City,* 309 U.S. 50 (1970).

70. *Abate* v. *Mundt,* 403 U.S. 182 (1971).

71. *Mahan* v. *Howell,* 401 U.S. 315 (1973).

72. *White* v. *Weiser,* 412 U.S. 783 (1973).

73. *Gaffney* v. *Cummings,* 412 U.S. 735 (1973).

74. *Whitcomb* v. *Chavis,* 403 U.S. 124 (1971).

75. *White* v. *Regester,* 412 U.S. 755 (1973).

76. See Stephen L. Wasby, "Welfare Policy and the Supreme Court: An Era of Uncertainty," *Public Welfare,* 30 (Spring 1972), 16–27.

77. *Wyman* v. *James,* 400 U.S. 309 (1971).

78. *See* v. *City of Seattle,* 387 U.S. 541 (1967), decided along with *Camara* v. *Municipal Court of San Francisco,* 387 U.S. 523 (1967), warrantless building code search of apartment house. Those decisions overruled an earlier Warren Court case, *Frank* v. *Maryland,* 359 U.S. 360 (1958), upholding administrative (health) searches without a warrant.

79. *King* v. *Smith,* 392 U.S. 309 (1968); *Lewis* v. *Martin,* 397 U.S. 552 (1970).

80. See also *Townsend* v. *Swank,* 404 U.S. 282 (1971), regulation allowing AFDC benefits to those eighteen- to twenty-year-olds in high school or vocational school, but not college, held invalid.

81. *California Department of Human Resources* v. *Java,* 402 U.S. 121 (1971).

82. *Dillard* v. *Industrial Commission of Virginia,* 416 U.S. 783 (1974).

83. *Shapiro* v. *Thompson,* 394 U.S. 618 (1968).

84. *Graham* v. *Richardson,* 403 U.S. 376 (1971), also invalidating Pennsylvania's allowing payment of general assistance benefits only to U.S. citizens; *Memorial Hospital* v. *Maricopa County,* 415 U.S. 250 (1974).

85. *Goldberg* v. *Kelly,* 397 U.S. 254 (1970); *Wheeler* v. *Montgomery,* 397 U.S. 280 (1970).

86. *Richardson* v. *Perales,* 402 U.S. 389 (1971).

87. *Ortwein* v. *Schwab,* 410 U.S. 656 (1973).

88. *U.S.* v. *Kras,* 409 U.S. 434 (1973).

89. *Boddie* v. *Connecticut,* 401 U.S. 371 (1971).

90. *Richardson* v. *Belcher,* 404 U.S. 78 (1971).

91. *Rosado* v. *Wyman,* 397 U.S. 397 (1970).

92. *Dandridge* v. *Williams,* 397 U.S. 471 (1970). See the comment by Samuel Krislov, "American Welfare Policy and the Supreme Court," *Current History,* 65 (July 1973), 42.

93. *Jefferson* v. *Hackney,* 406 U.S. 535 (1972).

94. *New York State Department of Social Services* v. *Dublino,* 413 U.S. 405 (1973).

95. *Levy* v. *Louisiana,* 391 U.S. 68 (1968); *Glona* v. *American Guarantee and Liability,* 391 U.S. 73 (1968); and *Weber* v. *Aetna Casualty and Surety,* 406 U.S. 164 (1972); *New Jersey Welfare Rights Organization* v. *Cahill,* 411 U.S. 619 (1972); *Gomez* v. *Perez,* 409 U.S. 535 (1972).

96. *Jimenez* v. *Weinberger*, 417 U.S. 628 (1974).

97. *Labine* v. *Vincent*, 401 U.S. 532 (1971). The law did not prevent such children from inheriting through the father's will, *if* he could have legally married the mother at the time of their conception, but not otherwise.

98. *Linda R.S.* v. *Richard D.*, 411 U.S. 614 (1973).

99. *Stanley* v. *Illinois*, 405 U.S. 645 (1972).

100. *Mourning* v. *Family Publications*, 411 U.S. 356 (1973).

101. *Sniadach* v. *Family Finance Corp.*, 395 U.S. 337 (1969).

102. *D.H. Overmyer* v. *Frick*, 405 U.S. 174 (1972); *Swarb* v. *Lenox*, 405 U.S. 191 (1972).

103. *Fuentes* v. *Shevin*, 407 U.S. 67 (1972).

104. *Mitchell* v. *W.T. Grant Co.*, 416 U.S. 600 (1974).

105. *Lindsay* v. *Normet*, 405 U.S. 56 (1972).

CHAPTER SEVEN

The First Amendment During the Transition

The two basic elements of the First Amendment are freedom of speech and press and the relation between church and state, to be discussed in this chapter. On free speech questions, both the Warren and Burger Courts were basically expansionist in their approaches, that is, they allowed more speech and speech-related activity than had previously been allowed. In so doing, they continued a trend that had begun in the 1930s. Yet under the Burger Court, the expansion slowed down and in some areas the justices even reduced allowable speech. In the church-state area, the Burger Court generally followed, reinforced, and expanded the doctrine utilized by the Warren Court.

FREEDOM OF SPEECH

The Warren Court's emphasis on equality has made us think that it is our most important civil liberties value. Yet freedom of speech and press are more central to a democracy—and to other civil liberties—because without them it is difficult to obtain and protect other rights. Many Americans assume that freedom of speech exists relatively unencumbered in their country. In fact, we *limit* speech in many ways. The justices themselves uphold restrictions on speech. Yet even when the Supreme Court defends free speech, we cannot be sure that such speech will exist unrestrained. At the community level, there are many extralegal encroachments, imposed by private individuals and groups, and government officials add to those infringements as well as instigating or initiating others themselves. Such facts forcefully remind us that First Amendment rights as stated by the Supreme Court are rights in *theory*, not always in practice.

With this in mind, we turn to the perennial problems of free speech, which come before the justices of the Supreme Court in many different forms. Some relate to the content of speech and others concern "free speech plus," speech connected with action. We look first at the critical problem of "prior restraint" upon freedom of speech and the press, advance limitations on speech or publication, which the Supreme Court has traditionally disfavored, and the closely connected question of whether laws attempting to limit speech are excessively vague or are overbroad.

We then turn to restrictions on sedition (speech critical of the government), libel, and obscenity, as well as speech connected with action, including the circumstances under which speech and such activity occur. The Burger Court tightened up in the area of obscenity. It also continued the policy of limiting libel suits as well as the Warren Court's proclivity for limiting the situations in which speech-related activity could be carried out. While some changes did occur, they were neither immediate nor radical, instead being the mixed results produced by a court in transition. This policy area was one in which the Nixon appointees were often unable to carry the Court in a conservative direction, because they were not always united and because the Chief Justice's position was sometimes strongly supportive of First Amendment rights.

Prior Restraint

The most feared limitation upon freedom of speech and press is restraint prior to publication. The law on this subject was thought to have been long settled,[1] yet the issue arose either directly or indirectly in a number of recent cases. The most noted case came to the Court when the administration sought injunctions against the *New York Times* and the *Washington Post* to prevent continued publication of stories based on the Pentagon Papers, documents taken from the government that told of behind-the-scenes foreign policy-making. Six justices voted in favor of refusing the injunction,[2] while the "unseemly haste" with which the case had been brought led Blackmun, Harlan, and the Chief Justice to dissent, and Burger chided the *Times* for not reporting stolen property. Three justices (Black [see p. 20], Douglas, Brennan) took broad freedom of speech positions, but the views of Marshall, Stewart, and White were far more limited. Marshall said the Court should not stop what Congress had declined to prohibit nor share the executive's responsibility for dealing with law-violators. Stewart focused on the executive's national security discretion, but he also stressed the need for the greatest possible disclosure of information if we were to have a public opinion that was informed and critical. He also felt that "secrecy

can best be preserved only when credibility is truly maintained."
Justice White felt that the government had simply failed to proceed in the proper way. Criminal publication could be dealt with
directly, he said, but he joined the majority because the government had not provided the unusually heavy justification required
for an injunction.

Related to prior restraint was the question of a newsman's
right not to testify to a grand jury about sources of information
given in confidence. Newsmen, from both newspapers and television, had either witnessed the manufacture, sale, and use of drugs
or had come in contact with Black Panthers in the course of carrying out investigative work for their stories; they had refused to
reveal their sources when asked to do so before grand juries. By a
vote of 5–4, the Court held that there was no *constitutional*
privilege against having to answer questions about the identity of
confidential news sources, but left open the way for "shield
laws,"[3] that is, laws that would provide that privilege. The justices did say that news*gathering* was subject to First Amendment
protections, but were unwilling to establish another privileged
relationship (like those between lawyer and client and doctor and
patient), that being the legislature's function. Specifically rejected by the Court was the reporters' claim that they should not
be forced to appear until the government showed they possessed
otherwise unobtainable information about specific criminal acts.
Stressing the broad investigative function of the grand jury, the
majority thought the case involved not prior restraint on publication nor compulsion to publish material but only whether reporters had to answer the same questions as other citizens; this was
particularly true where crimes had been *observed*. The justices
claimed "the evidence fails to demonstrate that there would be a
significant constriction of the flow of news to the public." Here we
see the idea that the First Amendment does not prevent any
burdens on the press from statutes that have other purposes—
here, the grand jury's investigation of crime—an example of the
First Amendment's *theory* not preventing restrictions *in fact*. For
the dissenters, Douglas argued for an absolute immunity for reporters and Stewart complained about "the Court's crabbed view
of the First Amendment," which "reflects a disturbing insensitiv-
ity to the critical role of an independent press in our society."
Stewart, emphasizing the public's right to know, felt that criminals would not be the only ones afraid to talk; office-holders and
bureaucrats who feared scorn or their associates' wrath might
now not reveal valuable information.

Prior restraint was also implicated in a 1973 case where a
city human relations commission had barred the grouping of

newspaper employment classified ads by male and female interest. Using a distinction between types of speech developed many years before, the Court held there was no First Amendment violation;[4] "commercial speech" could be limited more than noncommercial types of speech. Justice Powell said the press was not being disabled; even if the makeup of one section of the paper was affected and the paper's judgment as to where to place ads was limited, the paper remained free to comment editorially on the policies involved. In this case, Chief Justice Burger, who thought the commission order was prior restraint, voted with Justice Douglas. Using judicial self-restraint to reinforce freedom of the press, he felt the paper had "clearly acted within its protected journalistic discretion" and objected to judges defining which parts of the paper could be regulated and which could not. Stewart was even more forceful, calling the ruling the first "that permits a government agency to enter a composing room of a newspaper and dictate to the publisher the layout and makeup of the newspaper's pages."

When the question shifted from advertisements to the editorial page, the view that government should not interfere prevailed. Although the Court had earlier upheld the FCC's rules on responses to broadcast attacks (see pp. 104-105), in 1974 the Court unanimously invalidated laws requiring newspapers to publish candidates' responses to editorial attacks.[5] Burger noted the argument that the press was becoming progressively controlled by a small number of publishers with a substantial effect on public opinion, but rejected the claim that the statute's purpose was to add to the flow of information rather than to control it. The Court also denied access to advertising space in public transit after transit companies had refused to accept political ads, including some favoring impeachment of President Nixon.[6] Four justices ruled that the advertising space was not a public forum covered by First Amendment protections. Douglas, writing separately, said that no one had a right to inflict his views on a captive audience. The dissenters urged that the city, by allowing commercial advertising, had opened up the forum to communication and so could not then exclude one category of advertising, particularly where it was almost impossible to draw the line between ideological and nonideological advertisements.

Vagueness and Overbreadth

Because of the danger that protected speech would be restricted along with improper speech, the Warren Court had required the government to legislate in the area of speech in a particularly precise manner. In so doing, it used the concepts of "vagueness" and "overbreadth." While we find these terms used in other areas of the law, they have particular importance here because of the significance we attach to protecting free speech. Under these terms, laws must not be unclear (vague) and must not encompass more than is absolutely necessary (be overbroad). If a statute is found to have either defect in its language, it would be held unconstitutional *on its face* by the Warren Court, even if the statute might have been properly *applied*. The Court's rules about vagueness and overbreadth were strengthened during the transition. The decision setting aside an arrest for "offensive" conduct (see p. 19) was one example of the Court's application of the policy. Another involved invalidation of a statute making it a crime for three or more persons to assemble on sidewalks and act in an "annoying" manner, because the law hindered rights of assembly and association.[7] The Court noted that cities had other permissible ways of dealing with specific undesirable acts such as blocking sidewalks and littering. The Court also set aside a breach of the peace conviction based on the "abusive" and "opprobrious" language, "White son of a bitch, I'll kill you," and "You son of a bitch, I'll choke you to death," said to a policeman.[8] This case and several others that followed involved the "fighting words" doctrine, which stemmed from a much earlier case[9]—that speech could be constrained if it would provoke the audience to a breach of the peace. If such language could be controlled, the majority was saying, *only* such language—and no more—could be limited and statutes would have to be so written.

The new justices were clearly unhappy that convictions for speech that might be penalized under a narrowly written statute were being set aside. For example, they complained when the majority remanded a case in which "mother-fucker"—perhaps the last "fighting word" in the language—had been used at a school board meeting with both women and children in the audience.[10] Chief Justice Burger argued, "When we undermine the general belief that the law will give protection against fighting words and profane and abusive language . . . we take steps to return to the law of the jungle." Justice Powell was also unhappy, but he thought police should show restraint when faced with similar language.

Tension over this issue continued into 1973 and 1974. An example was a case involving a disorderly conduct conviction based on the words, "We'll take the fucking street later," said during an anti-war demonstration. The conviction was reversed as not involving fighting words or words that would have a tendency to lead to violence,[11] prompting Burger, Blackmun, and

Rehnquist to claim that the Court had substituted its impression of the facts for the lower courts' view. When the majority kept sending cases back to the lower courts for reconsideration, the three dissenters became particularly bitter:

> Apparently, not only must every statute regulating speech in the 50 states parrot the wording the Court desires, but a state court must play the role of a ventriloquist's dummy mouthing ceremonial phrases in order to obtain the seal of this Court's approval.[12]

Perhaps the most graphic example of the Nixon appointees' view of vagueness and overbreadth came in a case involving Captain Howard Levy, charged with urging blacks not to go to Vietnam as well as maligning and refusing to train Green Berets. He was convicted for "willfully disobeying a lawful command of his superior commissioned officer" and for "conduct unbecoming an officer and gentleman" as well as for "disorders and neglects to the prejudice of good order and discipline in the armed forces." Upholding Levy's court-martial, the Court, definitely drawing back from earlier policy as to overbreadth, said the language was not excessively broad, particularly in the military context.[13] The military provisions, which Justice Blackmun separately called "essential not only to punish patently criminal conduct but also to foster an orderly and dutiful fighting force," were said to have been given much specificity by custom and usage, military interpretations, and rulings of the Court of Military Appeals. Yet Stewart in dissent found it "hard to imagine criminal statutes more patently unconstitutional than these vague and uncertain General Articles." He said the provisions allowed prosecutions "for practically any conduct that may offend the sensibility of a military commander" and thought it an "act of judicial fantasy" to expect noncareer soldiers like Capt. Levy to understand the obscure and arcane meaning of the rules.

Employees' Rights

Free speech issues, including that of overbreadth, occurred regularly when employees' rights were at issue in the Burger Court; at times they were also intertwined with due process questions. One case involving a broad question of restrictions on free speech came as a major challenge to the Hatch Act's restrictions on government employees' political activity, prohibiting "tak[ing] part in the management of political affairs or in any political campaign." As had the Supreme Court many years before, the Court majority upheld the prohibitions, adding that the language was *not* overbroad.[14]

Other cases, however, involved the discharge of government employees, and thus raised the question whether government employment involved the same sorts of property interests, to be protected by due process, as we have seen in the welfare cases. The old position had been that one had no right to be a government employee, which meant in fact that one could only retain one's rights by ceasing to be an employee. The Warren Court had begun to touch upon this problem in dealing with penalties imposed on an employee for refusing to testify about political beliefs. The Court ruled that a professor could not be fired for asserting his constitutional rights (invoking the Fifth Amendment before a congressional committee), but then two years later said an employee who would not answer his superiors' questions about Communist affiliations was properly discharged for being of "doubtful trust and reliability."[15] In the Burger Court, the matter arose when a nonprobationary government employee was discharged for having made defamatory and false statements about other employees. Justice Rehnquist, in a plurality opinion, said that the phrase "efficiency of the service" was not impermissibly vague and there was sufficient protection for the employee against stigmatization by untrue and/or unsupported charges through post-termination proceedings.[16] Several justices were disturbed by Rehnquist's position that the right not to be discharged except for "cause" was dependent on the statute. Powell and Blackmun, although concurring in the Court's action, thought that employment could not be terminated without notice and a full evidentiary hearing, although the government must be able expeditiously to suspend employees who hindered efficient operation. Both White and Marshall, dissenting, wanted it firmly established that due process required notice and hearing before discharge *independent of the statute*. Douglas, also dissenting, was the one to stress the case's First Amendment policy aspects most directly: "Losing one's job with the Federal Government because of one's discussion of an issue in the public domain is certainly an abridgement of speech."

The Burger Court also decided cases on the rights of terminated college faculty; free speech was also involved because the terminations were allegedly made for unpopular statements. In line with prevailing practice, nontenured faculty had been given neither notice of reasons for dismissal nor an opportunity to have a dismissal hearing, and the Court found this acceptable; however, if damaging statements had been made about the professor, due process would require an opportunity to respond. If the faculty member had formal tenure or could show *de facto* tenure from lengthy experience, he was entitled to a hearing based on a statement of the grounds for nonretention. Nonrenewal for exercise of free speech was impermissible.[17] Marshall, dissenting, argued against arbitrary government action in employment. Going even further, he stated, "Every citizen who applies for a government job is entitled to it unless the government can establish some reason for denying the employment." What these cases seem to say is that employees, in academia and the regular civil service, are increasingly—although not fully—covered by norms of due process; they may be terminated for a wide variety of reasons, but exercise of free speech is considered *not* a valid reason.

Also related to employees' rights were cases on information obtained from employees under threat of job loss. The Warren Court had held such testimony to be improperly compelled and thus inadmissible in court; similarly, even though a public employee could be ordered to answer his superior's questions, he could not be dismissed for refusing to surrender his rights, for example, to immunity from prosecution.[18] The Burger Court continued these rulings, invalidating New York's requirement that a contractor who refused to waive immunity or to testify about his state contracts could have his contracts cancelled and could be debarred for five years from receiving other contracts. The state, in requiring information about the contractor's dealings, could do so only with a grant of immunity.[19]

Sedition

The Warren Court's position on speech critical of the government was established early. In 1957, the Court specified a tight "clear and present danger" test as the standard for judging seditious speech in connection with the Smith Act. Speaking through Justice Harlan, the Court ruled that the First Amendment protected abstract advocacy of overthrow of the government when the speaker did not also specifically incite his audience to acts of violence.[20] In its last term, the Warren Court reaffirmed this position. In a case involving a Ku Klux Klan leader, the Court invalidated a state criminal syndicalism law—outlawing advocacy of crime, sabotage, violence, and terrorism, and assembly to teach or advocate the same—because it punished mere advocacy and related assembly.[21]

In the interim, the Court had invalidated most loyalty oaths on the basis of a First Amendment freedom of association. The Court's ruling that a person not be prosecuted under the Smith Act except for active, knowing membership in organizations advocating overthrow of the government by force and violence led directly to invalidation of many disclaimer affidavits ("I have not now, nor have I ever been a member . . .") required in connection with one's employment.[22] The Court also voided an Arizona law providing prosecution for becoming or remaining a member of the Communist Party or other group intending to overthrow state government when the member knew of the unlawful purpose; *sharing* in the purpose would have to be shown, said the Court.[23] Stressing academic freedom and overturning an important Vinson Court case, the Court also struck down provisions making CP membership evidence of disqualification for employment and allowing dismissal for utterances that were "treasonable" or "seditious," holding the language unconstitutionally vague.[24]

The Burger Court somewhat unsettled this doctrinal development in narrowly upholding, against a charge of vagueness, a requirement that state employees "uphold and defend" the government. The justices ruled that the law required only that an individual not act disloyally.[25] The possibility that Warren Court doctrine might be overturned was shown by the dissent of the Nixon appointees when the Court later invalidated a loyalty oath required to get on the ballot because the oath reached too far.[26] The Burger Court also showed its conservative attitude on internal security matters when, in an extremely restrictive ruling, the justices upheld the Attorney General's refusal to admit a distinguished foreign professor (an acknowledged revolutionary Marxist) to the country to give lectures.[27] Congress' delegation to the executive branch of entry determinations was proper, said the majority, readily accepting the executive's claims. Douglas, seeing no national security threat and saying, "Those who live here may need exposure to the ideas of people of many faiths and many creeds to further their education," accused the government of thought control, while Marshall criticized the Court for giving unjustified and "unprecedented deference to the Executive."

The question of denying admission to the practice of law because of political beliefs also came before the Court. On this subject, the Warren Court had not shown much courage. The Court had allowed states to deny admission to the practice of law to those who would not provide information about their organizational memberships, as long as the inference was not directly drawn that the applicant was a Communist.[28] However, during the early Burger Court, the justices by a 5–4 vote voided state refusals to admit to practice those who would not provide complete information about their organizational affiliations.[29] In Justice Black's words:

> The First Amendment's protection of association prohibits a State from excluding a person from a profession or punishing him solely because he is a member of a particular political organization or because he holds certain beliefs. . . . Views and beliefs are immune from bar association inquisitions designed to lay a foundation for barring an applicant from the practice of law.

However, the justices were *un*willing to overturn the practice of screening applicants for the bar, despite claims of its "chilling effect" on free speech and association.[30]

Rights of association were also involved in a case where a college president refused to recognize a chapter of Students for a Democratic Society (SDS), partly because of the organization's views on violent protest. Justice Powell, asserting that "State colleges and universities are not enclaves immune from the sweep of the First Amendment," held for a unanimous Court that recognition of a group could not be denied without justification; *activities* that violated campus rules or were disruptive could, however, be prohibited.[31] Denial of recognition could not be based, he said, on the group's association with an unpopular organization or on its expressions about violence unless specific incitation were involved, although a group could be asked to affirm "its willingness to adhere to reasonable campus law." Both Douglas and Burger agreed that arguments over college matters should be settled on campus rather than in the courts. However, Douglas favored "ferment" in the university so it would not become a "useless appendage," while Burger was more concerned that there be a civil atmosphere in which divergent views might be expressed.

The thrust of these decisions was that the standards developed by the Warren Court for judging sedition had been left untouched. Individual's rights of association related to sedition—through membership in unpopular groups—were reinforced, but the new justices, like the President who had appointed them, seemed more favorably disposed toward restrictions imposed in the name of national security.

Libel

In 1964 the Supreme Court handed down its ground-breaking libel ruling in a case where black ministers and the *New York Times* had been sued for an advertisement about police brutality in the South. Setting a new standard for measuring libel, the Court said that a public official could win a libel judgment only if he showed that statements were made "with malice," that is, knowing they were false or with "reckless disregard" of whether or not they were false.[32] The purpose of the policy was to give greatest scope to political discussion, accepting the risks of false and damaging statements. The Court subsequently reinforced the policy and extended it to other situations, such as dismissal of a teacher for a letter-to-the-editor about the school board's use of funds. In setting aside the dismissal, the Court also stressed a teacher's rights as a citizen and his special competence to speak out on matters affecting education.[33]

The Court did allow Georgia football coach Wally Butts to recover for an article accusing him of turning over his "game plans" to Alabama coach "Bear" Bryant (a most grievous sin, football fans!).[34] Here the magazine reporter apparently had made little if any effort to check out the story, "highly unreasonable conduct constituting an extreme departure from the standards of investigation and reporting ordinarily adhered to by responsible publishers." Yet at about the same time the justices rejected the claim that a family's right to privacy had been invaded by a story that identified the family as the subject of a play about people held hostage in their own home.[35] Because "Exposure of the self to others in varying degrees is a concomitant of life in a civilized community," freedom of speech overrode the private citizen's interest.

The distinction between "public" and "private" was also at the heart of the libel cases that came before the Burger Court. The justices first reinforced and extended the *New York Times* v. *Sullivan* doctrine, but then backed off somewhat from their own work. In one case, a newspaper had mistakenly called a senatorial candidate "a former small-town bootlegger"; the lower court judge had awarded damages, because the libelous statement concerned the private portion of the candidate's personal life. The Supreme Court would not accept such an argument; statements about a candidate for office might be relevant in considering his fitness to hold the office for which he was campaigning, and the *New York Times* standards should apply.[36] The "clash of reputations" that was "the staple of election campaigns" should not be limited, said the justices. Although divided in their reasoning, they went even further when a radio station called a subsequently exonerated magazine distributor arrested in an obscenity raid a "smut peddler." Denying the distributor's libel claim, several justices said he could not recover where matters of *public interest* were involved, except under the *New York Times* standard, which applied in such situations whether public figures or private citizens were involved.[37]

Continuing its development of the law, the Court both extended and limited the *New York Times* rule in a pair of crucial 1974 rulings. In one, a non-union worker had won a $165,000 state judgment against a union that had (not falsely) listed him as a "scab." Here the justices held that federal labor law, which favored "uninhibited, robust and wide-open debate in labor disputes," superceded state libel law, and they denied the man's claim.[38] Justice Powell thought the Court was giving insufficient protection to defenseless individuals and feared that the ruling would make it easier for unions and employers to defame individual workers. In the other, more important, case, where an attorney had represented a family suing a policeman convicted of murdering their son, the John Birch Society had said the lawyer was part of a Communist conspiracy to discredit the local police. The Court ruled that the lawyer (a private citizen) could not recover *punitive* damages unless he could show that the statement had been made with malice, but that he could sue for *actual* libel damage without such a showing.[39] Justice Powell justified this because private citizens like the lawyer were both "more vulnerable to injury" and "more deserving of recovery" than public officials, who had not only voluntarily assumed some risks of being falsely defamed but also had better access to the media to respond. The Court did not dictate the libel standards the states could set with regard to suits by private citizens, thus seeming to give them flexibility, but did rule that liability could not be imposed without fault being shown. This was in reality a far *higher* standard than had existed in those states that had allowed recovery simply on a showing of false defamatory remarks; now a plaintiff would have to show that the person defaming him had engaged in *negligent* conduct. Similarly, where most states had *assumed* actual damages, a plaintiff would now have to *show* such damages.

Chief Justice Burger was opposed to these shifts in the direction of the Court's policy, and Justice White complained at length of the drastic nature of the Court's action, "scuttling . . . in . . . wholesale fashion" the libel law of most of the states. White said the Court had engaged without sufficient reason in what he called an "ill-considered exercise of the power entrusted to this Court." He was particularly distressed that the Court had shifted the burden away from those making defamatory statements and did not think the press, which he said was increasingly concentrated, vigorous, and not easily intimidated, would be restrained in its activities if it had to pay some libel judgments to private citizens.

Obscenity

Of all the free speech subjects considered by the Warren Court, obscenity probably gave the justices the most trouble. The basic approach used by the Court, after saying that obscenity was not protected, was to find almost nothing obscene—either by tightening up the definition of "obscene" or by ruling directly on the obscenity of an item. As this suggests, the Court, after enunciating its basic obscenity standard, kept tinkering with it, and was unsuccessful in clarifying it. The justices were so badly divided they often could not produce an opinion of the Court in obscenity cases,[40] and as a result they often resorted to summary *per curiam* rulings on the obscenity of particular items or to frequent denials of review. The situation meant that the Burger Court's 1973 obscenity rulings were the first in many years in which even five justices united behind a single opinion.

In 1957, the Warren Court said that obscenity was not entitled to First Amendment protection, because it did not have redeeming social importance.[41] Prior to this time, obscenity had been measured in terms of its effects on "those whose minds are open to immoral influences and into whose hands a publication of this sort may fall"; an isolated passage could be the basis of a conviction under this standard, sometimes referred to as the "mental sanitation" test. In the 1930s, in the *Ulysses* case, a lower federal judge had modified the definition by insisting that the work be viewed as a whole and that its literary and artistic merit be taken into account, but that case had not gone to the Supreme Court.

The Warren Court justices, indicating the basic elements of a new constitutional definition of obscenity, focused on thoughts rather than effects on behavior. Using the "average person" and applying "contemporary community standards," judge and jury were to decide whether "the dominant theme of the material taken as a whole" (not isolated purple passages) appealed to "prurient interest," a phrase not further defined except for the statement that the Court had in mind "material having a tendency to excite lustful thoughts."[42] (One is not helped by knowing that the Greek root of "prurient" is "to itch.") The new test lacked clarity, but the Court had clearly rejected the old *Hicklin* standard. Obscenity convictions were now to be much more difficult to obtain, and the Court shortly increased the difficulty by saying the prosecution must show that someone sold obscene material *knowing* it to be obscene.[43]

The justices quickly found that—as Justice Harlan had

suggested—obscenity is less easily recognizable in literature than poison ivy is among plants. (The degree of the Supreme Court's confusion was shown at one point in Justice Stewart's statement that while he could not define "hard-core pornography," "I know it when I see it.") Trying to clarify matters, the judges added two new elements: an item had to shock or be "patently offensive," and it had to be "*utterly* without redeeming social importance."[44] The Court also allowed appeal to prurient interest to be judged in terms of specific groups (sadists, fetishists, homosexuals) if materials were directed to those groups, and where material had been directed to children, states were also told they could judge the material by the standard of whether it was "harmful" to them. The way the material had been distributed could also be taken into account in prosecutions.[45] In 1964, a plurality of the justices, by suggesting that a *national* community standard was to be used in judging obscenity, caused further confusion.[46]

After all this effort, the Court seemed to stand obscenity law on its head. Reaching the question of the legality of mere possession of obscene literature, the Court ruled that a person could maintain his own collection of materials, no matter how raw, with *no* standards to be applied.[47] This ruling led some lower court judges to rule that obscene material, if not thrust offensively upon the general public or upon children, should be available to consenting adults. The Burger Court would not, however, follow this doctrinal development, reaffirming the federal government's powers over transfer of obscene material and later reinforcing Congress' power to ban importation of obscene material even if for private personal use as well as its interstate commerce power to ban the movement of obscene materials.[48] The individual's right to receive was held not to interfere with the government's ability to deal with commercial distribution. In a mailing case, the Court also upheld Congress' power to allow an individual receiving allegedly objectionable ("erotically arousing or sexually provocative") material to obtain a Post Office order to have his/her name removed from a company's mailing list, although Post Office censorship procedures were invalidated as not containing adequate procedural safeguards.[49]

The Burger Court's most important obscenity rulings came in 1973, when the justices tried to bring some coherence to the Court's obscenity definition(s). Speaking through Chief Justice Burger, the Court discarded the "*utterly* without redeeming social importance" test. An item could now be found obscene if it did not have serious literary, artistic, political, or scientific value, but to be banned, the regulated material had to portray sexual conduct in a patently offensive way *specifically defined by state law or state court rulings*. Material still had to be taken as a whole in judging for its appeal to prurient interest, but national community standards need not be followed; the "contemporary community standards" could be those of the state where the obscenity charges were brought.[50]

Justice Brennan, who had written most of the earlier opinions, objected strongly to the majority retrenchment. He felt "vagueness would still exist and that the Court's new standard would result in the striking down of virtually all state obscenity laws." More important, he thought the ruling would have the effect, "whether or not intended, of permitting far more sweeping suppression of sexually oriented expression. . . ."[51] He felt that the only way to deal with the problem was to prevent the states from dealing with more than distribution to adults where they did not desire the material or to juveniles. Noting that most of the obscenity cases coming before the Court involved close judgments, Brennan said that there would still be no really final ruling until the Supreme Court had acted—something that would require the justices to examine all the books and see all the movies as they had been doing.

Despite its efforts, the Court had failed to clarify matters completely, something that could be seen from the large number of obscenity cases coming to the Court. Then in 1974, upholding a conviction for mailing a brochure advertising an illustrated version of the report of the President's Commission on Obscenity,[52] the Court *attempted* to clear up the confusion by saying that in rejecting the requirement of a national standard, some other specific geographical area had not been prescribed. Rather, "A juror is entitled to draw on his own knowledge of the views of the average person in the community or vicinage from which he comes for making the required determination"; that distributors of literature would encounter different standards in different areas did not create a constitutional violation. Backing off from the Court's 1959 ruling on *scienter* (knowledge), the majority made prosecution easier by saying that the prosecutor need not show that the defendant knew the material was obscene, but only that he knew its "character and the nature of the materials."

In a companion case, the Court showed that it would in fact still have to make policy on a case-by-case, book-by-book (or movie-by-movie) basis, when it specifically held that the movie *Carnal Knowledge* was not obscene, because juries did not have "unbridled discretion in determining what is 'patently offensive.' "[53] The movie was not portrayal of "hard core sexual conduct for its own sake," said Justice Rehnquist, pointing out that cameras did not focus on genitalia or concentrate on "ultimate sexual acts." Despite the individual determination in this case, the Court refused review in roughly a dozen other obscenity cases, although Justice Brennan protested that an independent determination of the material's obscenity by the Supreme Court was required. His persistence finally provoked a protest from Justice White, who said the Court could exercise its discretion in accepting or rejecting obscenity cases just as with any other type of case.[54]

Earlier the Court had been faced with the question of whether a university could establish tighter obscenity standards than those in regular criminal prosecutions. The Court overturned the expulsion of a student for "indecent" speech for distributing an underground newspaper containing a cartoon of police raping the Statue of Liberty. No separate standard could exist for the campus, said the majority; disseminating ideas on campus could not be conditioned on "conventions of decency." Dissenting Justice Rehnquist stressed the need for administrators to have "control over the environment for which they are responsible," while Chief Justice Burger emphasized that a university was "an institution where individuals learn to express themselves in acceptable, civil terms," rather than "obscene and infantile" ones so that they "may learn the self-restraint necessary to the functioning of a civilized society. . . ."[55]

Related rulings on obscenity procedure actually reinforced rather than undercut Warren Court policy. Although the Warren Court had initially upheld the requirement that movies be submitted to censorship boards,[56] in its crucial procedural ruling the Court required protections for the exhibitor if film censorship were to exist. The censor had to make himself available and rule promptly; prompt review also had to be available with the burden on the censor to prove to a judge that portions to be deleted were obscene.[57] In the Burger Court, when a sheriff, without a warrant or any prior judicial determination of obscenity, seized a film he had seen at a drive-in for use as evidence, the Court held the seizure a prior restraint.[58] However, where a judge came to a theater to see a movie, the justices said there was no requirement of a pre-seizure adversary proceeding, although a prompt judicial determination on obscenity was required, as was an opportunity for the film to be shown prior to any final determination that it was obscene.[59] Douglas, Brennan, Stewart, and Marshall, dissenting, would have overturned the statutes.

"Free Speech Plus"

First Amendment claims for speech closely tied to action have come to be called "free speech plus." The largest component in this area is picketing and demonstrations; also included are other activities such as flag desecration and the wearing of armbands. The activity in these cases is important because without it people might not be able to express their views—or at least not be able to bring those views effectively to people's attention. However, the conduct with which the speech is intermingled may interfere with other legitimate activities, thus requiring regulation despite the resulting limitation placed on the communication itself.

The Warren Court clearly had been willing to place limits on *where* free speech could take place, as in demonstrations, as well as on activity only indirectly related to speech. (For example, when it was claimed that someone needed to travel abroad to increase his store of information on public matters, the Court was willing to allow restrictions.[60]) The Court's reluctance to adopt a liberal position was particularly clear with respect to civil rights demonstrators in the South. The Court protected a peaceful march to the State Capitol as part of the right to petition for redress of grievances, but upheld a state's right to ban courthouse and jailhouse picketing, in the latter situation upholding demonstrators' convictions.[61]

We might also note that the Warren Court had engaged in some "law-and-order" policy-making in some demonstration cases stemming from the 1963 Birmingham Good Friday march. The marchers had not applied for a parade permit nor attempted to dissolve the city's injunction against the march. The Court, although by a vote of only 5–4 and with Chief Justice Warren in dissent, upheld contempt convictions resulting from violating the injunction, so ruling even though the breadth of the city's ordinance, included in the injunction, opened the former to constitutional challenge. The important point is that one could not take the law into one's own hands by ignoring proper procedures, a point the Court reinforced two years later by overturning a march leader's direct criminal conviction under the ordinance, which the Court now said was excessively broad.[62] Such decisions support the observation that in freedom of communication cases the *situation* in which the communicator was located governed the Court's outcome.[63]

Despite its actions in civil rights demonstration cases, where labor picketing was involved the Warren Court's stance was different. The justices refused to ban union picketing in front of a store in a private shopping center, because the shopping center was a public place like the company towns of earlier days.[64] The Burger Court's position on labor picketing also seemed reasonably liberal. Where Illinois had tried to limit *all but* labor picketing near schools, the Court unanimously said the distinction between labor picketing and other peaceful picketing was impermissible.[65] Marshall remarked that just as the Court had protected school property for speech-related activity by students, "the public sidewalk adjacent to school grounds may not be declared off-limits for expressive activity by members of the public."

As to other picketing and related activity, the Burger Court at first took a liberal position in a case where a real estate broker obtained an injunction against the distribution, outside his suburban home, of leaflets accusing him of "blockbusting" in an integrated Chicago neighborhood. Here the Court held that the broker had not justified prior restraint on the peaceful distribution of literature, which Chief Justice Burger said involved no more than what would be said in a newspaper.[66] Then the justices said that the base commander at Ft. Sam Houston, an open military post, could not order off the public streets someone passing out leaflets any more "than could the city police order any leafletter off any public street."[67] However, in a case involving anti-war leafletting in a large, privately owned shopping center, the majority ruled the center, although open to the public, was not "dedicated to public use"; thus its owner need not permit handbilling not related to the shopping center's operation.[68] They so ruled even though the city had vacated several streets for the center, whose security guards were police deputies, and despite the dissenters' objections that the Warren Court ruling on picketing in private shopping centers was being attacked. Justice Marshall pointed out that other nonpolitical activity not related to the shopping center's operation had already been held; because people could obtain almost anything in the shopping center, he said, "if speech is to reach these people, it must reach them in Lloyd Center."

Other cases in this "free speech plus" area involved different types of activity. One was draft card burning. In another example of its imperfect liberalism, the Warren Court upheld the 1965 federal law punishing destruction of draft cards. Chief Justice Warren, ignoring the timing of the law's enactment (when anti-war protest was starting), said the law did not on its face abridge free speech any more than one requiring drivers to carry their driving licenses or taxpayers to keep records.[69]

In a more liberal vein, the Warren Court ruled in the *Tinker* case (see pp. 20, 31) that although "material disruption" could lead to limiting students' activities, mere fear by school officials that something *might* happen was not enough to warrant imposing such limitations.[70] Justice Fortas, reversing students' suspensions, said a student had a right to express his views on controversial subjects in the classroom and outside it: "We do not confine the permissible exercise of First Amendment rights to a telephone booth or the four corners of a pamphlet, or to supervised and ordained discussion in a school classroom."

A Burger Court issue closely related to the draft card and armband matters was flag desecration. Here the Court, over dissents from three Nixon appointees, threw out as vague a statute aimed at undefined "contemptuous treatment" of the flag.[71] Here Justice Powell joined the majority. While he thought it immature and silly to wear a flag sewn to the seat of one's jeans, he recognized that many treated the flag casually. Widely varying attitudes required the state to spell out what types of nonceremonial treatment of the flag were criminal, so that arrests and convictions would not be governed by individual police officers' views. Justice White also joined the majority, arguing that the behavior, while clearly contemptuous, involved communicating ideas and "Neither the United States nor any State may require any individual to salute or express favorable attitudes toward the flag." On the dissenters' side, Justice Rehnquist stressed limits on what a person could do with his own property, including the flag, "the one visible embodiment of the authority of the National Government . . . , not merely cloth dyed red, white, and blue, but also the one visible manifestation of two hundred years of nationhood. . . ." Shortly afterwards, the Court, *per curiam*, reversed a conviction for "improper use" of a flag with an attached peace symbol hung from an apartment window, saying there had been "prosecution for the expression of an idea through activity."[72]

One other matter bears mention here—the Selective Service System's actions punishing those who had engaged in various forms of protest, such as destroying their draft cards or sitting in at Selective Service System offices. The Warren Court had invalidated reclassification to I-A of those held delinquent under the regulations, as well as their accelerated induction for such activity, on the narrow statutory ground that a person statutorily entitled to his exemption could not be reclassified as a delinquent by his draft board.[73] The Burger Court followed this up by ruling that the delinquency regulations were not prescribed by Congress, which intended to deal with delinquents through the criminal law, not by accelerated induction after the reclassification.[74]

Prisons

Prisons provided a new context for free speech for the Burger Court's consideration. Dealing with prison mail censorship, the Court at first avoided the question of prisoners' rights by redefining the issue into the First Amendment rights of those receiving or intended to receive prisoners' letters. On that basis, the Court struck down California regulations as unnecessarily broad to achieve prison officials' legitimate ends.[75] Later in the 1973 Term, the Court *upheld* California and federal regulations on newsman interviews of prisoners, rejecting requests by newsmen to interview specific individual prisoners and prisoners' demands for interviews.[76] (Newsmen were already allowed to enter prisons and to interview prisoners they encountered as well as those drawn at random by officials from the prison population.) The majority said the First Amendment did not *require* that newsmen be given greater rights than the public. Furthermore, a prisoner's status as prisoner could be taken into account in balancing an individual's First Amendment rights against state interests, with deference given to "institutional considerations" and matters "peculiarly within the province and professional expertise of corrections officials." If prisoners had alternative ways (the mails and friends) of communicating to the press, their demands for interviews could be rejected. The liberal dissenters thought an absolute ban on specific interviews was improper. Although Justice Powell would not sustain the prisoners' demands for specific interviews, he said alternatives to interviews were unsatisfactory for newsmen, whose rights to information were necessary for informing the public.

CHURCH AND STATE

The Warren Court's major church-state rulings, already noted, were on school prayer; the earlier Warren Court also handed down rulings upholding the validity of Sunday closing laws. The late Warren Court touched on only a few new church-state questions. In one, the Supreme Court said that the separation of church and state would be violated if regular civil courts were to decide cases requiring rulings on matters of theology, for example, whether a group had departed from church doctrine.[77] Another question was the validity of an anti-evolution teaching statute almost identical to the one in the famous Scopes trial. Holding the statute to be unconstitutional,[78] Justice Fortas said that the First Amendment "does not permit the State to require that teaching and learning must be tailored to the principle or prohibitions of any religious sect or dogma."

Parochial School Aid

The most crucial policy matter facing the Burger Court, entailing high financial stakes, was government aid to religion, especially parochial schools. The Warren Court had sustained a New York statute providing for free textbooks for parochial school students, over the objection that the parochial school administrators, not the secular officials, chose the books.[79] Other programs were, however, to be rejected. Laws providing for a 15 percent salary supplement for nonpublic school teachers teaching secular subjects and for the purchase of certain secular services (textbooks, instructional materials, and salaries) from nonpublic schools came before the Court first. Because excessive state supervision of the parochial schools would be necessary to enforce the law's restrictions on the money's use, the laws were struck down for producing an "entanglement" of church and state.[80] However, before the Supreme Court acted, $24,000,000 in services had been undertaken by Pennsylvania parochial schools relying on the laws. The justices, by a 5–3 vote, allowed the challenged payment to be made, because further entanglement would be needed to recover the money.[81] Chief Justice Burger thought that the possibility of constitutional harm from the payment was remote. Douglas vehemently disagreed and asserted that because "The rule of no subsidy has been the dominant one since the days of Madison," there was "clear warning" for the school officials that they were "treading on unconstitutional ground" and they should not be allowed to collect the payments.

Still other state attempts at parochiaid statutes were not to get favorable treatment. New York's provision of direct money grants for maintenance and repair of school facilities and equipment, tuition reimbursement to parents, and per-pupil grants for examination and test services were all held defective. Despite the state legislature's findings emphasizing secular purposes, the Court, not showing its usual deference, struck down the laws because aid devoted to secular functions was not identifiable and separable from sectarian activities.[82]

The Supreme Court also adopted a distinction between higher and lower education in some cases involving colleges. The Chief Justice thought religion was less likely to "permeate" secular subjects in higher than in lower education and felt religious indoctrination was not a substantial purpose of the colleges. Federal aid had been given for construction of college buildings (such as libraries and science buildings) at sectarian colleges under the Higher Educational Facilities Act of 1963. Under the program, title to the buildings was to vest completely in the college after twenty years. This title transfer provision was held an unconstitutional gift to religion,[83] but the construction grants were upheld, there being only minimal inspection and no continuing entanglement. Not all financial aid to church-sponsored activities was prohibited, said the majority, and a program was acceptable as long as a *principal* or primary effect was not benefit to religion. On the other hand, Douglas saw little difference between small amounts given over a long period and a large amount given at one time. He also felt that religion was being aided because money that the colleges did not spend for one purpose because of the construction grant would be spent on other, perhaps religious, items.

When the Court allowed state construction of college buildings,[84] Douglas' persistent objections were answered. Justice Powell stated that all aid is not forbidden "because aid to one aspect of an institution frees it to spend its other resources on religious ends." Revenue bonds for financing nonsectarian buildings at colleges, involving neither the taxing power nor a state obligation to pay the interest or principal, were said to have a secular purpose rather than to advance or inhibit religion. Brennan thought the school's freedom to engage in religious activities would be limited by inspections and that the law's restrictions on sectarian use, which had to be followed if benefits were not to be lost, would create mutually damaging church-state involvements.

The Court did sustain tax exemptions for property used by religious institutions.[85] Burger, walking the "tightrope" between establishing religion and autonomy for religious institutions, felt that eliminating the exemption would *increase* government involvement in the affairs of religious bodies because of problems from tax assessments, liens, and foreclosures. Even Justice Brennan, who generally held a more purist conception of church-state separation, agreed that "the exemptions were not among the evils which the Framers and Ratifiers of the Establishment Clause sought to avoid."

Taken together, these cases indicate the Court's policy by the mid-1970s to be that no state funds could be expended for the salaries of parochial school teachers or for services at those schools when they could not be identified as secular in nature, and easily so, so as to avoid entanglement of the state in the church. Free textbooks and school busing *appeared* to remain constitutionally legitimate, despite later negative parochiaid rulings, and indirect aid through the property tax exemption was certainly legitimate. So was federal and state aid for some building construction at the college level, if the buildings were not given to the institutions.

Conscientious Objection

One other topic to come before the Court was conscientious objection to military service. Dealing with Congress' requirement that, to obtain C.O. status, a person had to have a "belief in a Supreme Being," the Warren Court had adopted a policy of religious diversity.[86] If beliefs occupied a position like that which God filled for those from orthodox religions, they satisfied the "Supreme Being" requirement. (Examples were a "religious faith in a purely ethical creed," a "Supreme Reality" ultimately responsible for the existence of man, or a power in nature that orders man's life.) A draft board could only decide whether a belief—even if it didn't sound like religion to the board—was sincerely held and whether it occupied the place of religion within the person's scheme of thought.

This question was returned to the Burger Court. Congress had altered the Selective Service Act, exempting from military service those who were opposed to all wars as a result of "religious training and belief," that is, "belief in a relation to a Supreme Being involving duties superior to those arising from any human relation." Those whose objection to war stemmed from political, sociological, or philosophical views or purely personal ethical codes were still excluded from the exemption. In a ruling similar to the Warren Court's decision, the Burger Court held that C.O. status could not be given only to those whose opposition to war stemmed from orthodox religious beliefs; those whose "religious training" came from philosophical reading rather than orthodox church education would also have to be included.[87] Harlan complained about the preference Congress gave to the "religious" and those who worshipped a "Supreme Being"; he would have had the C.O. exemption, in order to be nondiscriminating, include "those whose beliefs emanate from a purely moral, ethical or philosophical source."

Despite these rulings expanding "religion" for C.O.'s, the Court did deny the claims of a selective C.O. (opposed to some but not all war) based on the idea that the Vietnam war was an "unjust" war under Catholic teaching. Justice Marshall showed deference to Congress in saying that recognizing the selective C.O. claim would compromise the government's interest in fair and even administration of the C.O. exemption and entangle the government in questions of theology.[88] He also suggested that a "more articulate, better educated or better counseled" objector might get selective claims recognized while less literate claimants would not, an ironic recognition because that charge had already been made against the Court's "religious training and belief" ruling. C.O.'s who had completed their alternative service also did not fare well in their quest to obtain G.I. Bill benefits. Congress' distinction between active-duty servicemen and the C.O.'s was held to be reasonable, because the former's risks were greater, they had a continuing reserve obligation, and Congress could have used the device to attract people to the service.[89]

Another matter of conscience that came before the Court was Amish parents' refusal to have their children go to school after the eighth grade. Balancing parental direction of a child's religious upbringing against the state's interest in universal education, the Court held that the state could not compel school attendance for the Amish.[90] In a ruling tailored so that it probably would not apply to other groups, Burger pointed out that religious claims had to be involved to block the state's interest; efforts to maintain "a way of life, however virtuous and admirable," based on "purely secular considerations," were not enough. The Chief Justice also stressed that because Amish children go to school through the eighth grade and are provided informal vocational education, they would miss little public education. Douglas, while generally in agreement with the Court's position, claimed that the *children's* rights—not just the parents' rights—should be examined and protected. That Burger thought little of children's rights was shown by his statement that non-Amish parents do not normally consult with their children about sending them to parochial school, so the Amish should not be required to do so.

CONCLUSION

Many of the Warren Court's freedom of speech policies survived intact and healthy through the transition. In the area of obscenity, where the Warren Court's rulings had been vague, unclear, and not supported by a strong majority, the Burger Court clearly took a step back in setting forth standards for determining whether an item was obscene, but on procedure the Burger Court reinforced the work of its predecessor. The tight Warren Court libel standard was not changed, but the Burger Court shifted its own position where libel suits by private individuals were involved. The Burger Court made relatively little new internal security law; the subject simply did not preoccupy the Court as it had in earlier years; however, the few rulings the new Court made were, on the whole, conservative. When "free speech plus" was before the Court, the resulting policy was as unclear in the Burger Court as it had been during the Warren Court; if the newer Court's doctrine seems somewhat conservative, one might make the same claim about the Warren Court's rulings on demonstrators. The Burger Court seemed most conservative in the area of access by individuals to publications, being unwilling to allow dissenting groups to purchase broadcast time, newspaper space, or transit ads, although these rulings can also be seen as liberal in protecting the media's freedom.

After several years of the transition, the overall picture is that many new subjects have now been considered, but with the possible exception of obscenity and some activity relating to passing out leaflets, the basic thrust of the Supreme Court's freedom of speech doctrine has not changed.

In the area of church-state relations, policy was developed concerning two issues of importance. The more important was aid to parochial schools, where the Burger Court adopted the Warren Court's approach of keeping church and state strictly separated and invalidated almost all attempts at such aid. The Court also continued earlier policy on conscientious objectors, both as applied to exemption from military service and as extended to school attendance by Amish children.

NOTES

1. *Near* v. *Minnesota,* 283 U.S. 697 (1931).
2. *New York Times* v. *U.S.,* 403 U.S. 713 (1971).
3. *Branzburg* v. *Hayes*, 408 U.S. 665 (1972).
4. *Pittsburgh Press Co.* v. *Pittsburgh Commission on Human Relations*, 413 U.S. 376 (1973).
5. *Miami Herald Publishing Co.* v. *Tornillo,* 418 U.S. 241 (1974).
6. *Lehman* v. *City of Shaker Heights*, 418 U.S. 298 (1974).
7. *Coates* v. *City of Cincinnati*, 402 U.S. 611 (1971). See also *Papachristou* v. *City of Jacksonville*, 405 U.S. 156 (1972), vagrancy.
8. *Gooding* v. *Wilson*, 405 U.S. 518 (1972). See also *Lewis* v. *City of New Orleans*, 415 U.S. 130 (1974).
9. *Chaplinsky* v. *New Hampshire*, 315 U.S. 568 (1942).
10. *Rosenfeld* v. *New Jersey*, 408 U.S. 901 (1972).
11. *Hess* v. *Indiana*, 414 U.S. 105 (1973).
12. *Lucas and Lucas* v. *Arkansas*, 416 U.S. 919 at 920–921 (1974).
13. *Parker* v. *Levy*, 417 U.S. 733 (1974).
14. *Civil Service Commission* v. *Letter Carriers*, 413 U.S. 548 (1973); *Broadrick* v. *Oklahoma*, 413 U.S. 607 (1973).
15. *Slochower* v. *Board of Higher Education*, 450 U.S. 551 (1956); *Lerner* v. *Casey/Beilan* v. *Board of Education*, 357 U.S. 468 (1958).
16. *Arnett* v. *Kennedy*, 416 U.S. 134 (1974). In another case, the Court ruled that a probationary government employee could not obtain court review of her discharge until administrative agency review was final, nor could the district

court grant relief not authorized by the Civil Service Commission. The government should be granted wide latitude in handling its personnel affairs, said Rehnquist; irreparable injury must be shown before the courts might intervene. *Sampson* v. *Murray*, 415 U.S. 61 (1974).

17.   *Board of Regents* v. *Roth*, 408 U.S. 564 (1972); *Perry* v. *Sinderman*, 408 U.S. 593 (1972).

18.   *Garrity* v. *New Jersey*, 385 U.S. 493 (1967); *Gardner* v. *Broderick*, 392 U.S. 273 (1968); *Sanitation Men* v. *Sanitation Commissioner*, 392 U.S. 280 (1968). *Held* not applicable to a corporation, to which the Fifth Amendment is unavailable, *Campbell Painting Corp.* v. *Reid*, 392 U.S. 286 (1968).

19.   *Lefkowitz* v. *Turley*, 414 U.S. 70 (1974).

20.   *Yates* v. *U.S.*, 354 U.S. 298 (1957), limiting the reach of the Vinson Court's major ruling in *Dennis* v. *U.S.*, 341 U.S. 494 (1951).

21.   *Brandenberg* v. *Ohio*, 395 U.S. 444 (1969), overruling *Whitney* v. *California*, 274 U.S. 357 (1957).

22.   See *Baggett* v. *Bullitt*, 377 U.S. 360 (1964).

23.   *Elfbrandt* v. *Russell*, 384 U.S. 11 (1966).

24.   *Keyishian* v. *Board of Regents*, 385 U.S. 589 (1967), overruling *sub silentio Adler* v. *Board of Education of City of New York*, 342 U.S. 485 (1952).

25.   *Cole* v. *Richardson*, 405 U.S. 676 (1971).

26.   *Communist Party of Indiana* v. *Whitcomb*, 414 U.S. 441 (1974).

27.   *Kleindeinst* v. *Mandel*, 408 U.S. 753 (1972).

28.   *Konigsberg* v. *State Bar of California*, 353 U.S. 252 (1957) ("*Konigsberg I*"); *Konigsberg* v. *State Bar of California*, 366 U.S. 36 (1961) ("*Konigsberg II*"); *Schware* v. *Board of Bar Examiners,* 353 U.S. 232 (1957); *In Re Anastaplo,* 366 U.S. 82 (1961).

29.   *Baird* v. *Arizona*, 401 U.S. 1 (1971); *In Re Stolar*, 401 U.S. 23 (1971).

30.   *Law Students Civil Rights Research Council* v. *Wadmond*, 401 U.S. 154 (1971).

31.   *Healy* v. *James*, 408 U.S. 169 (1972).

32.   *New York Times and Abernathy* v. *Sullivan*, 396 U.S. 254 (1964).

33.   *Pickering* v. *Board of Education*, 391 U.S. 563 (1968).

34.   *Curtis Publishing Co.* v. *Butts*, 388 U.S. 130 (1967).

35.   *Time, Inc.* v. *Hill*, 385 U.S. 374 (1967).

36.   *Monitor Patriot Co.* v. *Roy*, 401 U.S. 265 (1971).

37.   *Rosenbloom* v. *Metromedia*, 403 U.S. 29 (1971).

38.   *Old Dominion Branch, Letter Carriers* v. *Austin*, 418 U.S. 264 (1974). They also added that there could have been no recovery by the plaintiff because there was no falsity in the statement: the man was a non-union worker who continued to work (the definition of "scab").

39.   *Gertz* v. *Robert Welch, Inc.*, 418 U.S. 323 (1974).

40.   See Justice Clark's exasperated "My Brethren, like all Gaul, are divided into three parts." *Manual Enterprises* v. *Day*, 370 U.S. 478 (1962).

41.   *Roth* v. *U.S./Alberts* v. *California*, 354 U.S. 476 (1967).

42.   The American Law Institute definition, phrased in terms of a "shameful or morbid interest in nudity, sex, or excretion, [going] substantially beyond customary limits of candor in description or representation of such matters," was mentioned in a footnote; despite the statement that it did not differ from the "lustful thoughts" idea, it seems to have a different emphasis.

43.   *Smith* v. *California*, 361 U.S. 147 (1959).

44.   *Manual Enterprises* v. *Day*, 370 U.S. 478 (1962); *Memoirs* v. *Massachusetts*, 383 U.S. 413 (1966).

45.   *Mishkin* v. *New York*, 383 U.S. 502 (1966); *Ginsberg* v. *New York*, 390 U.S. 629 (1968); *Ginzburg* v. *U.S.*, 383 U.S. 463 (1966).

46.   *Jacobellis* v. *Ohio*, 378 U.S. 194 (1964).

47.   *Stanley* v. *Georgia*, 394 U.S. 557 (1969).

48.   *U.S.* v. *Reidel*, 402 U.S. 351 (1971), on the postal power; *U.S.* v. *37 Photographs*, 402 U.S. 363 (1971), and *U.S.* v. *12 200-Ft. Reels of Super 8 MM. Film*, 413 U.S. 123 (1973), on the customs power; and *U.S.* v. *Orito*, 413 U.S. 139 (1973), on interstate commerce.

49.   *Rowan* v. *Post Office*, 397 U.S. 728 (1970); *Blount* v. *Rizzi*, 400 U.S. 410 (1971).

50.   *Miller* v. *California*, 413 U.S. 15 (1973).

51.   *Paris Adult Theater I* v. *Slaton*, 413 U.S. 49 at 96 (1973).

52.   *Hamling* v. *U.S.*, 418 U.S. 87 (1974). Justice Douglas, dissenting, said, "Sex is more important to some than to others but it is of some importance to all. If officials may constitutionally report on obscenity, I see nothing in the First Amendment that allows us to bar the use of a glossary factually to illustrate what the Report discloses."

53.   *Jenkins* v. *Georgia*, 418 U.S. 153 (1974).

54.   White's statement is at *J-R Distributors* v. *Washington*, 418 U.S. 949 (1974). For Brennan's statements, see, e.g., *Watkins* v. *South Carolina*, 418 U.S. 911 (1974), appeal dismissed, or *Carlson* v. *U.S.*, 418 U.S. 924 (1974), certiorari denied.

55.   *Papish* v. *Board of Curators*, 410 U.S. 667 at 672 (1973).

56.   *Times Film Corp.* v. *City of Chicago*, 365 U.S. 43 (1961).

57.   *Freedman* v. *Maryland*, 380 U.S. 51 (1965).

58.   *Roaden* v. *Kentucky*, 413 U.S. 496 (1973).

59.   *Heller* v. *New York*, 413 U.S. 483 (1973).

60.   See *Zemel* v. *Rusk*, 381 U.S. 1 (1965), requesting validation of a passport to Cuba. But see the Court's later reversal of the Secretary of State's practice of invalidating passports of those traveling to nations on the prohibited list, which would be an indication or warning that the government might not protect someone going there. *U.S.* v. *Laub*, 383 U.S. 475 (1967).

61.   *Edwards* v. *South Carolina*, 372 U.S. 229 (1963); *Cox* v. *Louisiana*, 379 U.S. 539 and 379 U.S. 559 (1965); *Adderly* v. *Florida*, 385 U.S. 39 (1966).

62.   The cases are, respectively, *Walker* v. *City of Birmingham*, 383 U.S. 307 (1967), and *Shuttlesworth* v. *City of Birmingham*, 394 U.S. 147 (1969).

63.   Harold J. Spaeth, "Is Justice Blind?" *Law & Society Review,* 7 (Fall 1972), 129.

64.   *Food Employees* v. *Logan Valley Plaza*, 391 U.S. 308 (1968).

65.   *Grayned* v. *City of Rockford*, 408 U.S. 104 (1972); *Police Department of City of Chicago* v. *Mosley*, 408 U.S. 92 (1972).

66.   *Organization for a Better Austin* v. *Keefe*, 402 U.S. 415 (1971).

67.   *Flower* v. *U.S.*, 407 U.S. 197 (1972).

68.   *Lloyd Corporation* v. *Tanner*, 407 U.S. 551 (1972).

69.   *U.S.* v. *O'Brien*, 391 U.S. 367 (1968).

70.   *Tinker* v. *Des Moines School District*, 393 U.S. 503 (1969).

71.   *Smith* v. *Goguen*, 415 U.S. 566 (1974). The Warren Court's flag-burning case, *Street* v. *New York*, 394 U.S. 576 (1969), had not resulted in a broad ruling, although the particular conviction was reversed.

72.   *Spence* v. *Washington*, 418 U.S. 405 (1974).

73.   *Oestereich* v. *Selective Service*, 393 U.S. 233 (1968), involving a divinity student (IV-D). The Court engaged in a little activism to reach the ruling, allowing pre-induction judicial review, not available to those with exemptions, e.g., C.O., available only at the draft board's discretion. Someone denied C.O. status could challenge his induction only by defending in a criminal prosecution for

failure to report or by bringing a post-induction habeas corpus proceeding, a policy the Court was unwilling to disturb.

74. *Gutknecht* v. *U.S.*, 396 U.S. 295 (1970); see also *Breen* v. *U.S.*, 396 U.S. 460 (1970).

75. *Procunier* v. *Martinez*, 416 U.S. 396 (1974).

76. *Pell* v. *Procunier*, 417 U.S. 817 (1974); *Saxbe* v. *Washington Post*, 417 U.S. 843 (1974).

77. *Presbyterian Church in the U.S.* v. *Hull Memorial Presbyterian Church*, 393 U.S. 440 (1969).

78. *Epperson* v. *Arkansas*, 393 U.S. 97 (1968). The law made it unlawful "to teach the theory or doctrine that mankind ascended or descended from a lower order of animal."

79. *Board of Education* v. *Allen*, 392 U.S. 236 (1968).

80. *Lemon* v. *Kurtzman*, 403 U.S. 602 (1971) (*"Lemon I"*).

81. *Lemon* v. *Kurtzman*, 411 U.S. 192 (1973) (*"Lemon II"*).

82. *Levitt* v. *Committee for Public Education & Religious Liberty*, 413 U.S. 472 (1973); *Committee . . .* v. *Nyquist*, 413 U.S. 756 (1973).

83. *Tilton* v. *Richardson*, 403 U.S. 672 (1971).

84. *Hunt* v. *McNair*, 413 U.S. 634 (1973).

85. *Walz* v. *Tax Commission*, 397 U.S. 664 (1970).

86. *Seeger* v. *U.S.*, 380 U.S. 163 (1965). This policy was not well communicated to Selective Service boards; those seeking C.O. status still encountered considerable difficulty in achieving their goal. See Robert Rabin, "Do You Believe in a Supreme Being—The Administration of the Conscientious Objector Exemption," *Wisconsin Law Review*, 1967, 642–684; James Davis and Kenneth Dolbeare, *Little Groups of Neighbors* (Chicago: Markham, 1968).

87. *Welsh* v. *U.S.*, 398 U.S. 333 (1970).

88. *Gillette* v. *U.S.*, 401 U.S. 437 (1971).

89. *Johnson* v. *Robison*, 415 U.S. 361 (1974); *Hernandez* v. *U.S.*, 415 U.S. 391 (1974).

90. *Wisconsin* v. *Yoder*, 406 U.S. 205 (1972).

CHAPTER EIGHT

Criminal Procedure During the Transition

The late Herbert Packer once suggested that there were two competing models of law enforcement. In one, the Due Process Model, the focus is on the trial, and procedural rights are emphasized; in the other, the Crime Control Model, efficiency and processing of cases is stressed. Where the latter is administrative and managerial, the former emphasizes the adversary process in a judicial proceeding. As Packer put it, "If the Crime Control Model resembles an assembly line, the Due Process Model looks very much like an obstacle course."[1] Neither model actually describes reality, but both are helpful as we attempt to see what the Warren and Burger Courts did with respect to criminal procedure.

The Warren Court clearly tried to implement the Due Process Model, particularly with respect to defendants' rights at the trial. These rulings were left relatively undisturbed by the Burger Court. Because of the effect of pre-trial events on rights at the trial, the Warren Court also extended the Due Process Model to cover search and seizure, lineups, and confessions. However, in doing so, the justices were more sensitive to the Crime Control Model and the needs of the law enforcement community. It was on such matters that the Burger Court, far more strongly attuned to the Crime Control Model, most seriously limited the Warren Court's criminal procedure work. The Warren Court rulings on police practices prior to trial were the ones that had most exercised the law enforcement community, and they were the main object of the Burger Court's retrenchment. Criminal procedure was and is definitely the area in which the Burger Court turned furthest away from the Warren Court's policy. Its success is shown by the considerably more favorable attitude toward the Court that police now have. Law officers, although they don't necessarily think the new Court's work has affected crime levels and although they dislike the death penalty decision as removing a deterrent to crime, feel less restrained than they felt under Warren Court rulings.[2] The change in direction is also shown by the fact that "the U.S. solicitor general and . . . the attorneys general of the states . . . show an increased confidence in pressing issues on appeal" in criminal cases.[3]

APPROACHES

Prior to the 1960s, most Supreme Court criminal procedure policy was closely tied to the facts of the cases through which it was developed. Even when the Court regularly decided for the defendant, the result was not doctrine of broad application. In the 1960s, the Warren Court changed this, and the justices accomplished much of their criminal procedure revolution through use of broad rules, of wide application. The Burger Court, in siding with law enforcement officials, did not overrule those broad rules but undermined many of them. This refusal to enforce them was accomplished through use of the "totality of circumstances" approach and the "harmless error" rule. The "totality" approach meant that the Court decided on each case on the basis of the entire set of facts in a case; thus only particularized rulings resulted. For example, the Nixon appointees and Justice White used a totality of circumstances test in upholding the identification of a defendant because a broad rule on suggestive identifications would not increase the validity of the trial.[4] In so doing, they undercut a Warren Court ruling against "unnecessarily suggestive" identifications.[5]

The totality of circumstances test does not *always* result in decisions against defendants, but that is often its effect. Thus the rule can be used to excuse prosecutorial sloppiness. For example, a prosecutor required a mistrial because of defectively drawn indictments, and the judge granted his request, over the objections of the defendant, who wanted to present his case. A five-man Supreme Court majority allowed retrial of the defendant, denying his double jeopardy claim.[6] Showing their favorable inclination toward the prosecution, the justices said there was no sense in going forward when the trial could have been set aside later because of the faulty indictment. Defendant's interest in presenting his case to the jury was "outweighed by the competing and equally legitimate demand for public justice."

Despite their preference for the totality approach, the Nixon justices did not always avoid broad rules, particularly when such rules would support their generally conservative position. Thus Justice Rehnquist wrote a broad rule that a guilty plea entered with advice of counsel precluded defendant's later challenges to events occurring prior to the plea (such as improper searches or coerced confessions); here dissenting Justice Marshall, an advocate of broad rules during the Warren Court, argued for use of the totality of circumstances test on the question of counsel's competence.[7]

The totality approach was reinforced by the "harmless error" rule, originally developed by the Warren Court.[8] As the Burger Court used the rule, a violation of a constitutional right would not be used to reverse a conviction if other evidence against an individual were considered overwhelming. This differed from the Warren Court justices' position that an error could not be harmless if it could reasonably have contributed to the finding of guilt. An example of harmless error came when a policeman posed as a fellow prisoner, then testified at a murder trial about a damaging statement the defendant had made. Admission of the statement was allowed, in view of the defendant's other voluntary confessions and the overwhelming evidence of his guilt,[9] over Justice Stewart's claim that it was improperly obtained because the circumstances meant that defendant was denied assistance of counsel. In another case, the majority, using the same approach, would not upset a murder conviction where the prosecutor made concededly improper remarks, because of what to them was an overwhelming case against defendant. Here an incensed Douglas argued:

> The function of the prosecutor under the Federal Constitution is not to tack as many skins of victims as possible to the wall. His function is to vindicate the right of people as expressed in the laws and give those accused of crime a fair trial.[10]

The approaches we have noted here were applied in a variety of criminal procedure policy areas. We now turn to those areas, beginning with search and seizure, then turn to questions of right to counsel and confessions, and finally examine a host of other questions involving trial and post-trial matters.

SEARCH AND SEIZURE

The first specific policy area we examine is that of unreasonable searches and seizures under the Fourth Amendment. This was a central area for the Burger Court, as it had been for the Warren

Court. This was true in terms of volume, for in the 1972 Term alone, the Court decided *ten* cases with opinion (5.6 percent of the term's total) on that subject alone. And, more important, it was true in terms of substance. This area of criminal justice policy is the one in which the Burger Court moved furthest away from the Warren Court's work.

There are essentially two aspects of search and seizure law. One entails the substantive laws of search—when and where searches can be carried out, how they can be performed, and what can be seized. Here the basic rule is that a search can be carried out only with a warrant, which must be obtained from a disinterested (neutral) magistrate; to obtain the warrant, the officer must have "probable cause" to believe the item(s) for which he is searching are present in the location he wishes to search. As stated in the Fourth Amendment, which protects against *unreasonable* searches and seizures, "no Warrants shall issue, but upon probable cause, supported by Oath or affirmation, and particularly describing the place to be searched, and the persons or things to be seized." The requirement for a search warrant is, however, only the starting point in the law of search and seizure and there are many exceptions to the rule, probably accounting for most searches and seizures in this country. Included are searches of an individual without a warrant subsequent to a valid arrest or of an automobile after its driver/owner has been arrested, the scope of such searches and conditions under which such searches may take place, and what may be taken in the searches.

The rules on these subjects are often complex and confusing, but some clear policy can be identified. The use of informants to obtain evidence is permitted, as is the stop-and-frisk of individuals acting suspiciously; so are more intrusive searches of persons arrested for automobile violations. When people are arrested, searches are limited to the area under the person's control and "mere evidence" may now be taken in searches. Searches of automobiles are allowed in some situations in which searches of other locations would not be permitted. Protection against wiretapping now extends to any place where a person might expect privacy, not only his home or office, but wiretapping and electronic surveillance may be carried out pursuant to properly obtained warrants within the scope of congressional legislation.

The Exclusionary Rule

The other major element of search law covers the question of how improperly (or illegally) seized material is to be dealt with. Until the Warren Court, the rule covering the states, deriving from the common law, was relatively straightforward. Evidence could be admitted even if improperly seized; it was the validity of the evidence itself, not the propriety of the search that produced it, that was at issue. But the Warren Court changed that. The Warren Court began its criminal procedure revolution by imposing on the states the exclusionary rule—that improperly seized evidence cannot be admitted in state courts—which had been in effect in federal trials for almost fifty years. The addition of this requirement in state trials made far more important the substantive rules of search and seizure developed both earlier and later by the Supreme Court.

The Warren Court's ruling on the exclusionary rule, which began its criminal procedure revolution, came as a response to the police misconduct frequently and forcefully brought to the Court's attention. The ruling also came only after several justices had clearly indicated their unhappiness with outrageous police searches and had warned they would change the old rule. In the *Mapp* case, they were faced with a search for a fugitive in which the police, falsely claiming to have a warrant, forced their way into a home and found obscene pictures. This way of conducting searches almost forced the Court to act.[11] Justice Clark's forceful statement made clear the Court's reason for applying the exclusionary rule to the states:

> The criminal goes free, if he must, but it is the law that sets him free. Nothing can destroy a government more quickly than its failure to observe its own laws, or worse, its disregard of the charter of its own existence.

The rule's purpose was to clean up police practices; it was intended to deter law enforcement officers from further improper searches on the theory they would search properly in order to be able to use evidence in courts. The rule extended to evidence seized improperly and, as well, to other evidence obtained derivatively—that is, from leads from the original evidence. This latter extension of the rule is known as the "fruit of the poisonous tree" doctrine: if the tree is tainted, so are its products.

The exclusionary rule became the subject of repeated attacks, particularly by Chief Justice Burger, who felt the rule both ineffective and costly because of "the release of countless guilty criminals."[12] In a line of argument substantiated by studies of police behavior,[13] Burger argued persuasively that the *prosecutor,* not the policeman, is penalized for the latter's noncompliance with search and seizure rules; that the potential effect of negative sanctions on the policeman has vanished by the time suppression of evidence occurs; and that the rule's impact is further diminished because the police use seizures for reasons other than convictions—to obtain informants, to harrass, to destroy contraband. However, he hedged as to whether the rule should be eliminated before some other method could be found to deal with police improprieties.

Despite Chief Justice Burger's criticism, the rule has not been repealed. However, the Court did find an opportunity to reduce its scope. Information about loan-sharking had been found during a search for gambling material; only the latter was specified in the search warrant. The loan-sharking evidence became the basis for asking questions to a witness before a grand jury. When he protested that improperly seized material (beyond the warrant's scope) could not be the basis for such questions, the Court said that grand jury witnesses may *not* refuse to answer questions based on evidence from improper searches.[14] The lineup was a familiar 6–3 (the Nixon Four, Stewart, and White v. Douglas, Brennan, and Marshall). Justice Brennan, arguing the position that courts should not get entangled in illegal acts of government, thought "The door is again ajar" for the use of improperly seized evidence. Thus, while improperly seized material still cannot be used in trials, it can be used to obtain indictments—a serious retraction from the full scope of the exclusionary rule.

Informants

As we noted above, the ever-present need to explain what constituted reasonable and unreasonable searches under the Fourth and Fourteenth Amendments increased after the exclusionary rule was applied to the states. In some areas of search law, the Warren Court showed strong support for law enforcement. One such policy question involved the use of undercover agents and informants, used increasingly to deal with gambling, gun, and drug cases. Here the Warren Court legitimated their use,[15] with Chief Justice Warren himself writing that preventing their use "would . . . severely hamper the Government in ferreting out those organized criminal activities that are characterized by covert dealings with victims who either cannot or do not protest." The Court also affirmed use of a Teamsters official as a paid government informant in obtaining Jimmy Hoffa's conviction for jury-tampering, where the informant was able to be present at conversations between Hoffa and his associates.[16] Here Warren dissented; he thought the government's action an "affront to the quality and fairness of federal law enforcement" and felt neither prosecution nor defense should intrude into the other side's preparation of its case; even the majority said that had the informant intruded into lawyer-client relationships, the result in the case would have been different.

Use of informants was reinforced by the Burger Court,[17] although over the objection of the usually conservative Harlan that recording of conversations by such persons helped "undermine that confidence and sense of security in dealing with one another that is characteristic of individual relationships between citizens in a free society." Where the Warren Court had placed limits on the use of information from informants as a basis for obtaining warrants, these limits were somewhat removed by the Burger Court.[18] The Burger Court further upheld the use of undercover agents and "illegal acts of the government" in a case where entrapment was the issue. A federal narc had supplied difficult-to-obtain (but obtainable) drug ingredients to a person who at other times had manufactured the drug without assistance and had arrested him when he made the drug. The Court said infiltrating the group in drug-related crimes was proper, as was supplying "some item of value" required by the drug ring.[19] Agents were not to instigate acts in otherwise innocent persons, but the defense of entrapment was held not available to those disposed to commit the crime. "Only when the Government's deception actually implants the criminal design in the mind of the defendant" could the entrapment defense be used. Because the defendants, who would have committed a crime when arrested, could always be said to be disposed to do so, Justice Stewart strongly preferred a test based on the *agents'* activity.

Scope of Searches

The Warren Court had limited *where* the police could search subsequent to a valid arrest. In the lead case, police, armed with an arrest warrant, had arrested the suspect in his house and then searched not merely the room in which he was arrested but the entire house. Setting aside Vinson Court rulings, the Court limited such searches to the person arrested and the area "under his control"; broader searches required a search warrant.[20] A year later, the Burger Court reinforced that ruling by throwing out a house search after police arrested a man on his front steps, then took him inside so they could search the house.[21] However, the Court did uphold a warrantless search of a room upon the consent of the woman living there with the man who was a suspect,[22] thus reinforcing the general rule that searches conducted with consent are valid.

In dealing with "street searches," long carried out by the

police, the Warren Court had both sustained and limited police authority. Where several men had been "casing" a jewelry store and had been evasive in answering a policeman's questions, the officer, without arresting them, had carried out a stop-and-frisk pat-down of outer clothing, which produced a gun. The justices upheld the officer's action as necessary to protect him from danger, even where probable cause to make an arrest might not exist. At the same time, however, the Court invalidated a more extended search in which a policeman saw (but did not hear) a conversation between a man and a known addict; the search had produced drugs, but the judges found no adequate basis for either a pat-down or more thorough search.[23] Through this pair of cases, the police had obtained constitutional approval for a long-used practice of "field interrogations," but found that the approval also carried limits on what they could do.

The Burger Court severely eroded the limitations imposed in these cases. A policeman, acting on an informant's tip, approached a car; when the driver opened the window at the officer's request, the officer reached into the car and removed from the defendant's waistband a loaded revolver not visible from outside the car; a subsequent search of the car produced drugs. The Court, saying that stop-and-frisk need not be based only on the officer's personal observation, upheld the entire process—both the frisk and the later search.[24] Marshall, pointing to the lack of preliminary inquiry by the officer and the absence of obviously criminal activity about to take place, noted the departure from previous search rulings and argued that the subsequent search was invalid because the officer could not have known that the defendant had his gun illegally, as the state allowed individuals to carry guns without a permit.

If stop-and-frisk pat-downs were acceptable, how much further could an officer go in searching a person? A policeman had made a valid arrest without a warrant for driving without a license. He then not only patted down the driver's coat but searched inside a pocket. Looking inside a cigarette package he found, he discovered heroin. Upholding the resulting drug conviction, the Burger Court refused to extend the Warren Court stop-and-frisk limitations to situations where an arrest had occurred. Sustaining the search, the justices further supported the police's position by indicating that there need not be case-by-case adjudication of whether the officer had a reason for making the search.[25] Sympathy for the policeman's work was clear in Justice Rehnquist's statement:

A police officer's determination as to how and where to search the person of a suspect whom he has arrested is necessarily a quick *ad hoc* judgment which the Fourth Amendment does not require to be broken down in each instance into an analysis of each step in the search.

The dissenters were particularly disturbed at how far the Court had gone, and were afraid that police would use traffic arrests as a pretext for full searches of a person.

Also involved in searches of the person were questions as to whether someone could be compelled to give certain personal evidence—such as fingerprints or hair samples—even though he would not have to testify directly about his involvement. The Court generally sustained demands for such "nontestimonial evidence," in cases involving both Fourth Amendment (search) and Fifth Amendment (self-incrimination) policy. The Warren Court had ruled that a person could be compelled to appear at a police lineup; however, the justices split over whether a defendant could be compelled to speak the words allegedly uttered by the person committing the crime.[26] Then the justices invalidated fingerprint evidence obtained from a "dragnet" of Mississippi black youths after a rape, saying the Fourth Amendment applied to such preliminary stages of an investigation. However, the justices showed a willingness to accept procedures for obtaining fingerprints that were short of a full warrant requirement as long as protections were provided.[27] In 1973, the Court moved from fingerprints to fingernails. When a man voluntarily came to the station house in connection with his wife's murder, a policeman noticed dried blood under the man's fingernails. Without an arrest, the police held the man and over his protest took scrapings from under his fingernails. By a 7–2 vote, the Court admitted the evidence.[28]

The Burger Court, asked to rule on grand jury requests for voice and handwriting exemplars for identification purposes, overruled Fourth and Fifth Amendment challenges. The justices said that a subpoena, however inconvenient, was not a Fourth Amendment seizure and the request was not unreasonable just because many were asked to give exemplars.[29] Justice Douglas argued in response that the prosecutor would be able to obtain through the grand jury what he could not obtain directly, and Justice Marshall thought the majority had "lost touch with the Constitution's concern for the "inviolability of the human personality.'"

The Warren Court, in ruling on *what* the police could seize, had helped law enforcement officers. The old rule was that police were limited to seizing "tools of the trade" and fruits of the crime (contraband), *not* "mere evidence." The Court eliminated this rule; all, including mere evidence (like a coat thought to be worn by the defendant during a robbery), could now be taken.[30] The Burger Court went even further. By a 5–4 vote, the warrantless seizure of clothes from a defendant, *ten hours* after his arrest, was upheld.[31] The majority accepted the police claim that no substitute clothes were available when the defendant was arrested and jailed late at night and rejected Stewart's argument that no emergency existed and that the police had ample time to seek a warrant. Stewart, who felt the Court was disregarding "established Fourth Amendment principle firmly embodied in many previous decisions of this Court," thought that the fact the police were not acting in bad faith nor engaging in shocking activity was irrelevant: "The Fourth Amendment . . . was not designed to apply only to situations where the intrusion is massive and violation of privacy shockingly flagrant."

Automobiles

The Court also ruled on car searches, one of the principal exceptions to the previously noted warrant required. Here policy on searches is generally less strict than for searches of persons or buildings, because a car can be moved. Warrantless searches of automobiles have been allowed in some situations where a home could not be searched.[32] A warrantless search of a car parked in a driveway next to a defendant's home, carried out over an extended period, was, however, too much for the judges[33] and prompted Justice Stewart's remark, "The word 'automobile' is not a talisman in whose presence the Fourth Amendment fades away and disappears." However, a warrantless search of the exterior of an impounded car was held to be valid, even when it took place several hours after the arrest of the owner.[34]

The Burger Court's flexible approach to car searches was quite evident in a case where an off-duty Chicago policeman had wrecked a rented car. Local police, knowing that Chicago policemen carry service revolvers at all times, searched the car the next morning for the gun and found evidence of a murder. A five-man majority found the search not unreasonable; the police had taken custody of the car, and the search of the trunk was standard procedure to protect the public from someone else's taking the gun.[35] Justice Rehnquist conceded the unevenness of the Court's auto search policy, but his opinion indicated the new appointees' affinity for the Crime Control Model:

> These officers in a rural area were simply reacting to the effects of an accident—one of the recurring practical situations that result from the operation of motor vehicles and with which local police officers must deal every day.

The issue of consent was also involved in automobile searches. A car had been stopped for traffic violations, and a search, allowed by the driver, produced an unlawfully possessed check. The Court did say that the state would have to show there was voluntary consent and that the search was not the result of duress. However, voluntariness could be determined from the circumstances of the case, and there was to be no requirement that a person giving permission knew he had a legal right to withhold his consent.[36] Such a requirement would place "artificial restrictions" on searches with no coercive atmosphere. In an argument reminiscent of an older position where improper searches were justified from what was obtained, Stewart went so far as to say that the search, by producing valid evidence, "provided some assurance that others, wholly innocent of the crime, were not mistakenly brought to trial." The dissenters felt the Court was allowing police to take advantage of uninformed citizens. Justice Marshall, in addition to arguing that the Court was out to uphold the police at all costs, said the majority was reinforcing their "continued ability . . . to capitalize on the ignorance of citizens so as to accomplish by subterfuge what they could not achieve by relying only on the knowing relinquishment of constitutional rights." As Justice Brennan put it, "It wholly escapes me how our citizens can meaningfully be said to have waived something as precious as a constitutional guarantee without ever being aware of its existence."

Statutory Searches

Congress, attempting to deal with increased criminal activity and particularly with organized crime, provided in its statutes for more searches. This shifted the Court's search-and-seizure policy-making somewhat from direct constitutional rulings to statutory interpretation. The Court said that statutory authority must be reasonably confined, but Congress' action certainly made it easier for the Court to uphold searches. For example, the Court upheld a federal agent's warrantless search of a pawnshop's locked gun storeroom under the 1968 Gun Control Act as part of a valid regulatory inspection system.[37] The justices said that invasion of the owner's privacy was at a minimum because the businessman operated in a field he knew to be well regulated. Despite the flexibility for Congress this suggests, the justices were, however, willing to impose limits on statutory searches, particularly in terms of the *application* of the laws. Although they recognized that the government had valid authority to conduct border searches, they said that a warrantless border search of an automobile, without probable cause or consent, more than twenty miles north of the U.S.-Mexico border, was *not* justified by the Immigration and Naturalization Act.[38]

Surveillance

The area of search law that became most heavily statutory was that on wiretapping and electronic surveillance, which provided perhaps the toughest search-and-seizure problems for the Court. Prior to 1967, the Court tried to use its old rule that wiretapping was not a search because no physical penetration of a person's house or place of business occurred. With the use of sophisticated electronic equipment, new and more consistent policies were needed. In 1967, the Court decided to dispense (at least for federal cases) with the old idea that *places* where people might be were to be protected; the *people* themselves were to be the focus. Invalidating the placement of an electronic listening device on a telephone booth, the Court said that what a person seeks to keep private is protected, at least if it occurs in a place where he might have a reasonable expectation of privacy.[39] This ruling seemed to abandon the distinction between electronic eavesdropping and cutting into a wire for wiretapping purposes.

Faced with eavesdropping under an extremely broad state statute, the Court, in *Berger* v. *New York*, invalidated the law but said that telephone conversations could be intercepted under some circumstances if proper protections were provided.[40] The conversations sought had to be shown with particularity; there could be only a limited period of initial surveillance; renewal of the tap could be allowed only if the initial search had produced some results. In this case, interestingly, the dissenting justices would have allowed *more*, not less, surveillance. As Justice Black put it:

Crimes, unspeakably horrid crimes, are with us in the country, and we cannot afford to dispense with any known method of detecting and correcting them unless it is forbidden by the Constitution or deemed inadvisable by legislative policy.

The policy resulting from these cases and then-existing statutes was that state officials could bug a telephone booth but could not tap the wires to the booth. That inconsistency was eliminated and policy greatly clarified when Congress, drawing on the *Berger* opinion, passed the Omnibus Crime Control and Safe Streets Act of 1968. This law permitted federal and state officials to tap telephone wires and to intercept oral communications under a court order obtained with *Berger*-type protections. Use of the seized material as evidence was now permitted. The statute provided the basis for much of the subsequent electronic surveillance litigation.

The Warren Court did not deal directly with the statute but did hand down an important related procedural ruling. The case, which had a particularly bumpy career, shows the problems the Court occasionally faces in coming to grips with an issue. In an appeal of convictions said to be based on government wiretapping, the Court had initially denied review. The justices granted a rehearing petition, an unusual action, and held that the Justice Department's own determination that overheard conversations were not relevant to a case was insufficient: relevancy could only be determined in an adversary court proceeding, even if it were of limited scope.[41] The government, dissatisfied, asked the Court to modify its ruling. The case was then argued *twice*. The Court then finally handed down a major ruling. The justices first held that surveillance could be challenged only by "those whose rights were violated by the search itself," that is, those directly involved in the conversation and those present where the conversations took place, but *not* those mentioned in the conversations or co-conspirators or co-defendants.[42] Then the Court said that those with proper standing were to be able to examine surveillance records directly; examination by a judge was insufficient. The majority recognized that the government might have to forgo some prosecutions rather than reveal all that was in the records, but insisted that fairness to defendants required the ruling. (Justice White did suggest that judges could order the defense not to divulge what they had seen and also pointed out that the defense could not "have an unlimited license to rummage in the files of the Department of Justice.") The Nixon Administration's hostile reaction in asking for a rehearing included the suggestion that the government might not reveal national security wiretapping. Not intimidated, the justices refused the rehearing and remanded a number of cases, including that of Muhammad Ali, for hearing on the surveillance issue.[43]

When the Burger Court came to interpret the 1968 statute, its first two rulings were setbacks for the administration and carried a clear message: the act's limitations were to be imposed strictly. The statute had provided exceptions to regular surveillance procedures in *national security* and intelligence cases, but electronic surveillance without a court order had been carried out in a *domestic* security case. The Court unanimously held such surveillance impermissible.[44] Speaking through Nixon appointee Powell, the Court made clear that the statute's requirements had to be followed, and Powell made strong statements both about the fear induced by electronic surveillance and about the need for judicial oversight of such law enforcement methods. (See p. 23.) A second setback for the administration came when a five-man majority said the statute's provision forbidding grand jury use of wiretap evidence was a valid defense to contempt charges.[45] Witnesses could not be forced to testify before a grand jury when the questions were based on intercepted conversations; in short, they could not be made to give up information that could not properly be introduced directly. Here Justice Rehnquist, who would have upheld the questioning because of the broad scope generally allowed in grand jury proceedings, complained that too much access to the government's files was being allowed; he felt witnesses were being allowed to rummage around in them.

In 1974, the Court again returned to interpretation of the statute, the administration coming off only somewhat better than it had earlier. After allowing the use of conversations of someone not named in a warrant application,[46] the Court then unanimously strictly enforced the act's clear instructions that surveillance authorizations be signed by the Attorney General or a specifically designated Assistant Attorney General, thus invalidating warrant applications in *several hundred* gambling and narcotics cases authorized by the Attorney General's Executive Assistant.[47] However, when the majority threw out extensions of the initial orders on the basis of the "fruit of the poisonous tree" doctrine, the Nixon appointees disagreed; they thought the extensions were valid because based on independently obtained evidence. Where the issue was only improper *identification* of an authorizing official, rather than improper authorization, the dissenters thought Congress had not intended to allow *any* flexibility, but the majority refused to throw out surveillance orders so obtained.[48]

COUNSEL AND CONFESSIONS

At Trial

Gideon v. *Wainwright* had provided for right to counsel *at trial* for serious offenses. The Warren Court had then extended the right-to-counsel rule into both the pre- and post-trial periods as well as to juvenile proceedings. Yet it was the Burger Court that further extended trial right to counsel. Wiping out the major-minor offense distinction, the Court unanimously said that right to counsel should be provided if imprisonment were to result.[49] Because counsel was not yet required every time that prison was *possible*, Chief Justice Burger wondered whether excessive time would be spent determining whether a person would be entitled to counsel. He also thought new burdens would be placed on the legal profession, but "the dynamics of the profession have a way of rising to the burdens placed upon it." Justice Powell, who would have allowed judges to determine counsel rights on a case-by-case basis, thought the Court's rule too inflexible; some nonjailable offenses, like drunk driving, were serious enough to warrant a lawyer. While he was concerned that the Court favored the indigent over those with only a little bit of money, he wished to protect judges' sentencing flexibility and to keep the justice system from becoming overburdened, which he thought would result from zealous young lawyers trying all the issues in a case.

The Warren Court had not dealt with whether a state could later recover funds used to defend indigents. In 1974, the Burger Court, over only two dissents, upheld a recoupment statute calling for reimbursement of attorney and investigator fees and expenses.[50] The Court was careful to stress that recoupment applied only to those later able to pay and that one could be exempted from the law on a showing of "extreme hardship"; if one remained indigent, the state could not recover. The justices asserted that knowledge that one would have to repay costs did not affect ability to obtain legal services, and that no "chilling effect" had been imposed on the right to counsel. These rulings were somewhat like those in which the Court had kept poor people from going to jail because they were unable to pay fines. After saying that a person given a jail-and-fine sentence could not be kept in jail beyond the maximum statutory sentence because of failure to pay the fine, the justices unanimously said the state could not turn a fine into a prison term for those who could not pay. One could not be jailed for failure to pay a fine where only the fine was imposed (the $30 or thirty days situation); instead the state had to provide means of spreading the payments.[51]

Pre-Trial

The Warren Court, in one of its more important rulings on criminal procedure prior to trial, had extended the right to counsel to police lineups. The purpose was to avoid suggestive lineups and the contaminated identifications of the defendant that would result at the trial.[52] However, as to identifications themselves, the Warren Court also said that eyewitness identification at trial could be set aside only where pre-trial procedures were so suggestive as to produce very strong likelihood of irreparable misidentification.[53] This was hardly a pro-defendant policy, and the Court used the totality of circumstances approach in reaching it.

When the Burger Court was faced with additional questions involving right to counsel at lineup, the protections of the Warren Court were seriously cut back. Saying that the Warren Court's ruling involved *post-indictment* lineup proceedings, a plurality of four justices held that the counsel right did not attach until commencement of judicial proceedings such as indictment.[54] The Burger Court also held there was no right to counsel where a witness was being shown a display of pictures, even after defendant had been indicted.[55] The dissenters felt the risks of misidentification were as great at a photographic display as at a lineup and argued that the Court was trying to destroy completely the constitutional principles underlying the earlier *Wade/Gilbert* rule.

Among the most significant of all Warren Court rulings were those applying counsel rights to interrogation both after indictment[56] and before it. The pre-indictment stationhouse situation first produced *Escobedo* v. *Illinois*.[57] After taking Escobedo to the stationhouse for questioning, police had refused his requests and those of his lawyer to see each other and had obtained a confession. Throwing out his conviction, Justice Goldberg indicated that when the focus of law-enforcement officers' attention shifted from investigation to accusation, the right to counsel applied; that meant a person had to be allowed access to his lawyer. *Escobedo* did *not*, however, require that a lawyer be appointed for those who could not afford one.

Such a requirement came soon, however, in the famous case of *Miranda* v. *Arizona*,[58] really a combination of five cases in which police interrogations had taken place without the suspects knowing or being told of their rights; the resultant confessions had led to convictions—in Miranda's case for a rape-kidnap. The central element in the Court's ruling was the validity of confessions. The justices said no confession from in-custody interrogation was to be considered valid and admitted in evidence unless the person interrogated was warned of and understood his rights. The rights stipulated by the Court were those to remain silent; to know that what the person said can and will be used against him in court; to have his lawyer present; if he could not afford a lawyer, to have one appointed; and to discontinue the conversation at any time.

Miranda had a political significance far beyond its legal particulars. The case seemed to combine all of the Warren Court's basic criminal procedure approaches. As Graham states it, *Miranda*

> . . . provided a concise catalogue of the features of the Warren Court's criminal-law decision-making that had most rankled its critics: It saddled the police with what appeared to be drastic new restrictions, based upon a reinterpretation of constitutional provisions that had been on the books for most of the nation's history. It overturned well-established precedents by a vote of 5 to 4. It was frankly "legislative," containing a detailed code of post-arrest procedure, similar to a statute that a legislature might enact. It implied that local police, judges and juries would violate suspects' rights unless hemmed in by the Supreme Court. Finally, it appeared to undermine the truth-finding role of criminal courts in order to carry out the Supreme Court majority's concept of a social good.[59]

Following *Mapp, Gideon,* and *Escobedo,* the *Miranda* ruling produced strongly negative police reaction—that they were being forced to fight criminals "with two hands tied behind their back" and "with three strikes against them."[60] As if this were not enough, the case also seemed to exacerbate the problem of rising crime rates and increasing racial tension.

The Court's position vis-à-vis the law enforcement community was further damaged by the *Miranda* opinion itself as well as by the follow-up to the case. The Court established a firm rule with respect to confessions ("no warnings, no admissibility"). However, the justices did not provide clear standards for the "intelligent waiver" of rights that had to occur before someone could be interrogated. Trial judges were thus still left much discretion to determine if the waiver had occurred. The Court had stopped short of requiring the presence of a lawyer before rights could be waived, but had not made this or the waiver flexibility clear. This omission left police feeling that the Court had gone further than it had actually gone.

Out of "a desire not to frighten the public with the spectre of emptying the jails of convicted murderers and rapists,"[61] the Court did not make *Miranda* fully applicable to all past confessions cases. The rule was, however, made applicable to *trials* begun after the date of the decision instead of to *interrogations* conducted after that date.[62] Through this ruling, the justices did allow some who had given confessions before *Miranda* the opportunity to overturn their convictions. As Graham remarked, no one benefited but "a few confessed criminals and the most ruthless of the court's enemies."[63] Perhaps trying to cure some of the damage from having made the *Miranda* rule partly retroactive, the Court later held that *Miranda* did not apply to those whose retrials began after *Miranda* if their original trial began before it.[64] (Taking essentially this position, the Arizona Supreme Court refused to apply the *Miranda* rule to Miranda himself and would not reverse his conviction on retrial.) Despite the severity of the criticism, the Warren Court did not retreat from the *Miranda* rule itself. In fact, the ruling was reinforced by applying it to tax investigations and to an interrogation without warnings in the suspects' bedroom after the police broke in.[65]

Just as one would have expected the Burger Court to overturn the exclusionary rule, so one might well have expected it to overturn *Miranda*. However, *Miranda* was not repealed, but it was weakened. That came when a prosecutor was allowed to use a confession, obtained without the warnings, to impeach the testimony of a defendant who had decided to take the stand;[66] however, the prosecutor still could not use such a confession in his basic presentation (or case-in-chief). The Burger Court also held that the standard for judging voluntariness of pre-*Miranda* confessions at the required separate judicial hearing was only "preponderance of the evidence," not the stronger standard of "beyond a reasonable doubt."[67]

Then in June 1974, it appeared that the Court had said police failure to inform a defendant of *all* his rights did not bar use of all evidence obtained from him.[68] A defendant had not been told he had a right to a free lawyer. However, once the reader looked further than the newspapers,[69] he found that the case, which produced a nearly unanimous decision, involved a statement made *before Miranda*, and the police could hardly be said to have violated a rule not yet announced; the decision thus did not weaken *Miranda* itself, although it carried the potential for doing so in the future. We are now in a position where the Court has not yet dealt with post-*Miranda* incomplete warnings nor has it adopted the idea that "trial judges would be permitted to admit otherwise untainted confessions in the interest of justice when the failure to give the correct warnings was inadvertent, or could otherwise be explained."[70]

Post-Trial

The Warren Court extended the *Gideon* right-to-counsel rule to a number of post-trial situations and this movement was carried forward—but not much—by the Burger Court. Included in the Warren Court's extensions were first appeal[71] and probation-revocation where sentencing had been deferred; this was covered by the rule because sentencing was considered a critical stage of the trial proceedings.[72] The right was even extended into the jail. When a prisoner was disciplined for violating regulations against helping other prisoners with legal documents, the Court said that he had to be able to help others prepare legal materials *unless* the prison provided alternative assistance for illiterate or poorly educated inmates.[73] The Burger Court extended attorney assistance to prisoners. A ban on the use of law students or legal paraprofessionals assisting lawyers in the prison context was set aside because it would dilute prisoners' right to access to the courts.[74] In ruling on probation-revocation procedures (see below), the justices held that presumptively a lawyer should be provided when requested but that the hearing board should make such determinations on a case-by-case basis; grounds for refusal should be clearly stated.[75] Although the Court said nothing about the right to counsel at parole-revocation hearings,[76] the justices were unwilling to extend the right to apply to hearings on penalizing prisoners for infractions of prison rules. The majority felt providing counsel "would inevitably give the proceedings a more adversary cast and tend to reduce their utility as a means to further correctional goals."[77]

Refusing to extend Warren Court policy on right to counsel during appeal, the Burger Court held that indigents were *not* entitled to appointed counsel on discretionary state appeals or petitions for certiorari to the U.S. Supreme Court.[78] While a defendant had to have an attorney at trial "as a shield to protect him against being 'haled into Court' by the State and stripped of his presumption of innocence," he was not entitled to one on appeal to act "as a sword to upset the prior determination of guilt." "Unfairness," said the majority, "results only if indigents are singled out by the State and denied meaningful access to that system because of their poverty." Because transcripts, appellate briefs, and the defendant's own statements would provide higher courts with sufficient material from which to determine whether or not to take a case, that access was not being impeded. (Justice Rehnquist also asserted that "the State need not provide any appeal at all," making clear that a right we presume exists has little constitutional foundation.)

A closely related appeal right was the right to a transcript. The Warren Court, in one of its earliest criminal procedure rulings, had begun to establish indigents' rights to a free transcript on appeal.[79] In contrast, the Burger Court held that alternatives to a full free transcript could be considered, although the burden was on the state to show such alternatives were adequate; there could also be no distinction between felony and nonfelony cases as the basis for providing transcripts.[80]

Adequacy of Counsel

When considering the *right* to counsel, the Supreme Court seldom considered counsel's *adequacy*. The rulings handed down by the Burger Court did not hold much hope for the inadequately represented defendant. A guilty plea based on "reasonably competent advice" could not be challenged, the Court said, even though defendant's lawyer misjudged the admissibility of his confession and failed to attack it.[81] There was no requirement, Justice White said, that "all advice offered by the defendant's lawyer withstand retrospective examination. . . . " However, the Court would not interfere even when a lawyer did not raise a basic constitutional claim deriving from clear law, a challenge to a grand jury from which blacks had been systematically excluded. As we will see, the adequacy of the plea itself might be challenged; however, a counseled guilty plea precluded a habeas corpus attack on matters prior to the plea unless a prisoner could show that advice he received was not "within the range of competence demanded in criminal cases."[82] A defendant, said Justice Rehnquist, did not have to be advised of "every conceivable constitutional plea in abatement he might have to the charge" nor did his counsel have to pursue certain factual inquiries far enough to uncover possible constitutional infirmities. Excusing his fellow lawyers' incomplete representation of their clients, Rehnquist said their work frequently involved not only their specialized legal knowledge but also practical considerations that might lead to decisions not to bring all possible procedural challenges. Justice Marshall, however, felt competence *in terms of the law* was the proper and fair standard for judging adequacy of representation. That lawyers did not as a general practice raise claims—for example, systematic exclusion of blacks from Tennessee grand juries in the mid-1940s—did not make their inaction acceptable to Marshall. He also argued that a defendant could not be said to have intelligently pleaded if he did not know his rights. If lawyers were not compelled to consult with their clients, "the representation of criminal defendants becomes only another method of manipulating persons in situations where their control over their lives is precisely what is at stake."

Juveniles

Right-to-counsel questions also appeared in connection with juvenile proceedings, which had generally been said to be civil rather than criminal in nature. The Warren Court first held that waiving juveniles over to criminal court for trial as adults could not take place without assistance of counsel.[83] Then the Court held that a juvenile was entitled to the right to counsel if he might be institutionalized as a result of a juvenile proceeding.[84] The Court also insisted that other major procedural protections—notice, protection against self-incrimination, and the right to confront witnesses—be made available. As Justice Fortas put it, "Under our Constitution, the condition of being a boy does not justify a kangaroo court. . . . Juvenile court history has demonstrated that unbridled discretion, however benevolently motivated, is frequently a poor substitute for principle and procedure."

The Burger Court would not add a right to jury trial to those rights.[85] Reflecting much the same approach he used with respect to welfare, Justice Blackmun was bothered by the thought of making the juvenile proceeding into a fully adversary matter instead of an "intimate, informal protective" one, although he did note, "The fond and idealistic hopes of the juvenile court proponents and early reformers of three generations ago have not been realized." The Court did hold, however, that the "beyond a reasonable doubt" standard, not the weaker "preponderance of the evidence," must be used in juvenile proceedings, and made that rule fully retroactive.[86]

RETROACTIVITY

The problem of applying new criminal procedure policy to earlier convictions arose not only with confessions but also with most other new rules. If we believed that the Supreme Court *finds* pre-existing constitutional rules instead of making policy, the rule on retroactivity would be automatic: a rule, once found, would apply to all past cases. However, we have come to reject as mythology the idea that the Court only finds the law. In making policy on the application of criminal procedure rules to past cases, the Court has come to recognize a practical problem: reversing all previous convictions that had been improperly obtained in terms of the new rule would produce a large "jail delivery" and substantial new inputs for the courts as the defendants were retried; in addition, locating witnesses and refreshing their dimming memories would be difficult. The result of recognizing these practicalities was a general stance of not applying new criminal procedure rules to past cases. Such a stance underscored the symbolic nature of the new rules—they were nice statements of principle, but seldom helped those already in jail.

Although the Court's general stance against retroactivity is clear, the process of developing retroactivity policy plagued the Court because it seemed unfair or even legislative not to apply the new rules to all past cases. To aid in determining whether to make new rules retroactive, the Court developed three criteria: (1) What was the rule's effect on the reliability of the fact-finding process at trial? (2) Had law enforcement officials relied on the earlier rule? and (3) What would be the impact on the administration of justice? Applying these criteria was by no means easy, and the uneven results produced the complaint that the Court had "yet to produce any considered, coherent statement" on the subject, with rulings "almost as difficult to follow as the tracks of a beast of prey in search of his intended victim."[87]

Full retroactivity, applying a rule to all convictions even where appeals were exhausted, was seldom used. Its basic application came in situations affecting either the jurisdiction of a court over a case (as in double jeopardy) or the trial's reliability (right to counsel).[88] The Court occasionally ordered partial retroactivity. This meant applying the new rule where cases were not complete. For example, the justices opted for partial retroactivity with respect to *Mapp*, applying the exclusionary rule to cases pending on appeal;[89] this type of partial retroactivity was used only once more.[90] The start of the *trial* was also used as a point for partial retroactivity, as with the *Miranda* doctrine. Generally, new rules were applied only prospectively, that is, to situations, incidents, or events arising after the Supreme Court's new rule was announced. This was particularly true where the purpose of the rule was largely to deter or clean up police behavior. However, some justices protested this refusal to grant retroactivity. Justice Fortas perhaps stated the argument best. He said that to hold new criminal procedure rules nonretroactive would be to "add this Court's approval to those who honor the Constitution's mandate only where acceptable to them or compelled by the precise and inescapable specifics of a decision of this Court" and to "award dunce caps to those law enforcement officers, courts, and public officials who do not merely stand by until an inevitable decree issues from this Court . . . but who generously apply the mandates of the Constitution as the developing case law elucidates them."[91] In this comment, he was suggesting that the Court's new rules were not surprises but were almost inevitable and could have been anticipated by the law enforcement community. If Fortas represented a pro-retroactivity position, the Nixon appointees were clearly indisposed to granting it and were far less willing to do so than the Warren Court majority had been. They showed their bitterness over retroactivity most fully when right-to-counsel rules were applied to cases occurring long before the Warren Court's *Gideon* rule was enunciated.[92]

The Warren Court's rulings on retroactivity were doctrinally inconsistent. More than that, however, the unwillingness to rule in favor of retroactivity was also inconsistent with the Court's basic thrust on criminal procedure. Far fewer retroactivity rulings were favorable to the defendant than were the basic criminal procedure rulings (40 percent compared with 72 percent, between 1962 and 1968).[93] Perhaps the Court used its (non)retroactivity rulings to respond to the hostility with which its criminal procedure rules were received. This interpretation is reinforced by evidence that the Court gave retroactivity only to its more popular—or at least less unpopular—rulings. Whatever the reason, the rulings meant that the Supreme Court was not only not uniformly liberal as to criminal procedure doctrine, but was also willing to retreat or modify the thrust of its opinions when its liberalism was more than the public (and particularly important publics like the law enforcement community) could take.

OTHER ISSUES

Search and seizure, right to counsel, and confessions may have been the most spectacular of the criminal procedure areas with which the Court dealt. There were obviously many others as well. After *Mapp* and *Gideon*, the Warren Court proceeded to incorporate most of the remaining Bill of Rights provisions into the Fourteenth Amendment Due Process Clause as prohibitions against the states. Although the idea of "selective incorporation" of portions of the Bill of Rights was continued, by the time the Warren Court was finished, most all of the Bill of Rights applied to the states. After each incorporation, the Court continued its development of the substantive law on the newly incorporated provisions. Particular attention was given to the Fifth and Sixth Amendments.

Fifth Amendment

"No person . . . shall be compelled in any criminal case to be a witness against himself," says the Fifth Amendment. After incorporating this basic element into the Fourteenth Amendment, the Warren Court reinforced its action by invalidating a prosecutor's comment to a jury on the defendant's failure to testify.[94] Clearly it would do the defendant little good not to testify if the prosecutor could use that fact to his disadvantage. Many Fifth Amendment claims faced the Burger Court. One involved notice-of-alibi rules that required a person to give advance notification to the prosecutor if he were to use an alibi. Such rules were upheld over the objection that they allowed the prosecutor to question defendant's witnesses widely and forced the defendant to release his case before he had seen the prosecutor's; the majority said the rule was a reasonable way to eliminate surprise from the trial.[95] Three years later, however, the Burger Court unanimously overturned a notice-of-alibi provision not explicitly allowing the defendant discovery rights with respect to the prosecutor's case prior to trial.[96] The justices felt that "discovery must be a two-way street. The State may not insist that trials be run as a 'search for truth' so far as defense witnesses are concerned, while maintaining 'poker game' secrecy for its own witnesses."

A central Fifth Amendment question involved immunity. The Warren Court, repeating the doctrine of earlier cases, had said that because the Fifth Amendment's purpose was not to prevent testimony but to prevent *prosecution* from that testimony, one could be compelled to testify if sufficient immunity were granted.[97] The Burger Court then dealt with the necessary *scope* of immunity. In a case under the 1970 Organized Crime Control Act, the majority held in 1972 that the statute's "use immunity" —a proscription against the use or derivative use of compelled testimony—was sufficient protection under the Fifth Amendment.[98] "Transactional immunity"—forbidding prosecution for any activity implicated in the testimony—gave broader protection than the Fifth Amendment required and was not mandated, although Congress could grant it if it wished.

Sixth Amendment

"In all criminal prosecutions, the accused shall enjoy the right to a speedy and public trial, by an impartial jury . . . , and to be informed of the nature and cause of the accusation; to be confronted with the witnesses against him. . . . " The Warren Court, after incorporating the Fifth Amendment, upheld incorporation of the Sixth Amendment right to confront witnesses, a ruling that lost some vitality during the Burger Court.[99] The Warren Court also finally ruled that jury trials were guaranteed in the states.[100]

The old issue of systematic exclusion of minorities from juries, where policy was by now relatively routinized, arose only infrequently, and did not pose major questions. However, important jury trial issues did face the Court. One of the most important was related to publicity surrounding a trial. Here questions of criminal procedure and free speech intersected. The notable cases were *Estes* (televising courtroom proceedings) and *Sheppard* (massive pre- and during-trial publicity).[101] In both cases the Court was willing to limit press freedom to insure the competing value of fair trial. In *Estes*, the justices banned courtroom television; the public trial requirement of the Constitution could be satisfied without opening the court to the distractions the justices thought television caused. In *Sheppard*, where the media had demanded the defendant's conviction in a murder trial and where there was a carnival-like courtroom atmosphere, excessive publicity was held to be grounds for reversing a conviction. The Supreme Court felt the effect of publicity and the atmosphere *during* the trial were well within the trial judge's control; he could have run his courtroom in a more controlled manner and could have sequestered the jury to isolate it from media reports. All this was not "new law." However, the Court's ruling with respect to prejudicial *pre*-trial publicity, which stimulated the development of American Bar Association guidelines, was new:

> The trial court might well have proscribed extrajudicial statements by any lawyer, party, witness, or court official which divulged prejudicial matters, such as the refusal of Sheppard to submit to interrogation or take any lie detector tests; any statement made by Sheppard to officials; the identity of prospective witnesses or their probable testimony; any belief in guilt or innocence. . . .

The Supreme Court under Earl Warren *extended* the right to a jury trial in the states to all situations involving authorized sentences of six months or more. According to a plurality of three, however, petty offenses could be tried without a jury.[102] The most important Burger Court jury questions dealt with jury size and the vote necessary to convict. The Court sustained state six-person criminal juries in noncapital cases and federal six-person civil juries imposed by district court rule,[103] although the latter ruling brought objections that the Federal Rules of Civil Procedure allowed reduction in jury size only by stipulation of both parties. The dissenters also made the more serious claim that the Court was mounting a "frontal assault on the very nature of the civil jury as that concept has been understood for some seven hundred years."

Nonunanimous (10–2 and 9–3) verdicts in twelve-person state criminal juries were also upheld. Four majority justices said the Sixth Amendment did not require unanimous jury verdicts, while Powell, concurring, claimed that unanimity was required in *federal* juries.[104] The basic argument was over whether the standard of "beyond a reasonable doubt," used in criminal trials, itself implied—and thus compelled—unanimity. The majority ruled that it did not, because each of the jurors would be applying the standard in reaching his own decision. Justice White stated, "The fact of three dissenting votes to acquit raises no question of constitutional substance about either the integrity or the accuracy of the majority verdict of guilt." The dissenters, however, felt that the jury majority would be unwilling to listen to those of opposing views because the vote rule did not require them to do so.

Death Penalty

The death-penalty question is really an Eighth Amendment (cruel and unusual punishment) problem, but it appeared first and was initially resolved as a jury rights matter. The first death penalty issue before the Warren Court involved the Lindberg (kidnapping) Act death penalty provision, which allowed the jury but not the judge to impose capital punishment. The Court invalidated the provision because it discouraged use of a jury trial.[105] Also struck down was the systematic exclusion of those opposed to the death penalty, because it left a "hanging jury" that could not be used to impose the penalty;[106] the judges felt a person opposed in general to capital punishment could still carry out his proper role as a juror.

The death penalty jury case before the Burger Court involved both the standard single trial proceeding in which a jury decided both guilt and punishment and California's split trial (one trial on guilt, then a separate one on punishment); the primary question was that in both, sentencing was left to the jury's absolute discretion. The majority, emphasizing the virtual impossibility of identifying factors to be taken into account in applying the death penalty, held there was no violation of the Constitution in either procedure.[107] Brennan, dissenting, wanted the jury's unbridled discretion channeled even if it could not be fully controlled. This could be done by requiring juries to indicate their findings and their reasons for imposing a penalty, as well as by having legislatures indicate the factors juries should take into account.

By thus dealing with death penalty–related jury questions, the Court had been developing policy incrementally. These rulings had also led the Court to a position where it had to confront the death penalty itself. Here the Court had little guidance from its own precedents, as it had decided very few cases under the Eighth Amendment. In addition to an early ruling on deprivation of citizenship, the Warren Court had found it to be cruel and unusual punishment to make it a crime to be a narcotics addict. However, in one of its last decisions, the Warren Court had also said it was *not* an Eighth Amendment violation to prosecute a chronic alcoholic for public intoxication.[108]

The basic death penalty ruling, one of the most controversial during the Burger Court, came in a *per curiam* opinion of less than a page, in which the Court said that capital punishment *as applied* was improper. *All nine* justices then wrote separate opinions, five supporting the judgment, each for different reasons, the four Nixon appointees opposing it.[109] Only Brennan and Marshall were opposed to the penalty as a direct violation of the Eighth Amendment under all circumstances. Douglas found it invalid as "pregnant with discrimination . . . ," while Stewart's opposition was to the penalty's present application:

> These death sentences are cruel and unusual in the same way that being struck by lightning is cruel and unusual. . . . The petitioners are among a capriciously selected random handful upon whom the sentence of death has in fact been imposed. . . . The Eighth and Fourteenth Amendments cannot tolerate the infliction of a sentence of death under legal systems that permit this unique penalty to be so wantonly and so freakishly imposed.

Given the lack of certainty about the punishment and its effects, the dissenters would have left matters to the judgment of the state legislatures. For Justice Powell, the question of assessing the penalty was "the very sort of judgment that the legislative branch is competent to make and for which the judiciary is ill-equipped." Justice Blackmun, who indicated his intense personal opposition to capital punishment (see pp. 22–23), and Chief Justice Burger felt similarly, Burger indicating that "If we were possessed of legislative power," he would either join Brennan and Marshall in their outright denunciation of capital punishment "or, at the very least, restrict [its] use . . . to a small category of the most heinous crimes."

Speedy Trial

Another Sixth Amendment right is that of a speedy trial. The speedy trial requirement was applied to the states in a late Warren Court ruling, where the justices said that a prosecutor could not hold a case over the defendant's head but either had to bring it to trial or dismiss it totally.[110] Then the Court, following its pattern of establishing a rule and then developing the substance of policy, began to elaborate and reinforce the speedy trial right. Prisoners awaiting trials in other jurisdictions were allowed to get to trial quickly, and the Court imposed firm remedies—dismissal of charges—when speedy trial was not provided.

When a federal prisoner against whom state charges were pending made a demand for a state trial, the Warren Court had said that the state was required to make a good faith effort to bring him to trial.[111] The Burger Court, stressing that "the duty of the charging authority is to provide a prompt trial," extended this doctrine. The justices did this by reversing the state conviction of a federal prisoner who had tried for *seven years* to get a state trial only to find that witnesses had died or had become unavailable and relevant police records were lost or destroyed.[112] In another case, which the justices conceded was close, there had been *sixteen* continuances, the first eleven of which received no defense objection, and a murder trial *five years* after the initial trial date. The Court unanimously held that, on the facts, the speedy trial right had not been denied but they used the opportunity to stress again that the burden was on the prosecutor to get a case to trial quickly.[113] In keeping with the Court's new approach in criminal procedure cases, Justice Powell did not adopt a fixed time period for determining when the speedy trial right had been denied but only specified factors to be taken into account. Powell also emphasized *society's* rights even though the constitutional rights of a *defendant* were basically at issue; he noted that when speedy trial was not provided, rehabilitation during incarceration was delayed, backlogs in criminal courts reinforced defendants' plea-bargaining advantage, and those out on bail pending trial might commit more crimes. Further reinforcement of the speedy trial right occurred in 1973, when the Court ruled that a defendant need not show actual prejudice to the defense in order to sustain his claim of denial of speedy trial. Equally if not more important was the ruling that while violations of other rights (for example, public trial, impartial jury) could be cured by a new trial, denial of a speedy trial could *only* be remedied by dismissal of the case.[114] Congress added substantially to speedy trial rights in the federal courts when it passed the Speedy Trial Act in 1974, to go into effect in 1975.

Double Jeopardy

In addition to its more familiar language about self-incrimination, the Fifth Amendment also states, " . . . nor shall any person be subject for the same offense to be twice put in jeopardy of life and limb. . . ." It was in a double jeopardy case, *Palko* v. *Connecticut,* that the basic theory of selective incorporation, that only those portions of the Bill of Rights would be applied to the states that were "necessary to a concept of ordered liberty," had been announced.[115] It was therefore noteworthy that the Warren Court criminal procedure revolution ended with the application to state defendants of the protection against double jeopardy.[116] The Court did not, however, feel that its ruling was earthshaking, Justice Marshall noting that *"Palko's* roots had . . . been cut away years ago. We today recognize the inevitable."

Some prohibitions against double jeopardy may always have applied to the states because they were considered fundamental. For example, to retry someone after an acquittal probably would not have been allowed. However, with the prohibition now applicable to the states, new double jeopardy questions came to the Burger Court. In one, when a crime, for example, a robbery, against several people took place at one time, a prosecutor, instead of trying the defendant once, would treat as separate crimes the acts against each individual and would try the defendant serially until he got a guilty verdict. The Court held that, after an initial acquittal, new trials created double jeopardy if the only issue were identification of the defendant.[117] Another issue involved separate federal and state, or state and municipal, charges from a single act. The Burger Court held the state-local duplication to be double jeopardy because the local government was an arm of the state, and thus the state was trying the person twice; in short, the two governments were not "two sovereignties."[118] On the federal-state issue, the Court's explicit policy remained that it was *not* double jeopardy for both jurisdictions to try the defendant.[119] However, the thrust of the Court's other rulings suggests this is no longer good law, and Department of Justice policy since the Eisenhower period has been *not* to try a person on federal charges if he has already been tried and acquitted on state charges.

Closely related to these double jeopardy issues were certain questions on sentencing. The Warren Court had said that when sentence is imposed on retrial for the same offense, time already served must be credited. To avoid judicial vindictiveness, a higher sentence on retrial must be justified by the judge on the basis of objective information about defendant's conduct after the original sentencing.[120] The Burger Court, however, quickly restricted the scope of the rule to *judicial* resentencing. Protecting "flexibility and discretion in the sentencing process," the Court upheld a higher sentence by a *jury* on retrial if the jury had not been informed of the prior sentence. Also shifting the burden of proof, the justices said the *defendant* would have to show the new sentence to be the product of vindictiveness.[121] Although Stewart pointed out the possibility for prosecutorial and judicial vindictiveness,[122] Powell, who conceded the jury was likely to know about the prior trial, said it would have "no motivation to engage in self-vindication" and no institutional interest in discouraging appeals by imposing higher sentences.

Contempt

The Burger Court, in addition to dealing with many of the same criminal procedure problems as had the Warren Court, dealt with a wide range of sentencing and related issues, breaking much new ground because the policy questions were virtually untouched. Included were the issues of disruptive defendants and contempt for misbehavior in court. The Burger Court's disruptive defendant case did not involve a "political trial" like the Chicago Eight case, but its applicability to that sort of situation was clear. A judge, after warning a defendant about disruptive behavior and vile and abusive language, had excluded him from the courtroom. Supporting the judge, the Court said he must be given "sufficient discretion to meet the circumstances of each case" and had three permissible choices: keep the "obstreperous defendant" present but bound and gagged; cite him for contempt; or remove him "until he promises to conduct himself properly."[123] (Where a defendant left the trial voluntarily, the Court later held, the judge had the right to continue with the trial.[124])

In another case, a defendant insisting on representing himself had called a judge a variety of mostly unpleasant names, and the judge had waited until the end of the trial to impose contempt sentences. The Supreme Court said he could have sentenced immediately for the improper acts to keep order in the court. However, when sentencing was delayed, the contempt charges had to be heard by a different judge,[125] because at the end of the trial the judge might be supersensitive and particularly vindictive. Dealing with the length of contempt sentences, the Court said that a contemnor was entitled to a jury trial "whenever a strong possibility exists that he will face a substantial term of imprisonment upon conviction, regardless of the punishment actually imposed"; here, sentences each less than six months but adding to more than six months had been assessed.[126] Another type of limit on judges' power to hold people in contempt was also imposed when the Court reversed a contempt conviction where the only misbehavior had been a single instance in which a defendant had used the word "chickenshit" in referring not to the judge but to an alleged assailant.[127]

Guilty Pleas

We have already noted the problems faced by a prisoner trying to challenge events prior to a counseled guilty plea. Many more questions concerning the practice of plea-bargaining remained to be answered. As to the plea itself, the Warren Court had said that an affirmative showing of the plea's voluntary nature had to be made in both state and federal cases.[128] However, the most basic issues surrounding plea-bargaining did not reach the Court until 1970. This allowed the Burger Court to write on a largely blank slate. In so doing, the justices, showing they wanted to enforce plea-bargaining, validated the practice. The Court first refused to hold that guilty pleas were compelled when they had been entered to avoid going to jury trial and facing the death penalty.[129] A plea, said the justices, was not coerced even if made to avoid the death penalty if it involved an intelligent and counseled choice among alternatives.[130] The defendant always had some choices to make, the majority said, and existence of some pressure to make those choices would not invalidate the plea, even where the threat of death was involved.

In more explicitly legitimating plea-bargaining, the Burger Court injected some requirements of fairness into the process. A prosecutor had promised the defendant he would make no recommendation about sentence to the judge, but a new prosecutor then recommended the maximum sentence. The judge, refusing to allow withdrawal of the plea, imposed the maximum. Here the justices finally agreed unfairness had occurred; however, they could not agree as to whether the defendant should be allowed to withdraw the plea or be granted the specific bargain he had been promised.[131] And the Chief Justice took the occasion to stress that plea-bargaining was "an essential component of the administration of justice," which, "properly administered . . . is to be encouraged," partly because it protects the public from criminal behavior during defendants' pre-trial release and speeds the beginning of the rehabilitative process.

Probation and Prisons

We have noted the Court's rulings on double jeopardy–related sentencing matters. In addition, the Court also dealt with special sentencing provisions for sex offenders. The Warren Court had first ruled that prisoners could not be kept in a *corrections* facility past the end of their prison terms without a particular showing that they were dangerous, and when being considered for commitment as mentally ill, were entitled to the same protections as other citizens.[132] The Court then held that a person sentenced to an indeterminate sentence under a state sex offenders act was entitled to the protections (the right to be heard, the offering of evidence, confrontation and cross-examination, counsel, and a finding adequate for meaningful appeal) in connection with his psychiatric examination.[133] Here the Burger Court followed up by unanimously requiring procedural protections at each stage at which commitment under a state sex offenders statute was reviewed and continued.[134]

The Burger Court also disposed of some cases involving sentencing under new congressional statutes. Here the justices' posture was to interpret the statutes so as to leave judges' sentencing discretion unfettered, even though the rehabilitative goals of the statutes might be hindered.[135] These latter rulings did not, however, establish broad policy. Such policy *was* forthcoming in cases on probation- and parole-revocation procedures. Breaking new ground and abandoning the idea that people on probation and parole were subject to almost total control by the officials to whom they were assigned, so that they could easily be sent (back) to jail, the Burger Court surrounded both probation and parole with basic procedural safeguards. Burger first said the parolee's liberty, even if conditional, was valuable. Thus, "Its termination calls for some orderly process, however informal."[136] To revoke parole, some minimal inquiry must be carried out at the time of arrest or quickly thereafter, perhaps by an administrative officer, with a further hearing required before final revocation. At the hearing, the parolee must have notice of violation, disclosure of evidence, an opportunity to be heard and to present witnesses and evidence, and the right to cross-examine; there was no ruling on right to counsel. The hearing body must be neutral and detached and must make written statements about evidence used and reasons for the revocation. Brennan and Douglas thought counsel should be provided, and Douglas thought a parolee with no new offense should not be arrested or jailed until parole had been revoked. The following year, these protections were extended to probation-revocation.[137]

The Court then finally reached the controversial issue of prison regulations and conditions, made all the more visible by events like Attica in 1971. The Court first dealt with some First Amendment questions like mail censorship and interviews (see p. 158) and then turned to within-prison discipline. The importance of these rulings cannot be underestimated, because the notion that prisoners have rights *as* prisoners is itself new, and to see it implemented shows the extent of the forward march of legalization in areas previously untouched by the law or by the idea of due process. Such rulings also indicated that the Court was willing to make inroads on the doctrine that the courts would keep their hands off internal prison matters.

In its most important prison case, the Court considered procedures for imposing within-prison penalties.[138] Justice White started with the position that because "A prisoner is not wholly stripped of constitutional protections when he is imprisoned for crime," the state could not act arbitrarily in attaching sanctions for major misconduct. Although the state did not have to allow for "good time," once it had been created, the state had to be fair. Yet the protections provided by the Court were constantly hedged in terms of the special situation of a state prison disciplinary proceeding. Advance written notice of a violation and a written statement of the discipline board's findings of facts and reasons for its actions were required. However, calling of witnesses and presentation of evidence was allowed only where "not . . . unduly hazardous to institutional safety or correctional goals." Prison officials were to be able to refuse to call witnesses who might engage in reprisals or be insubordinate. Confrontation and cross-examination could be limited because they were felt to contain greater dangers to the interests of those in charge of the prisons. Prisoners might not be "able to cope with the pressures and aftermath of the battle" of an adversary hearing or trial, said Justice White. Such an atmosphere would clearly be produced if lawyers were to be permitted at the hearing.

Even though White had left the door open to future rule changes, Marshall thought prisoners had been given "little more than empty promises" in a ruling that "deprives an accused inmate of any enforceable constitutional right to the procedural tools essential to the presentation of any meaningful defense. . . ." The prisoner would be left without much more than his own word and would be engaged in a "swearing contest" he would invariably lose. Marshall, like White, recognized the demands prison security imposed, but clearly gave more weight to prisoners' rights than did the majority.

CONCLUSION

The Warren Court's race relations, school prayer, obscenity, and reapportionment rulings had all drawn severe criticism and resistance; the greatest controversy, however, came over the Court's criminal procedure rulings. The justices' shift to broad rules made the law enforcement community feel severely restricted. Police officers' previous autonomy with respect to searches was limited and if the police did search improperly, the evidence would not be admissible. Suspects had to be warned of their rights if their confessions were to be used. And lawyers would be present, not only at trials in most important cases but also at earlier "critical stages of the proceedings." As one might expect, the rhetorical reaction was substantial. However, that rhetoric about the Warren Court's consistent pro-defendant ("pro-criminal") stand masked the fact that the Court was certainly *not* uniformly pro-defendant. The justices had, for example, provided legitimation of the use of informants and of stop-and-frisk, and had provided Congress a method by which wiretapping and electronic eavesdropping could be properly carried out. In addition, the Warren Court had generally refused to apply its new rulings retroactively.

One might well have expected the Supreme Court under Warren Burger to engage in substantial retrenchment from Warren Court policy, particularly because Burger's criticisms of the new rules were clear even before he arrived at the high court. Yet both the exclusionary rule of *Mapp* and the warning requirement of *Miranda*, although suffering some erosion, remain essentially intact. Right to counsel at trial was extended. Remedies for deprivation of speedy trial were firmly enforced. Despite those actions, the Burger Court was clearly more conservative than the Warren Court. The new Court tended to focus more on the total law enforcement situation than had the Warren Court, with results generally favorable to the police rather than the defendant. Particularly on search-and-seizure questions, the new justices' deference to and support for the work of law enforcement officers was clear; limitations on stop-and-frisk were removed, and automobile searches were made easier. When Congress supplied law enforcement officers with new tools, the Court generally sustained the legislative action, although it held the executive branch to the procedures provided in those statutes. In addition to retreating from Warren Court policy in the search area, there were areas where the Burger Court refused to extend new protections, for example, the right to counsel in some post-trial situations, where it was likely the Warren Court would have done so.

Despite the Warren Court's seemingly exhaustive treatment of criminal procedure, there were areas of the criminal justice system that had not been touched by Supreme Court litigation. In these new areas, for example, prisoners' rights, the Burger Court's basic posture was generally one that favored the individual less than the earlier justices would have. Yet even here the policies upheld were often conservative only by comparison with the Warren Court; where state or federal officials had adopted a moderate posture, the Supreme Court did not necessarily undercut it.

Thus the Burger Court was unwilling to "push to the frontier," but that did not mean it adopted reactionary positions or was unremittingly and explicitly pro-law enforcement. The picture is not one of stark across-the-board withdrawal from the Warren Court's work, but of some retreat, albeit more severe in some areas than in others, coupled with advances in some areas already marked out by the Warren Court and moderate policy developed in new areas.

NOTES

1. Herbert Packer, *The Limits of the Criminal Sanction* (Stanford, Cal.: Stanford University Press, 1968), p. 163. Others have talked of a variant called the Bureaucratic Model, where agencies' operational needs predominate, and a Rehabilitative Model, in which social workers and psychiatrists "treat" defendants.

2. "Cops Like Burger Court," *Southern Illinoisan* (Carbondale), July 29, 1973.

3. Norman Dorsen, "The Court of Some Resort," *Civil Liberties Review*, 1 (Winter–Spring 1974), 99.

4. *Neil* v. *Biggers*, 409 U.S. 188 (1972). See also *Cupp* v. *Naughten*, 414 U.S. 141 (1973), a single instruction to a jury "may not be judged in artifical isolation, but must be viewed in the context of the overall charge."

5. *Stovall* v. *Denno*, 388 U.S. 293 (1967).

6. *Illinois* v. *Somerville*, 410 U.S. 458 (1973). See also *Alo* v. *U.S.*, certiorari denied, 414 U.S. 919 (1973), claimed failure to grant a speedy trial after suppression of an earlier indictment because of wiretaps on defendant's lawyer.

7. *Tollett* v. *Henderson*, 411 U.S. 258 (1973).

8. *Chapman* v. *California*, 386 U.S. 18 (1967).

9. *Milton* v. *Wainwright*, 407 U.S. 371 (1972).

10. *Donnelly* v. *DeChristoforo*, 416 U.S. 637 at 648–649 (1974).

11. *Mapp* v. *Ohio*, 367 U.S. 643 (1961).

12. *Bivens* v. *Six Unknown Federal Narcotics Agents*, 403 U.S. 388 at 416 (1971). Argument over the effects of the rule is substantial. See Dallin H. Oaks, "Studying the Exclusionary Rule in Search and Seizure," *University of Chicago Law Review*, 37 (Summer 1970), 655–757, and Bradley C. Canon, "Is the Exclusionary Rule in Failing Health? Some New Data and a Plea Against a Precipitous Conclusion," *Kentucky Law Journal*, 62 (1973–1974), 681–730.

13. See, for example, Jerome Skolnick, *Justice Without Trial* (New York: John Wiley, 1966).

14. *U.S.* v. *Calandra*, 414 U.S. 338 (1974).

15. *Lewis* v. *U.S.*, 385 U.S. 206 (1968).

16. *Hoffa* v. *U.S.*, 385 U.S. 293 (1966).

17. *U.S.* v. *White*, 401 U.S. 745 (1971).

18. Compare *Spinelli* v. *U.S.*, 393 U.S. 410 (1969)—police, to show probable cause to obtain a warrant, need to support an informant's tip—with *U.S.* v. *Harris*, 403 U.S. 573 (1971)—tax investigator's affidavit for a warrant accepted, although based on a tip with no assertion that the informant had previously given correct information. *Spinelli* author Harlan, dissenting, would have required "corroboration of [the] trustworthiness" of an informant.

19. *U.S.* v. *Russell*, 411 U.S. 423 (1973).

20. *Chimel* v. *California*, 395 U.S. 752 (1969); the overruled cases were *Harris* v. *U.S.*, 331 U.S. 145 (1947), and *Rabinowitz* v. *U.S.*, 339 U.S. 56 (1953).

21. *Vale* v. *Louisiana*, 399 U.S. 30 (1970).

22. *U.S.* v. *Matlock*, 415 U.S. 164 (1974).

23. *Terry* v. *Ohio*, 392 U.S. 1 (1968); *Sibron* v. *New York*, 392 U.S. 40 (1968).

24. *Adams* v. *Williams*, 407 U.S. 143 (1972).

25. *U.S.* v. *Robinson*, 414 U.S. 218 (1973); *Gustafson* v. *Florida*, 414 U.S. 260 (1973).

26. *U.S.* v. *Wade*, 388 U.S. 218 (1967); *Gilbert* v. *California*, 388 U.S. 263 (1967).

27. *Davis* v. *Mississippi*, 394 U.S. 721 (1969).

28. *Cupp* v. *Murphy*, 412 U.S. 291 (1973).

29. *U.S.* v. *Dionisio*, 410 U.S. 1 (1973); *U.S.* v. *Mara*, 410 U.S. 19 (1973).

30. *Warden* v. *Hayden*, 387 U.S. 294 (1967).

31. *U.S.* v. *Edwards*, 415 U.S. 800 (1974).

32. See *Chambers* v. *Maroney*, 399 U.S. 42 (1970), occupants of car arrested and car taken to police station.

33. *Coolidge* v. *New Hampshire*, 403 U.S. 443 (1971).

34. *Cardwell* v. *Lewis*, 417 U.S. 583 (1974).

35. *Cady* v. *Dombrowski*, 413 U.S. 433 (1973).

36. *Schneckloth* v. *Bustamonte*, 412 U.S. 218 (1973).

37. *U.S.* v. *Biswell*, 406 U.S. 311 (1972).

38. *Almeida-Sanchez* v. *U.S.*, 413 U.S. 266 (1973). The Court denied certiorari in a case involving a body (vaginal) search at the border. Justice Douglas, dissenting, pointed out that "80% to 85% of all those subjected to body cavity searches at the border are innocent of the suspected wrongdoing," and said that warrants should be required for these "intrusive and degrading" searches. *Mason* v. *U.S.*, 414 U.S. 941 at 942 (1973).

39. *Katz* v. *U.S.*, 389 U.S. 347 (1967).

40. *Berger* v. *New York*, 388 U.S. 41 (1967).

41. *Kolod* v. *U.S.*, 390 U.S. 136 (1968).

42. *Alderman* v. *U.S.*, 394 U.S. 165 (1969).

43. *Giordano* v. *U.S.*, 394 U.S. 310 (1969). However, at about the same time, the Court did say that an adversary hearing was not necessary to resolve *all*

issues. An in-chambers proceeding might be sufficient to resolve points such as whether the government had turned over all tapes involving the claimant. *Taglianetti* v. *U.S.*, 394 U.S. 316 (1969).

44.   *U.S.* v. *U.S. District Court for the Eastern District of Michigan*, 407 U.S. 297 (1972).

45.   *Gelbard* v. *U.S.*, 408 U.S. 41 (1972).

46.   *U.S.* v. *Kahn*, 415 U.S. 505 (1974).

47.   *U.S.* v. *Giordano*, 416 U.S. 505 (1974).

48.   *U.S.* v. *Chavez*, 416 U.S. 562 (1974).

49.   *Argersinger* v. *Hamlin*, 407 U.S. 25 (1972).

50.   *Fuller* v. *Oregon*, 417 U.S. 40 (1974). See also *James* v. *Strange*, 407 U.S. 128 (1972), turning on equality of treatment for different kinds of debtors.

51.   *Williams* v. *Illinois*, 399 U.S. 235 (1970); *Tate* v. *Short*, 401 U.S. 395 (1971).

52.   *U.S.* v. *Wade*, 388 U.S. 218 (1967); *Gilbert* v. *California*, 388 U.S. 263 (1967).

53.   *Simmons* v. *U.S.*, 390 U.S. 377 (1968).

54.   *Kirby* v. *Illinois*, 406 U.S. 682 (1972). Even with this ruling, there could have been protection against "unnecessarily suggestive" identifications, under *Stovall* v. *Denno*, 388 U.S. 293 (1967), but this was undercut by *Neil* v. *Biggers*, 409 U.S. 188 (1973).

55.   *U.S.* v. *Ash*, 413 U.S. 300 (1973).

56.   *Massiah* v. *U.S.*, 377 U.S. 201 (1964).

57.   378 U.S. 478 (1964).

58.   384 U.S. 436 (1966).

59.   Fred Graham, *The Self-Inflicted Wound* (New York: Macmillan, 1970), p. 7.

60.   Many police are now aware that confessions are used in only a small percentage of cases and are essential in even fewer, and that defendants will continue to cooperate with police even after being given the warnings. See Stephen L. Wasby, *The Impact of the United States Supreme Court: Some Perspectives* (Homewood, Ill.: Dorsey Press, 1970), pp. 147–169, and Neal Milner, *The Court and Local Law Enforcement* (Beverly Hills, Cal.: Sage Publications, 1971).

61.   G. Gregory Fahlund, "Retroactivity and the Warren Court: The Strategy of a Revolution," *Journal of Politics*, 35 (August 1973), 591. He also suggests that "one of the reasons for the *Johnson* decision was the fact that most state and federal judges had anticipated it by denying retroactivity to *Escobedo*."

62.   *Johnson* v. *New Jersey*, 394 U.S. 719 (1966).

63.   Graham, p. 192.

64.   *Jenkins* v. *Delaware*, 395 U.S. 213 (1969).

65.   *Mathis* v. *U.S.*, 391 U.S. 1 (1968); *Orozco* v. *Texas*, 394 U.S. 324 (1969).

66.   *Harris* v. *New York*, 401 U.S. 222 (1971).

67.   *Lego* v. *Twomey*, 404 U.S. 477 (1972). The hearing was required by *Jackson* v. *Denno*, 378 U.S. 368 (1964).

68.   *Michigan* v. *Tucker*, 417 U.S. 433 (1974).

69.   On problems of communicating Supreme Court rulings, see Wasby, pp. 83–98, and David L. Grey, *The Supreme Court and the News Media* (Evanston, Ill.: Northwestern University Press, 1968).

70.   Graham, p. 184.

71.   *Douglas* v. *California*, 372 U.S. 535 (1963).

72.   *Mempa* v. *Rhay*, 389 U.S. 128 (1967).

73.   *Johnson* v. *Avery*, 393 U.S. 483 (1969).

74.   *Procunier* v. *Martinez*, 416 U.S. 778 (1973).

75.   *Gagnon* v. *Scarpelli*, 411 U.S. 778 (1973).

76. *Morrissey* v. *Brewer*, 408 U.S. 471 (1972).

77. *Wolff* v. *McDonnell*, 418 U.S. 539 (1974).

78. *Ross* v. *Moffitt*, 417 U.S. 600 (1974).

79. *Griffin* v. *Illinois*, 351 U.S. 12 (1956).

80. *Mayer* v. *City of Chicago*, 404 U.S. 189 (1971).

81. *McMann* v. *Richardson*, 397 U.S. 759 (1970).

82. *Tollett* v. *Henderson*, 411 U.S. 258 (1973).

83. *Kent* v. *U.S.*, 383 U.S. 541 (1966).

84. *In Re Gault*, 387 U.S. 1 (1967).

85. *McKeiver* v. *Pennsylvania*, 403 U.S. 528 (1971).

86. *In Re Winship*, 397 U.S. 358 (1970); *Ivan V.* v. *City of New York*, 407 U.S. 203 (1972).

87. *Mackey* v. *U.S.*, 401 U.S. 667 at 685, 676 (1971), Justice Harlan.

88. Also given full retroactivity was the rule in *Barber* v. *Page*, 390 U.S. 719 (1968), no use of preliminary hearing testimony at trial without good faith effort to produce the witness, held retroactive, *Berger* v. *California*, 393 U.S. 315 (1969).

89. *Linkletter* v. *Walker*, 361 U.S. 618 (1965).

90. *Tehan* v. *Shott*, 382 U.S. 406 (1966), on the retroactivity of *Griffin* v. *California*, 380 U.S. 609 (1965).

91. *Desist* v. *U.S.*, 394 U.S. 233 at 276–278 (1969).

92. *Loper* v. *Beto*, 405 U.S. 473 (1972); compare *Burgett* v. *Texas*, 389 U.S. 109 (1967).

93. Fahlund, 573.

94. *Malloy* v. *Hogan*, 378 U.S. 1 (1964); *Griffin* v. *California*, 380 U.S. 609 (1965).

95. *Williams* v. *Florida*, 399 U.S. 78 (1970).

96. *Wardius* v. *Oregon*, 412 U.S. 470 (1973).

97. *Ullman* v. *U.S.*, 350 U.S. 422 (1956).

98. *Kastigar* v. *U.S.*, 406 U.S. 441 (1972); *Ziccarrelli* v. *New Jersey State Commission of Investigation*, 406 U.S. 472 (1972), is the companion state case.

99. *Pointer* v. *Texas*, 380 U.S. 400 (1965), reinforced by *Barber* v. *Page*, 390 U.S. 719 (1968); *Mancusi* v. *Stubbs*, 408 U.S. 204 (1972). But see *Davis* v. *Alaska*, 415 U.S. 308 (1974), allowing cross-examination of a witness about his probationary and juvenile delinquent status, which the State did not wish to reveal.

100. *Duncan* v. *Louisiana*, 391 U.S. 145 (1968).

101. *Estes* v. *Texas*, 381 U.S. 532 (1965); *Sheppard* v. *Maxwell*, 384 U.S. 333 (1966).

102. *Baldwin* v. *New York*, 399 U.S. 66 (1970).

103. *Williams* v. *Florida*, 399 U.S. 78 (1970); *Colgrove* v. *Battin*, 413 U.S. 149 (1973).

104. *Johnson* v. *Louisiana,* 406 U.S. 356 (1972); *Apodaca* v. *Oregon,* 406 U.S. 404 (1972).

105. *Jackson* v. *U.S.*, 390 U.S. 570 (1968).

106. *Witherspoon* v. *Illinois*, 391 U.S. 510 (1968).

107. *McGautha* v. *California*, 402 U.S. 183 (1971).

108. *Robinson* v. *California,* 370 U.S. 660 (1962); *Powell* v. *Texas,* 392 U.S. 514 (1968).

109. *Furman* v. *Georgia*, 408 U.S. 238 (1972).

110. *Klopfer* v. *North Carolina*, 386 U.S. 213 (1967).

111. *Smith* v. *Hooey*, 393 U.S. 374 (1969).

112. *Dickey* v. *Florida*, 398 U.S. 30 (1970).

113. *Barker* v. *Wingo*, 407 U.S. 514 (1972).

114. *Moore* v. *Arizona*, 414 U.S. 25 (1973); *Strunk* v. *U.S.*, 412 U.S. 434 (1973).

115. 302 U.S. 319 (1937).

116. *Benton* v. *Maryland*, 395 U.S. 784 (1969).

117. *Ashe* v. *Swenson*, 397 U.S. 436 (1970).

118. *Waller* v. *Florida*, 393 U.S. 387 (1970). After the Florida court on remand ruled that a municipal ordinance violation and state grand larceny charges were not the same offense, the Court denied certiorari. *Waller* v. *Florida*, 414 U.S. 945 (1973).

119. *Bartkus* v. *Illinois*, 359 U.S. 121 (1959).

120. *North Carolina* v. *Pearce*, 395 U.S. 711 (1969).

121. *Chaffin* v. *Stynchcombe,* 412 U.S. 17 (1973). See also *Colten* v. *Kentucky,* 407 U.S. 104 (1972), upholding heavier fine in general trial court in a *de novo* appeal of petty court convictions.

122. When a defendant appealed a misdemeanor conviction and the prosecutor then obtained a felony indictment for the same incident, the Court did throw out the felony charge because it was retaliation for bringing an appeal. *Blackledge* v. *Perry,* 417 U.S. 21 (1974).

123. *Illinois* v. *Allen*, 397 U.S. 337 (1970).

124. *Taylor* v. *U.S.*, 414 U.S. 17 (1973).

125. *Mayberry* v. *Pennsylvania*, 400 U.S. 455 (1971).

126. *Codispotti* v. *Pennsylvania*, 418 U.S. 506 (1974).

127. *Eaton* v. *City of Tulsa*, 415 U.S. 697 (1974).

128. *Boykin* v. *Alabama*, 395 U.S. 238 (1969); *McCarthy* v. *U.S.*, 394 U.S. 459 (1969).

129. *Brady* v. *U.S.*, 397 U.S. 742 (1970).

130. *North Carolina* v. *Alford*, 400 U.S. 25 (1970).

131. *Santobello* v. *New York*, 404 U.S. 257 (1971).

132. *Baxstrom* v. *Herold*, 383 U.S. 107 (1966). See the later *McNeil* v. *Director, Patuxent Institution*, 407 U.S. 245 (1972), in which the Court ordered the release of a person who, after being turned over to a state institution for examination for commitment under the Defective Delinquent Statute, was retained for longer than his basic criminal sentence because he refused to talk to psychiatrists—who therefore would not evaluate him.

133. *Specht* v. *Patterson*, 396 U.S. 605 (1967).

134. *Humphrey* v. *Cady*, 405 U.S. 504 (1972).

135. *Marshall* v. *U.S.*, 414 U.S. 417 (1974); *Warden* v. *Marrero*, 417 U.S. 653 (1974); *Dorszynski* v. *U.S.*, 418 U.S. 424 (1974).

136. *Morrissey* v. *Brewer*, 408 U.S. 471 (1972).

137. *Gagnon* v. *Scarpelli*, 411 U.S. 778 (1973).

138. *Wolff* v. *McDonnell*, 418 U.S. 539 (1974).

CHAPTER NINE

The Transition to the Burger Court: A Final Look

RETROSPECTIVE

The Supreme Court under Warren Burger followed one of the most activist Supreme Courts in our nation's history, thus reinforcing its role as a transitional court. Perhaps all courts are courts in transition, changing personnel, and through personnel, orientations; the Supreme Court in the very late 1960s and early-to-mid-1970s seemed to fit particularly well in that category. One observer has noted, "After the Marshall era, a period of great constitutional creativity, the Court experienced a period characterized by limitation and modification but not by major departure from established precedent."[1] We cannot yet tell fully to what extent the Burger Court will "play Taney to Warren's Marshall," but we have been able to see that the new Court is playing a more limited role in the American political system.

In looking at the transition from the end of the Warren Court to the first years of the Burger Court, we have seen a mixed picture instead of clearly defined results. Looking back from the mid-1970s, we see a Court that, after completing the most immediate years of the transition, was close—or at least closer—to the dominant national alliance, more in tune with the nation than its predecessor. However, perhaps because America was troubled and uncertain and beset by many problems, the Court had not settled down to a fully predictable decisional pattern, and we may find that just as there were early, middle, and late Warren Courts, the years through 1974 were simply the early Burger Court.

President Nixon by no means obtained all the policy results he may have desired from the Court's rulings, and the Court unanimously handed down the decision that led to his resignation. However, Nixon had appointed like-minded men who voted together with an extremely high rate of cohesion and who generally set the Court's tone, although occasional differences helped produce moderate-to-liberal decisions when one or more of the justices joined the holdover liberal members of the Court and maintained a high surprise level for the observer.

The policies of the Court Nixon helped compose have not been uniformly conservative, just as the Warren Court's rulings had not been consistently liberal. By comparison with its predecessor, the Burger Court has showed greater restraint toward legislative action, lower court judges' rulings, and state policy in some areas. However, judicial review has also been frequently exercised to overturn state and federal statutes or to intervene in the internal workings of the Congress and the presidency. The new justices, in short, have not been consistently self-restrained; instead, they have used restraint when it was helpful but at other times abandoned it to reach particular policy goals. While respecting clear, firm precedent, the justices have been willing to trim back or override precedents, particularly where Warren Court rulings were ambiguous.

We have also seen that, despite the Court's evident increasing conservatism, the Burger Court did not repeal the Warren Court's doctrinal output. Access to the courts was limited. Warren Court advances in some areas, perhaps most notably school desegregation, were ended. And the new justices seriously eroded Warren Court policy on reapportionment and some aspects of criminal procedure and free speech. The Burger Court also broke new ground in areas barely covered by the Warren Court and maintained or advanced earlier doctrine on right to counsel and church-state relations.

If we perceive the Warren Court as uniformly liberal, the Burger Court looks conservative. However, measured against a more accurate picture of the Warren Court, including its hesitancy to protect certain rights and its retreats in the face of public opinion, the Burger Court's retrenchment seems far less clear. We thus find substantial doctrinal continuity between the two Courts, their relation being characterized generally by an absence of the next step forward rather than by any sharp break or discontinuity. Reinforced by the shift from the use of broad rules to case-by-case adjudication in some policy areas, the change from the one court to the other was predominantly incremental. Like "other revisionist tribunals," the Burger Court has relied heavily on "the cumulative force of incremental changes."[2]

Despite this gradualism, a change in tone or atmosphere cannot be ignored. The Burger Court gave less emphasis to equality and the rights of the individual, prominent Warren Court

themes, particularly where the poor were involved; more weight
was given to the government's interests and to the concerns of the
law enforcement community in particular. The new Supreme
Court fit in well with changes in public opinion on how to deal
with minorities, obscenity, and "law 'n order," and the justices
now are generally far from the forefront of social change. Thus,
despite a lack of major policy shifts, we are not likely to see many
advances of the types to which we became accustomed in the
Warren Court years. Chief Justice Burger and his colleagues,
who have frequently said that the Supreme Court is not meant to
cure all that ails America, have been engaging in a self-fulfilling
prophecy.

THE COURT AND CIVIL LIBERTIES

If no sharp cutbacks in Warren Court policy have taken place,
why have some observers stressed the degree to which the Burger
Court retreated from Warren Court policy? Perhaps the most
basic reason is that many observers had come to expect the type of
change the Warren Court seemed to produce, as well as that
Court's strong attachment to the rights of the individual. Thus
people who looked to the Warren Court for protection of their civil
liberties had come to ignore decisions inconsistent with its basically liberal approach, just as liberal decisions of an essentially
more moderate Burger Court have been ignored.

At least since the New Deal, those defending the Court have
said that its exercise of the power of judicial review was most
proper when used to protect civil liberties. In fact, such protection
is necessary so people can participate fully in our political system.
By reinforcing the minority rights part of the majority rule–
minority rights formula, the Court makes judicial review by
nonelected judges consonant with democracy. When the Court
does not fully uphold minority rights—as the Burger Court did
not in failing to continue the Warren Court's civil libertarian
posture—many people become disappointed. That disappoint-
ment is not relieved by the knowledge that the Burger Court was
liberal by comparison with earlier Supreme Courts.

The perception that the Court had changed considerably did
not require any direct overruling of Warren Court precedent. Because of expectations of the Warren Court, developed over fifteen
years, those who became aware of the Burger Court's slowing of
the civil liberties advance began to magnify its effects. Change
was further magnified by a lack of realization that the Court is
establishing only *minimum* standards in an area, for example,

criminal justice. The states (or the federal government) are not prevented from establishing higher standards if they wish to do so. However, the generally held erroneous belief that Court-established standards, for example, allowing police greater lee-way in conducting searches, are mandatory for all the states may blunt efforts to develop tighter rules legislatively.[3] This may mean that any retrenchment by the Court is seen to have even more negative effects on civil liberties than if people understood the Court's actions more accurately. Resulting was a multiplier effect to the Burger Court's tendency not to go forward, leading lawyers seeking social change to be more hesitant in bringing cases while government attorneys were more willing to test their causes before the justices.

Former Justice Goldberg, claiming, "The Court has never overruled precedent to any significant degree in order to facilitate a significant contraction of human liberties," has noted that

> No carefully worded opinion can lessen the momentousness of an unprecedented reversal of the trend of expanding constitutional rights. Nor can its effects be limited to a single civil right or a single area of civil liberties. Any overruling acts as an admission that some right the Court had formerly called "fundamental" was not so fundamental after all; the admission will undermine the public belief that the other rights labelled fundamental in the past retain their status. For any contraction by overruling, the Court may pay a huge premium in lost force of those decisions that it wishes to retain as "good constitutional law."[4]

Such a position, held by many, suggests an inevitability and moral propriety of movement only in the liberal direction; once individual rights are established by judicial interpretation, there can and should be no turning back. However, to adopt such a posi-tion would cause trouble for a Supreme Court wishing to have some effect on the real political environment in which it is inevit-ably embedded. If the Court must remain in touch with political reality, forward movement on civil liberties can hardly be inevit-able when public opinion on civil liberties turns conservative. Thus, despite some Court-watchers' discomfort with the Burger Court, we must remember the even greater discomfort many people felt when the Warren Court was trying to protect minori-ties and those with little political power. Uncomfortable with the Warren Court, they are now far more comfortable with the Burger Court. And the favorable reception accorded the Burger Court suggests as well the very real political virtues of judicial self-restraint.

That the Court has been inconsistent in its constraint and

has engaged in judicial activism when that assisted in achieving conservative ends has meant, however, that the attractiveness of judicial self-restraint has recently increased for many American liberals. This shift is noteworthy because liberals favored self-restraint in the 1930s when the Supreme Court was invalidating New Deal economic legislation but disavowed it and applauded the Court's activism in the 1950s and 1960s when civil rights goals were aided. The Burger Court's posture of activism in support of conservative policy may lead liberals to direct more energy toward legislative solutions to problems and to the *substance* of policy and less to judicial remedies against policies they dislike. If this is so, the result may well be an increase in democracy's vitality. The irony of that development's having been prompted in any measure by the Burger Court and particularly by President Nixon will make it no less important.

Despite the importance of the justices' not losing complete touch with what is going on around them, and of their acting so as to achieve their goals as fully and effectively as possible,[5] one may seriously question whether keeping in touch with political reality should be the Court's predominant task. Because of the substantial political and bureaucratic obstacles that hinder the implementation of the Court's decisions and blunt their impact, the justices' rulings will seldom be fully implemented in any event. Therefore one might demand that the Court lean harder in the direction of emphasizing our nation's constitutional ideals, model itself on the Warren Court, and thus serve as a major source of our aspirations and ideals. This is particularly necessary because no other individual or institution in our political system is likely to perform that crucial function. While acting on some matters like privacy, Congress is not equipped to establish broad ideals for the nation, and the presidency's reputation after Watergate makes it difficult to look there for succor. In short, if full compliance is unlikely regardless of the Court's attempts to attune itself to political reality, the justices can at least provide a beacon light for the nation by setting high standards for others to follow.

Perhaps most important, because the statements in the Bill of Rights are only rights in theory, they need all the help they can get if they are to survive in fact. As an historian recently remarked about the 1940s, "Since the man in the street is always ready to do his own balancing of First Amendment and other freedoms, usually forcefully, the Supreme Court's willingness to pursue the same philosophy was a civil liberty disaster."[6] The pressures in the real world against the Bill of Rights are substantial; if our civil liberties are whittled down before they ever leave the Supreme Court, they will be reduced even more thereafter, the Supreme Court's hesitancy and reluctance serving as an excuse. This further increases the need for the Court itself to apply the civil liberties of our Constitution with the greatest possible force, so that they will have a chance to persist. As we move further into the Burger Court's time in history, we will have to see whether the justices continue to move away from such a posture or whether they begin to give greater recognition to its importance.

NOTES

1. Richard Funston, "Foreword: The Burger Court: New Directions in Judicial Policy-Making," *Emory Law Journal*, 23 (Summer 1974), 656.

2. J. Woodford Howard, Jr., "Is the Burger Court a Nixon Court?" *Emory Law Journal*, 23 (Summer 1974), 752.

3. See Stephen Arons and Ethan Katsh, "Reclaiming the Fourth Amendment in Massachusetts," *Civil Liberties Review*, 2 (Winter 1975), 82–89.

4. Arthur Goldberg, *Equal Justice: The Warren Era of the Supreme Court* (Evanston, Ill.: Northwestern University Press, 1971), pp. 90, 93–94.

5. See Martin Shapiro, *Law and Politics in the Supreme Court* (Glencoe, Ill.: Free Press, 1964).

6. William Preston, Jr., "The 1940s: The Way We Really Were," *Civil Liberties Review*, 2 (Winter 1975), 34.

Epilogue: The 1974 Term

The Supreme Court's October 1974 Term did not bring major doctrinal surprises. Decisions on economic policy, to which the Court devoted more attention, were more conservative. However, there was little change in civil liberties policy, and some Warren Court doctrine and earlier Burger Court rulings were extended. The Court's internal dynamics remained much the same. Only slightly more than one-third of the Court's rulings were unanimous, and about 13 percent (including several major rulings) were decided by 5–4 votes. The Nixon appointees remained cohesive; at least three of the four voted together in all but ten cases. Although occasional divisions kept them from total domination of the Court, the Nixon Four were in dissent only two times when they voted together. The liberals were also cohesive, although their cause was weakened by Justice Douglas' nonparticipation in nearly twenty cases, a result of the stroke that was to lead to his departure from the Court early in the 1975 Term.

ECONOMIC REGULATION

The Court's continued deference to Congress on economic regulation was clear. By reading the availability of certain compensation remedies into the 1973 Regional Rail Reorganization Act, the majority sustained the statute. Claims that the law, passed to solve the severe economic problems of the major Northeastern railroads, took property without just compensation were rejected.[1] The Court also ruled that the Economic Stabilization Act and the resulting Pay Board wage guidelines were constitutional as applied to state employees.[2]

The Court also continued to sustain national power against state claims, for example, upholding the national government's ownership of Atlantic Ocean offshore oil rights and ruling that Mississippi's effort to collect the wholesale markup on liquor sold to military installations was an unconstitutional tax on the United States.[3] State power to tax was also limited. The justices ruled invalid New Hampshire's tax on nonresidents' income earned in the state because the state did not tax its own residents' income.[4]

Showing its conservatism, the Court narrowly interpreted "commerce" in federal statutes. Extending an earlier ruling, the Court ruled that the attempt by an association of stevedoring companies to prevent union picketing of a foreign-flag ship over foreign seamen's wages was not within commerce and thus was not subject to federal labor provisions, so the companies could obtain state antipicketing injunctions.[5] In the antitrust field, the Court ruled that companies manufacturing material for construction of interstate highways did not come within the Clayton and Robinson-Patman Acts; similarly, one of the nation's largest suppliers of janitorial services was not "engaged in commerce" within the meaning of the Clayton Act, which was said not to reach all corporations potentially subject to the federal commerce power.[6]

Not all the Court's antitrust rulings were as narrow. For example, the justices unanimously invalidated bar association minimum legal fee schedules, at least in connection with practices like title searches on homes that affected interstate commerce.[7] Other antitrust rulings, however, went against the government, including decisions that Congress had kept stockbrokers' fixed commissions and restrictions on the transfer of mutual fund shares beyond the reach of the antitrust laws in order to enforce the securities statutes.[8] The Court also handed down several rulings that prevented people from bringing fraud suits under the Securities Exchange Act.[9] Demonstrating the same attitude in a case brought to prevent issuance of government permits for the trans-Alaska pipeline, the Court ruled that, in the absence of statutory authorization, attorneys' fees were not recoverable in federal litigation, thus making it more difficult for "private attorneys general" to challenge business depredations upon the environment.[10] Also protecting business from environmental claims was the decision that those wishing to build steam-operated power plants did not need to obtain a license from the Federal Power Commission even when they used considerable water from the nation's navigable rivers, because the agency's jurisdiction was limited to those plants that directly converted water power to electricity.[11]

The Court's rulings affecting employees present a mixed picture. The "while employed" standard of the Federal Employers Liability Act (on employee injuries) was defined narrowly, provoking Justice Blackmun to complain that the Court was changing a "mature and highly developed legal standard . . . without explaining" its actions.[12] The efforts of farmworker organizations to exclude low-paid immigrants from the country were hurt by a 5–4 ruling that the need for the labor of aliens commuting to work here on a daily or seasonal basis did not have to be certified because the Immigration and Naturalization Service had properly classified them as "lawfully admitted for permanent residence . . . returning from a temporary visit abroad."[13] Another ruling put the burden on unions to invoke the NLRB's election procedure when management refused to recognize the union despite its presentation of authorization cards showing its majority status.[14] Unions were also held subject to antitrust action (rather than to the labor laws) for picketing to get general contractors to subcontract with firms that bargained with unions, and were held not entitled to a jury trial when charged with contempt for picketing, which was improper under the labor laws.[15] Departing from this posture, the Court, with the Nixon appointees split, upheld an NLRB policy that the right of employees to act in concert included an employee's right to have a union representative present at employer "investigative interviews" where the employee feared the interview would result in disciplinary action.[16]

SEPARATION OF POWERS

In many of the above cases, the Court showed its continued willingness to sustain the work of administrative agencies. For example, the justices unanimously upheld the ICC's use of emergency powers to issue, without notice and hearing, a Service Order on the return of empty freight cars, and also found adequate ICC consideration of the environmental factors affected by railroad freight rate increases.[17] The Court also strengthened the executive's hand by ruling against disclosure of various internal memoranda when withholding was challenged under the Freedom of Information Act (FOIA). The Court said the public could not have access to documents that were not final opinions, but when the materials were final they had to be made available. The Court also interpreted another FOIA provision to allow the FAA Administrator to withhold analyses of airline operation and maintenance performance.[18]

With respect to the presidency itself, the Court brought to an end the impoundment controversy President Nixon had initiated. Using statutory interpretation, the justices held that there was no congressional intent to give the executive discretionary authority over water pollution control allotments.[19] However, the Court strengthened the President's discretion in another area by holding that he might impose conditions when granting pardons. Here the justices upheld President Eisenhower's 1960 commutation of a court-martial-imposed death sentence in which he substituted life imprisonment without the possibility of parole, rejecting the arguments that the President had violated the separation of powers by imposing a condition not available in the law and that the Court's death-penalty decision had nullified the soldier's sentence.[20] (The Court had been expected to issue a further ruling on the constitutionality of the death penalty but instead set the case for reargument in the 1975 Term.)

In its only ruling on congressional procedure, the Court refused to interfere with a Senate subcommittee subpoena to a bank for the records of an organization's account because an investigation was essential to legislating and because the protection afforded by the Speech and Debate Clause was absolute. Thus the subpoena could not be challenged on grounds of invasion of privacy.[21]

VOTING RIGHTS

Despite its earlier avoidance of the 1972 Democratic National Convention delegate-selection controversy, the Court now ruled that a state court had interfered with the national party's right of association by issuing an injunction to prevent the seating of the Illinois "reform" delegation, which had successfully challenged the "regular" elected Illinois delegates at the convention.[22] Concerning reapportionment, the Court said federal courts should avoid imposing multimember districts on a state without "persuasive justification"; courts ordering districting also had to meet tighter standards on population variances than did legislatures.[23] At the local level, the Court sustained county commissioner districts of widely varying population where, although each commissioner came from a separate district, all were elected on a countywide basis.[24]

Following up Warren Court rulings on property requirements for voting, the Court, invalidating laws limiting voting in city bond issues to those who had "rendered" property for taxation, said that residence, age, and citizenship were the only valid requirements in local elections of general interest unless a com-

pelling state interest were shown.[25] However, the Court seemed
to step back from its earlier strong reinforcement of the Voting
Rights Act. Land had been annexed to Richmond, Virginia to
dilute the black vote (decreasing the black population from 52
percent to 42 percent), but the justices found no violation of the
act because the city council election system fairly reflected the
black presence in the post-annexation population.[26]

EMPLOYMENT DISCRIMINATION

There were two important rulings on racial job discrimination. In
one, although the union was pressing their claims, employees
who felt union grievance procedures inadequate had picketed
their employer protesting racial discrimination and had been
fired. Despite Douglas' charge that minority employees were
being made captives of the union, the Court, speaking through
Justice Marshall, rejected the claim that the discharge was for
protected "collective action" and ruled that national labor law
requiring the union to represent all employees meant that the
employees had to use the grievance procedure; the employer was
not to be expected to bargain separately with each group of dissi-
dent employees.[27] Aiding minority workers, the Court extended
its 1971 *Griggs* v. *Duke Power Company* decision. Placing great
weight on Equal Employment Opportunities Commission (EEOC)
guidelines, the justices ruled that for employment tests that
eliminated blacks to be valid, they had to be shown by "profes-
sionally acceptable methods" to be job-related. Furthermore,
those discriminated against could collect back pay without having to prove that the employer had acted in bad faith.[28] The provision of a financial remedy was of particular significance; in imposing it, the seven-justice majority said the injury to the worker
was real even when not intentionally inflicted.

GENDER DISCIMINATION AND WELFARE

The Court continued its earlier mixed pattern on gender discrimination. A federal statute allowing female officers to remain
in the armed services longer than men before discharge for not
having been promoted was upheld; the legislative classification,
said to recognize differences between male and female officers in
promotion opportunities, was found completely rational.[29] On the
other hand, exclusion or automatic exemption of women from jury
service was struck down where the result was almost totally male

jury pools. States could not justify the exclusion on the ground that women as a class serve a distinctive societal role with which jury service would interfere.[30] The Court also said the "age of majority" (when one could sign contracts and marry without permission) must be the same for both sexes, thus invalidating a state rule setting the age at twenty-one for males but only eighteen for females.[31]

In a gender-discrimination welfare case, the justices unanimously invalidated part of the Social Security Act that granted benefits to surviving mothers caring for a child but not to such surviving fathers. The law was unconstitutional because women wage-earners were afforded less protection for their survivors than was provided for survivors of male wage-earners.[32] Child care given by the father was no less important than that given by the mother, said Justice Brennan. Continuing its heavy use of statutory interpretation in the welfare area, the Court said the phrase "dependent child" did not include unborn children, who therefore did not have to be provided with benefits.[33] And the Court also ruled that Congress, in order to deter sham marriages intended only to secure financial benefits, could legitimately deny mother's insurance benefits to wives and stepchildren not related to a dead wage-earner for at least nine months.[34]

Seeming to reverse its earlier position on durational residence requirements, the Court sustained a one-year requirement for obtaining a divorce, saying that only delay, not a total denial of access to the courts, resulted.[35] The majority issued its ruling although the woman who had brought the case—the only named plaintiff—had already obtained a divorce, because the case had been brought as a class action and thus the controversy was still alive. The residence rule, justified by the state's desire to protect divorces from collateral attacks by other states and to avoid becoming a "divorce mill," was attacked by Justice Marshall for imposing a penalty on interstate travel and for locking a couple into "what may be an intolerable, destructive relationship." The Court's refusal to use mootness here provides a clear example of the abandonment of self-restraint in the interest of a conservative result.

CONSUMER RIGHTS

Two crucial consumer rights cases in this term involved notice and hearing. In one, the Court continued the process of narrowing the reach of "state action" begun in the *Moose Lodge* case. When a privately owned utility company had terminated electric service for nonpayment without notice to the customer, the majority said the company's behavior was not "state action" and thus was not subject to due process requirements, even though the utility had monopoly status; was heavily regulated by the state; and had filed its termination procedures with the regulatory agency.[36] The majority claimed the state agency had not specifically approved the termination procedure, but dissenting Justice Douglas said the utility was not even following its own rules (discontinuance on "reasonable notice").

The unsettled nature of garnishment and repossession law was obvious in the other case, when the Court invalidated a procedure in which a writ for garnishment was issued without a judge's involvement and with no provision for early hearing on the garnishee's claims.[37] The decision left the doctrine that garnishment and repossession statutes are valid only if they provide for prompt post-seizure hearings and clearly revived the earlier *Fuentes* ruling. Justice Blackmun, dissenting, wanted to have garnishment rules cover employee wages but not dealings between business enterprises; he also complained that the Court had been damaged by the confusion caused by deciding *Fuentes* with only seven justices instead of rearguing it with nine.

Another case affecting the poor came when city residents claimed that suburban zoning ordinances with low-density development requirements fenced out low-income people. Although Brennan and Douglas said the majority showed hostility to claims by the poor, the Court, by another 5–4 vote, refused to invalidate the zoning rules, saying those protesting must specifically assert how the ordinances would harm them and how judicial intervention would assist in protecting their rights.[38] In so doing, the majority extended earlier rulings upholding local government zoning authority and limiting housing rights.

STUDENT RIGHTS

Prior to this term, the Court had said nothing about due process for students, but 1975 brought two important rulings. In the first, over the objections of the four dissenting Nixon appointees that the Court was inappropriately intervening in the activities of school officials, the Court said that public school students were entitled to notice and hearing before being suspended from school even for periods of up to ten days. In such situations both the notice and the hearing could be informal, for example, a statement by the principal to the student and an opportunity for the student to tell his side of the story, although longer suspensions might require more formal procedures.[39] In the second case, the Court extended its doctrine on personal liability of state officials by holding that school board members were liable for damages if they denied a student's rights maliciously or did so when they knew or *should have known* they were doing so; this prompted the dissenters to wonder whether people would any longer be willing to serve on school boards.[40]

FIRST AMENDMENT

There was relatively little First Amendment activity in this Term. In a ruling clearly restricted to the facts of the case, the justices sustained a $60,000 verdict for a woman who said a newspaper had invaded her family's privacy through false portrayal that subjected them to ridicule. However, they did rule that news media could not be barred from printing the name of a rape victim when the information came from court documents open to the public.[41] The majority also said an advertisement in a Virginia newspaper for abortion services in New York (where they were legal) could not be punished under a statute forbidding "encouraging or prompting" abortions, because speech was not stripped of its First Amendment protection by being in a paid commercial advertisement.[42]

Upsetting a Chattanooga, Tennessee ban on the musical "Hair," the Court extended Warren Court doctrine by ruling that procedures for movie censorship must be followed for censorship of stage productions; the censor had the burden of showing that material was obscene, and prompt judicial review had to be available.[43] Then the Court struck down an attempt under nuisance law to protect citizens from unwilling exposure to offensive material. Drive-in theaters had been prohibited from showing movies with nude scenes if the movies could be seen from outside the theater. The Court said otherwise protected speech could not be prohibited even if some people were offended. Justice Powell also pointed out that nudity could not be deemed obscene even when viewed by minors and that the law had not kept other distracting elements of films from public view.[44]

In the church-state area, the Court reinforced its earlier work, striking down still another effort to aid parochial schools. This time, Pennsylvania statutes providing "auxiliary services" for children and loans directly to the schools for instructional materials were invalidated. Only the loan of textbooks to parochial school children, which the Court had allowed in the past, was sustained.[45]

CRIMINAL PROCEDURE

The Burger Court handed down a number of important criminal procedure rulings during the year; on the whole, they did not alter the trend of basic doctrine. The Court both limited and extended the government's search powers. The *Almeida-Sanchez* ruling on roving border searches was extended to invalidate fixed traffic checkpoints away from the border; the Court also said that someone's appearing to be Mexican was insufficient cause for roving border patrols to stop them; at the border itself, a brief stop for questioning about immigration status and suspicious circumstances was acceptable under loose standards, but there could be no further detention without probable cause or consent.[46] Then, expanding search authority, the Court upheld Internal Revenue Service use of "John Doe" summonses to search bank records for the identity of persons involved in suspicious transactions.[47] Because the summonses were not issued to aid an investigation of a particular person, Justices Douglas and Stewart called this a "breathtaking expansion of the summons power" and "a sharp and dangerous detour . . . from precedent."

In another Fourth Amendment ruling, the Court unanimously said that when an arrest was based on information filed by a prosecutor, no extended restraint could be imposed without a judicial determination of "probable case"; however, this judicial preliminary hearing need not be adversary. Weakening the decision's force, the majority reaffirmed the rule that an illegal arrest or detention was *not* a reason for voiding a subsequent conviction.[48] The Court dealt with another aspect of detention when it ruled unanimously that a person could not be committed to a mental institution for custodial care if he were not likely to harm himself or others.[49]

Several *Miranda*-related issues arose. Extending its 1971 ruling in *Harris* v. *New York*, the Court allowed use of a damaging statement made to the police after the defendant was warned of his rights and indicated he would call a lawyer but before he actually talked to the attorney. As in *Harris*, the statement could be used only to impeach the defendant's trial testimony, but not in the prosecutor's principal argument.[50] The opinion is also important because the justices stated strongly that state courts could not read the U.S. Constitution more strictly than had the Supreme Court in order to impose a higher standard on the police, although they might use state law for that purpose. Here we see an assertion of the supremacy of Supreme Court constitutional interpretation in order to reinforce the Court's pro-law enforcement stand. Later the Court rejected a prosecutor's attempt to use a defendant's earlier *silence* to impeach the alibi he later offered.[51] And the justices did weaken police reliance on use of the *Miranda* warnings by saying that where someone had been illegally arrested, merely giving the warnings did not by itself remove the taint from subsequent statements; because of the "fruit of the poisonous tree" doctrine, more would have to be done to show that the statements were voluntary.[52]

Right to counsel questions were resolved in several cases. For one thing, despite the aphorism that "One who defends himself has a fool for a client," the Court extended federal law to the states by ruling that one had a constitutional right to reject court-appointed counsel and represent oneself.[53] The Court also reinforced effective representation. When a lawyer in a civil case advised his client not to produce demanded material the lawyer thought might incriminate the client, the lawyer had been held in contempt of court. Unanimously overruling the contempt charge, the Court said that to do otherwise would weaken the client's Fifth Amendment rights, which would be ineffective without the technical advice only a lawyer could provide.[54] The justices distinguished this situation from a refusal to obey a court order issued during a trial, which could be dealt with through the contempt power. Shortly afterwards, the Court underlined this point by holding subject to summary contempt a person who persisted in his refusal to answer questions during a trial after a grant of immunity; in effect, he was disrupting the progress of the trial and therefore was hindering the orderly administration of justice.[55]

Double jeopardy questions facing the Court included whether the government could appeal from trial court dismissal of indictments. The justices allowed the appeal when it would not result in a new trial for the defendant, for example, when the trial judge ruled against the government on a point of law after the trial had resulted in a finding of guilty. However, when more trial proceedings would have to occur after a successful appeal, the Double Jeopardy Clause barred the appeal.[56] The Court also ruled that double jeopardy had occurred when a juvenile alleged to have committed a criminal offense was first tried as a juvenile but, before institutionalization as a juvenile, was tried again as an adult. Here the Court stressed that protection against double jeopardy meant not only protection against being punished twice but against being *tried* twice.[57]

A five-man majority including Justice Blackmun carved a rather large hole in the Burger Court's earlier doctrine that guilty pleas foreclosed challenges to any matters prior to the plea. They did so by ruling that when state law allowed judicial review of certain matters (such as unreasonable searches) after a guilty plea, a person who had pled guilty in the state courts was not prevented from seeking habeas corpus in the federal courts.[58] The majority said that when the state had decided to allow post-guilty plea review to facilitate the trial process, the federal courts should aid rather than undercut the state policy by also allowing such review.

Other decisions concerning appeals were conservative. A ruling sustaining a Texas statute under which appeals by an escaped felon were automatically dismissed unless he voluntarily surrendered within ten days carried another recitation of the statement that "there is no federal constitutional right to state appellate review of state criminal convictions."[59] The Court also ruled that a serviceman charged by military authorities must exhaust his military court remedies before turning to civilian courts even when his claim was that the military courts cannot properly try him—for example, for a simple drug charge probably not service-connected.[60]

SUMMARY

What we see looking back at the Burger Court's 1974 Term is support for Congress' power to pass statutes regulating the economy and for national authority in conflict with state power, but narrow interpretation of those national statutes to achieve pro-business results. Both pro-union and anti-union rulings came from the Court, but when unions were not involved those with claims of racial discrimination in employment were treated well. Administrative agencies continued to receive deference as well as protection from having to release internal information. The President's impoundment power was restricted, but his discretion in the use of the pardon power was affirmed.

The Court strongly opposed property restrictions on the right to vote, but lessened its support for minorities under the Voting Rights Acts, just as it changed its position on durational residence requirements, upholding those for divorces. Gender discrimination in and out of the welfare area produced some victories for equal treatment of the sexes. Consumers found some revived support in garnishment proceedings, but the Court's constrained interpretation of "state action" took away protection from utility practices, and the Court's sympathy for the poor was hardly overwhelming. A major boost was given to the rights of students, and those committed to mental institutions were also given increased protection. The Court's support for free speech was consistent, and it reinforced its position of strict separation of church and state.

The Court provided evidence of its continuing pro-law enforcement stance but also provided much support for defendants' rights. The former position was evident with respect to searches of bank accounts and in an extension of the Court's earlier position on *Miranda*, but defendants as well as prosecutors obtained sustenance from the *Miranda* cases. Defendants' rights to defend themselves were upheld, and their lawyers' ability to provide them with effective advice was reinforced. Double jeopardy decisions also benefitted defendants. The Court also provided greater appeal rights to those who had pled guilty but made appeal for military defendants a much longer process.

The picture one draws from the 1974 Term is thus the mixed picture one has seen earlier in the transition. Even if the 1974 Term seems too late to consider part of the transition, the Court still has a decisional pattern not clearly leaning in one direction or the other, but mixed and with much room for future development.

NOTES

1. *Regional Rail Reorganization Act Cases*, 419 U.S. 102 (1974).
2. *Fry* v. *U.S.*, 95 S. Ct. 1792 (1975).
3. *U.S.* v. *Maine*, 420 U.S. 515 (1975); *U.S.* v. *State Tax Commission of Mississippi*, 43 L.W. 4691 (1975), an extension of the earlier ruling at 412 U.S. 363 (1973).
4. *Austin* v. *New Hampshire*, 420 U.S. 656 (1975).
5. *American Radio Association* v. *Mobile Steamship Association*, 419 U.S. 215 (1974).
6. *Gulf Oil Corp.* v. *Copp Paving Co.*, 419 U.S. 186 (1974); *U.S.* v. *American Building Maintenance Industries*, 43 L.W. 4838 (1975).
7. *Goldfarb* v. *Virginia State Bar*, 43 L.W. 4723 (1975).
8. *Gordon* v. *New York Stock Exchange*, 43 L.W. 4958 (1975); *U.S.* v. *National Association of Securities Dealers*, 43 L.W. 4968 (1975).
9. *Blue Chip Stamps* v. *Manor Drug Stores*, 43 L.W. 4707 (1975); *United Housing Foundation* v. *Forman*, 43 L.W. 4742 (1975); *Rondeau* v. *Mosinee Paper*, 43 L.W. 4768 (1975).
10. *Alyeska Pipeline Service Co.* v. *Wilderness Society*, 421 U.S. 240 (1975).
11. *Chemehuevi Tribe* v. *F.P.C.*, 420 U.S. 395 (1975).
12. *Kelley* v. *Southern Pacific Co.*, 419 U.S. 319 (1974).
13. *Saxbe* v. *Bustos*, 419 U.S. 65 (1974).
14. *Linden Lumber Division, Summer & Co.* v. *N.L.R.B.*, 419 U.S. 301 (1974).
15. *Connell Construction Co.* v. *Plumbers Union*, 43 L.W. 4657 (1975); *Muniz* v. *Hoffman*, 43 L.W. 4895 (1975).

16. *N.L.R.B.* v. *Weingarten*, 420 U.S. 251, and *ILGWU* v. *Quality Manufacturing*, 420 U.S. 276 (1975).

17. *I.C.C.* v. *Oregon Pacific Industries*, 420 U.S. 184 (1975); *Aberdeen and Rockfish Railroad Co.* v. *S.C.R.A.P.*, 43 L.W. 4844 (1975).

18. *Renegotiation Board* v. *Grumman Aircraft*, 421 U.S. 168 (1975); *N.L.R.B.* v. *Sears, Roebuck*, 421 U.S. 132 (1975); *F.A.A. Administrator* v. *Robertson*, 43 L.W. 4833 (1975).

19. *Train* v. *City of New York*, 420 U.S. 35, and *Train* v. *Campaign Clear Water*, 420 U.S. 136 (1975).

20. *Schick* v. *Reed*, 419 U.S. 256 (1974).

21. *Eastland* v. *United Serviceman's Fund*, 95 S. Ct. 1813 (1975).

22. *Cousins* v. *Wigoda*, 419 U.S. 477 (1975).

23. *Chapman* v. *Meier*, 420 U.S. 1 (1975).

24. *Dallas County* v. *Reese*, 95 S. Ct. 1706 (1975).

25. *Hill* v. *Stone*, 421 U.S. 289 (1975).

26. *City of Richmond* v. *U.S.*, 43 L.W. 4865 (1975).

27. *Emporium Capwell* v. *Western Addition Community Organization*, 420 U.S. 50 (1975).

28. *Albemarle Paper Co.* v. *Moody*, 43 L.W. 4880 (1975).

29. *Schlesinger* v. *Ballard*, 419 U.S. 498 (1975).

30. *Taylor* v. *Louisiana*, 419 U.S. 522 (1975).

31. *Stanton* v. *Stanton*, 421 U.S. 7 (1975).

32. *Weinberger* v. *Weisenfeld*, 420 U.S. 636 (1975).

33. *Burns* v. *Alcala*, 420 U.S. 575 (1975).

34. *Weinberger* v. *Salfi*, 43 L.W. 4985 (1975).

35. *Sosna* v. *Iowa*, 419 U.S. 393 (1975).

36. *Jackson* v. *Metropolitan Edison*, 419 U.S. 345 (1974).

37. *North Georgia Finishing* v. *Di-Chem*, 419 U.S. 601 (1975).

38. *Warth* v. *Seldin*, 43 L.W. 4908 (1975).

39. *Goss* v. *Lopez*, 419 U.S. 565 (1975).

40. *Wood* v. *Strickland*, 420 U.S. 308 (1975).

41. *Cantrell* v. *Forest City Publishing Co.*, 419 U.S. 245 (1974); *Cox Broadcasting Co.* v. *Cohn*, 420 U.S. 469 (1975).

42. *Bigelow* v. *Virginia*, 43 L.W. 4735 (1975).

43. *Southeastern Promotions* v. *Conrad,* 420 U.S. 546 (1975).

44. *Erznoznik* v. *City of Jacksonville*, 43 L.W. 4809 (1975).

45. *Meek* v. *Pittinger*, 95 S. Ct. 1753 (1975).

46. *U.S.* v. *Ortiz*, 43 L.W. 5026 (1975); *U.S.* v. *Brignoni-Ponce*, 43 L.W. 5028 (1975). See also *U.S.* v. *Peltier,* 43 L.W. 4919 (1975), holding *Almeida-Sanchez* not retroactive.

47. *U.S.* v. *Bisceglia*, 420 U.S. 141 (1975).

48. *Gerstein* v. *Pugh*, 420 U.S. 103 (1975).

49. *O'Connor* v. *Donaldson*, 43 L.W. 4929 (1975). See also *Drope* v. *Missouri*, 420 U.S. 162 (1975), on the weight to be given to a defendant's incompetence to stand trial, a ruling also favoring those with mental problems.

50. *Oregon* v. *Hass*, 420 U.S. 714 (1975).

51. *U.S.* v. *Hale*, 43 L.W. 4806 (1975).

52. *Brown* v. *Illinois*, 43 L.W. 4937 (1975).

53. *Faretta* v. *California*, 43 L.W. 5004 (1975).

54. *Maness* v. *Meyers*, 419 U.S. 449 (1975).

55. *U.S.* v. *Wilson*, 95 S. Ct. 1802 (1975).

56. Compare *U.S.* v. *Wilson*, 420 U.S. 332 (1975), with *U.S.* v. *Jenkins*, 420 U.S. 358 (1975), bench trial had not resolved all the facts, and *Serfass* v. *U.S.,* 420 U.S. 377 (1975), dismissal of indictment before trial.

57. *Breed* v. *Jones*, 95 S. Ct. 1779 (1975).

58. *Lefkowitz* v. *Newsome*, 420 U.S. 293 (1975).

59. *Estelle* v. *Dorrough*, 420 U.S. 534 (1975).

60. *Schlesinger* v. *Councilman*, 420 U.S. 738 (1975); see also *McLucas* v. *DeChamplain*, 421 U.S. 21 (1975).

Index*

Only the most major cases are listed in the Index. Citations to cases are to be found in the footnotes at the end of each chapter.